ANDREA IMMER'S

2004
WINE
BUYING
GUIDE
for Everyone

ANDREA IMMER'S

2004 WINE BUYING GUIDE

for Everyone

FEATURING MORE THAN 600 TOP WINES
AVAILABLE IN STORES AND RESTAURANTS

Andrea Immer

Broadway Books / New York

BROADWAY

PRINTED IN THE UNITED STATES OF AMERICA

BROADWAY BOOKS and its logo, a letter B bisected on the diagonal, are trademarks of Broadway Books, a division of Random House, Inc.

Visit our website at www.broadwaybooks.com

First edition published 2002

The Library of Congress has cataloged the first edition as follows:
Immer, Andrea
    [Wine buying guide for everyone]
    Andrea Immer's wine buying guide for everyone /
Andrea Immer ; edited by Anthony Giglio.—1st ed.
       p. cm.
    Includes index.
    1. Wine and wine making. I. Title: Wine buying guide for everyone. II. Giglio, Anthony. III. Title.

TP548 .I4624 2002
641.2'2—dc21   2002023077

ISBN 0-7679-1544-5

10 9 8 7 6 5 4 3 2 1

CONTENTS

INTRODUCTION

Although enjoying a good glass of wine is easy, all the types, costs, and confusing labels can make *shopping* for a bottle pretty hard. For the typical wine consumer, buying guidance—in the form of critics' 100-point scores and elaborate tasting reports of rare and exclusive bottlings—isn't much help. That is why I wrote *Andrea Immer's Wine Buying Guide for Everyone*. It is your road map to the *real* world of wine buying—from restaurants and hotels to supermarkets, price clubs, wine shops, and websites. Here is what you'll find inside:

Real-World Wines

This guide showcases more than 600 of the most popular and available wines on the market. That includes everything from supermarket stalwarts to trade-up labels to superpremium "restaurant" brands (with plenty of boutique pedigree but without the you-can't-get-it frustration). Putting it plainly, if the wine is in your favorite neighborhood shops and eateries, at your supermarket or Costco, Olive Garden or Walt Disney World, Marriott or Carnival Cruises, Delta Airlines or wine.com, it's probably in this book.

Wine Reviews from the Trenches

I am indebted to the many consumers and wine pros who helped assess, for each of the wines in this book, what really matters to buyers at the point of purchase—taste and value for the money. For each wine, you'll also see their real-world reactions, as well as my impressions of how the wine stacks up in its grape or style category and in the marketplace overall. My tasters also contributed write-in candidates to the list of wines, and I've included those that received the highest number of positive mentions and have decent availability. There's also space in each listing for your notes, so you can keep track of the wines you try. (I hope you'll share your impressions with me for the next edition—read on to see how.)

Other Helpful Buying Tools in the Guide

Throughout the *Immer Guide,* I've included simple tools to address just about every major wine buying question I've ever been asked. They are:

Best-Of Lists—A quick reference to the top-performing wines in each grape or style category.

Andrea's Kitchen Fridge Survivor™ and Kitchen Countertop Survivor™ grades—"How long will a wine keep after it's opened?" Having heard this question more than any other from my restaurant customers and wine students, I decided several years ago that it was time to find out, so I started putting every wine I taste professionally to the "fridge/countertop test." The resulting report card should help both home wine drinkers and restaurateurs who pour wine by the glass make the most of the leftovers, by simply recorking and storing red wine on the kitchen countertop and storing recorked sparkling, white, and pink wines in the fridge.

Immer Best Bets—This is the book's "search engine" of instant recommendations for every common wine occasion and buying dilemma, from Thanksgiving wines to restaurant wine list best bets, party-crowd pleasers, blue chip bottles to impress the client, and more.

Wine List Decoder—This handy cross-reference chart will help you crack the code of different wine list terms, so you can quickly and easily find the styles you like.

Great Wine Made Simple Mini-Course—Mini-lessons covering wine styles, label terms, glassware, buying wine in stores and restaurants, and other housekeeping details to simplify buying and serving wine, so you can focus on enjoying it.

I had been in the restaurant wine business for more than a decade before I wrote my first book, *Great Wine Made Simple.* Having studied like crazy to pass the Master Sommelier exam (the hardest wine test you can imagine), I knew there were lots of great books out there. So why another? Because as I worked training waiters and budding sommeliers, I began to see that in practice those books weren't much help. Wine, like food, golf, the saxophone, and so many other sensory pursuits, is something you learn not by studying but by doing. So *Great Wine Made Simple* teaches wine not through memorization but the way I learned it—through tasting. It works, and it's fun, whether you are just a dabbler or a committed wine geek.

Similarly, I intend this guide to fill a gap. Most people around the country buy wine based on price and convenience. And whether it's restaurant guests, live callers on my CNN, Food Network, and radio appearances, or e-mail from users of my website, they all have the same questions: What are the good, cheap wines? And which wines are really worth the splurge? This buying guide is the first to answer those questions realistically, featuring wines and tastes in the broad marketplace, along with plenty of shrewd pro advice to help you make the most of every wine purchase. Food is one major way to do that, so as a professionally trained cook I've also included lots of pairing pointers.

What's New in This Year's Guide

Wow! What a difference a year makes. The new data on wine prices and popularity reveal a very different marketplace since publication of the last edition of the *Guide*. In addition, the profile of my tasting panel changed (more on this below), and with it the *opinions* about brands and prices reflected in the reviews. The result is a much bigger and better *Guide*. Here's why:

Technology dramatically expanded, and changed, the tasting panel. Almost all data for this edition was collected through my website. Because of the 24/7 convenience, I added thousands of reviewers, got hundreds of new write-in wines, and lots of great commentary.

Consumers dominated the tasting panel. *The bulk of new contributors were consumers*, about 70% of the total. This new panel makeup markedly altered the rankings from last year's *Guide*. Specifically, consumers were far more likely to be high on the big-brand wineries that offer genuine quality for the money. As such, the tables of top-rated wines in the front of the book are a who's-who of great wines you can actually find. Yay!

Down-under wines (Aussie, and Chilean, too) rose to the top of the value heap. The consumer-dominated panel also flushed out the new stars on the value scene. Aussie blends, in particular, got high marks; and Chilean Cabernet in the one-dollar-sign price point literally dusted the like-priced California competition.

Wine styles: cheers for Shiraz, Italian wines, and Riesling; snores for Merlot. Both the red grape Shiraz, and the white Pinot Grigio, are simply on fire, and it's easy to see why: there are plenty of tasty choices at everyday prices. I was thrilled to see major enthusiasm for Riesling and bubbly, too. But Merlots, even the dominant brands, took a lot of shots for being over-priced for the quality (I concur), and outside a few stars from Washington state, very few of them got top marks.

What's worth the splurge? Blue chip brands, and bubbly. Finally, the blue chip wineries—top names with a real track record for quality (as opposed to new-kid-on-the-block boutiques)—are where my tasters splurge. In other words, the wineries you've been hearing about for years—from Italy, Australia, France, and California—are still delivering the goods at palatable prices. And many tasters seemed to concur with my long-held view on bubbly—you get a lot of pleasure for the price.

How to Use This Buying Guide

Here is everything you need to know to get instant buying power from the *Immer Guide*.

Looking Up Wine Recommendations— by Wine Category or Winery Name

Wine Category—Grape, Region, or Type
The wine reviews are grouped by major grape variety, region, or type. For example:

Review
section
headings
look like this

WHITE WINES
Sparkling/Champagne

You'll probably recognize some of the main grape and style categories, because they lead the wine market in both quality and sales. These include what I call the Big Six grapes (the white grapes Riesling, Sauvignon Blanc, and Chardonnay; and the reds Pinot Noir, Merlot, and Cabernet Sauvignon), plus Pinot Grigio, Italian reds, Syrah/Shiraz, and some other popular categories. This is also the way most wine lists and many shops are set up. The "Other Whites" and "Other Reds" sections are used for less common grapes and proprietary blends.

Helpful to know: I've arranged all the wine categories from lightest to fullest in body, as a quick reference for when you are shopping or perusing a wine list. More and more, restaurant wine lists are being arranged by body style, too, because it helps both the guest and the server quickly determine which wines are lightest or heaviest, so they can match their personal preference or food choice if they wish.

Winery Name—Alphabetical Wine Listings
The wines in each category are in alphabetical order by winery name, so you can easily find the specific wine you're looking for. For example:

Wine category heading ———
Alphabetical wine listings ⟍

Chardonnay
Almaden Chardonnay, California
Beaulieu Vineyard (BV) Coastal Chardonnay, California

Helpful to know: If you are looking for a specific winery name rather than a grape or style category, the Winery Index at the back of the book will show you which producers' wines were reviewed for the guide and the page number for each wine review.

Key to the Ratings and Symbols in Each Wine Entry

This sample entry identifies the components of each wine listing.

1. Wine name and provenance (country or state)
2. Price category
3. Taste and value ratings
4. Symbols: These identify wines rated as
   ✓ best-of (rated most popular in their category) or
   ✗ worthy write-ins in their respective categories.

---

❷ ❸

❶ Chateau Andrea Rosé   PC   T   V
   New York $$ 26   28
❹ ✗ Tasters marvel at its "amazing quality for a
❺ bag-in-the-box." Pro buyers (including me) find
   it "every bit as good as the finest Cold Duck …
   and sometimes better!"
❻ *Kitchen Fridge Survivor™ Grade:* A
❼ Your notes: _____

_____

---

5. Reviewers' commentary, in quotation marks, along with my notes on the wine
6. My Kitchen Fridge/Countertop Survivor™ Grade
7. Space for your wine notes.

Price Category

Prices for the same wine can vary widely across the country. Here's why: individual states regulate the sale and taxation of wine within their borders, and sometimes local municipalities have further regulations and taxes. That means the price for any particular wine depends very much on where you live and shop. In general, wines are cheapest in large urban areas, where there's lots of retail competition. They are usually most expensive in so-called "control states," where there is zero competition because the state acts as the sole retailer (Pennsylvania is one example). In addition, some of the wines in the survey are available in a different size or in more than one size (e.g., half-bottles, standard 750 ml bottles, magnums, jugs, and larger). The price categories here, based on a standard 750 ml bottle, are intended as a guideline to help you compare relative prices of the different wines in the survey:

$ = up to $12
$$ = $12.01 to $20
$$$ = 20.01 to $35
$$$$ = above $35

NA indicates a wine not available in 750 ml bottles (sold only in jugs or bag-in-box format; prices for these are quite low).

Note: These are retail store prices, not restaurant wine list prices.

Taste and Value Ratings

Tasters (no pro credentials necessary, just an opinion) were asked to assess any of the listed wines that they'd tried in the past year on the following criteria:

- *Taste*—What did you think of the wine's taste?
- *Value for the Money*—Were you happy with what you got for the price you paid?

I kept the rating criteria simple, with scores listed on a scale of 0 to 30:

 0–9 = Poor
10–15 = Fair
16–19 = Good
20–25 = Very good
26–30 = Outstanding
   X = No data available

Certainly everyone has an opinion based on his or her own preferences and experience, and that is precisely what I sought to capture with this simple scale. I have also come to believe, from my years in the restaurant business and teaching wine classes, that most consumers can recognize inherent wine quality, regardless of their level of wine sophistication. I am pleased to say that the responses bore that out. Specifically, the wines that are consistently recognized by experts as quality and value leaders in their category were standouts among my tasters, too. Similarly, wines that have slipped, or whose price has risen unduly, were for the most part assessed accordingly. Other provocative attributes that influenced commentary and ratings included extreme prices (either high or low), an extreme reputation (either good or bad), and substantial inconsistency in the taste from one year to the next.

Symbols

Best-Of ✓—Identifies the top-rated wines in each category. (Rated "most popular" in the category—an average of the taste and value scores.)

Worthy Write-In ✗ —Denotes that a wine was added to the book listings by popular demand (as noted earlier, only those write-ins with decent availability were included). Because most tasters gave their write-ins verbal endorsements rather than scores, I haven't included scores here but will do so in future editions of the guide.

Reviewers' Commentary and My Notes

Along with their taste and value assessments, reviewers were asked to include comments on the wines—not tasting descriptions per se but "buyers' notes" reflecting their gut reactions to the wine. If they felt a wine was overrated, underappreciated, delicious, awful, in a beautiful (or ugly) bottle, or whatever, I asked them to say so and have passed along those impressions, as well as my own based on working every day with myriad wines, wine servers, and wine drinkers.

Andrea's Kitchen Fridge Survivor™ and Kitchen Countertop Survivor™ Grades

I think a great many people hesitate to open wine for everyday meals because they won't know what to do with leftovers. No wonder! It's wildly expensive to pour out unfinished wine. And the frustration of wondering and worrying whether your wine's over the hill, *after* the intimidation of shopping for the wine, is more than most of us can be bothered with.

Since I couldn't stand the idea of people pretty much giving up on wine with dinner, and "How long will it keep after I open it?" is one of the most common wine questions I'm asked, I decided it was time to give some real answers.

I'm a bit embarrassed to admit that I began to test how long wines hold up in the everyday kitchen not because I was on a quest to answer these big-picture questions but because I kept tasting some impressive leftovers. In my sommelier and writing duties, I taste multiple wines often, and rarely with enough company to finish them the day they're opened, or even the next. In going back to the leftovers—to see if they were as good (or as disappointing) as I'd remembered—I got some amazing surprises. Far more often than you'd think, the good wines stayed that way for days. Even more astonishing, some of the wines that were initially underwhelming actually came around and started tasting better after being open for a while (in the same way that some cheeses need to sit out at room temperature to show their best flavor or a pot of chili can taste better after a day or two in the fridge).

And thus were born the Kitchen Fridge Survivor™ and Kitchen Countertop Survivor™ experiments. I hope the grades will give you confidence to enjoy wine with dinner more often, or even multiple wines with one meal (I frequently do), knowing that you can have tastes or just a glass of many wines, over several days, without the wines going "bad."

To test the wines' open-bottle longevity, I handled them as follows:

Whites—Recorked with the original cork (whether natural or synthetic). Placed in the fridge.

Reds—Recorked with the original cork. Placed on the kitchen counter.

Sparkling wines—Opened carefully without popping (popping depletes carbonation faster). Closed with a "clamshell" stopper designed for sparkling wines—sold in housewares departments and sometimes wine stores. Placed in the fridge.

Bag-in-box wines—These were not tested, because the airtight bag inside keeps the wine from oxidizing as it's consumed—one of the major virtues of this type of packaging.

The same process was repeated after each daily retaste, until the wine's taste declined noticeably. As I said, some wines actually taste better after a day or two. They were handled the same way.

There's no science to this. My kitchen is just a regular kitchen, probably much like yours. Hopefully these grades, which showed the wines' staying power in an everyday setting, will give you the confidence to enjoy wine more often with your everyday meals:

Avg = a "one-day wine," which tastes noticeably less fresh the next day. This doesn't mean the wine is less worthy, just less sturdy— so plan accordingly by inviting someone to share it with you.

B = holds its freshness for 2–3 days after opening

B+ = holds *and gets better* over 2–3 days after opening

A = has a 3- to 4-day "freshness window"

A+ = holds *and gets better* over 3–4 days

To learn how to lengthen the survival rate of your wine leftovers, see "Handling Wine Leftovers" in the *Great Wine Made Simple* Mini-Course chapter of this book.

Your Notes

Would you join my tasting panel? Of course, I would love for you to record your wine impressions and share them with me for the next edition of the *Immer Guide* (you may do so at *www.greatwinemadesimple.com*). But even if you are not the survey type, do it for yourself. Whether you're at home or in a restaurant, the guide is a handy place to keep notes on what you drank, what you paid, what food you had with it, and what you thought. Don't you hate it when you've enjoyed a wine, then can't remember the name when you want to buy it again?

A Few Questions About the Wine Entries

How Were Wines Chosen for Inclusion in the Book?

The wines represented are top sellers in stores and restaurants nationally, in each style category. I featured mostly the top-selling premium, cork-finished wines because they outsell generics overall. However, I did include the dominant jug and bag-in-box wines, and my tasters did not ignore them. Don't see one of your favorite wines? Keep in mind that both popularity and availability of specific wines can vary a lot regionally, so a big brand in your area may not have the same sales and presence in other markets. This is especially true with local wines—for example, the Texas Chenin Blanc or New York Riesling that's on every table in your neck of the woods may not even be distributed in the next state. I also included worthy write-ins—those with decent availability that got the highest number of positive mentions from my tasters, although in some cases that availability may be skewed heavily to restaurants. Why? you ask. Many buyers have told me of their frustration at seeing the wines they'd like to purchase available only in restaurants. It's a phenomenon that became increasingly common in the wine boom of the 1990s. Simply put, wineries with a limited supply often concentrate on restaurant lists because of the image enhancement they can offer—good food, nice setting, and (usually) fewer competing selections than in a shop.

Why No Vintage Years?

This guide deals with the top-selling wines in the market, and so, for the most part, the year available in stores and restaurants is the winery's current release.

But I am also making a philosophical statement about vintages for the wines in the guide, and it is this: I believe that the leading wines in the market *should* be fairly consistent from one year to the next so that consumers, and the retail and restaurant wine buyers who serve them, need not sweat the vintage, as long as it's current and fresh. There are certain wine categories where vintage is a bigger consideration—among them expensive California reds, French Bordeaux and Burgundy, and upscale Italian reds. But even with these, if you do not intend to cellar the wines (very few buyers do), vintage isn't so critical. A few of the tasters mentioned the vintage issue, but most were comfortable with my approach.

> **IMMER INSIGHT**: Ninety-five percent of the quality wines on the market are meant to be consumed within one to three years of the harvest (the vintage date on the label), while they are young, fresh, and in good condition. Most wines do not get better with age, so why wait?

Can You Really Define "Outstanding" Wine?

Indeed I can. We all can. Broadly, it is a wine that captures your attention. It could be the scent, the taste, the texture, or all three that make you say first, "Mmm. . . ," and then, "Wow" as your impressions register in the moment, in the context of all your prior experience and the price you paid. If it all sounds very personal and subjective, you're exactly right—it is. That is why I felt a guide like this, showcasing the impressions of real-world buyers, was so important. The fact that the wines herein are big sellers is already an endorsement. The details put each wine in context—of price, similar-style wines, occasion, and whatever else buyers feel is important. No other wine buying guide does that.

Who Are the Tasters? You

Over a six-month period in 2002–2003 I collected tasting data on my website from thousands of American wine buyers—trade colleagues (retail and restaurant buyers, sommeliers, hoteliers, chefs, waiters, importers, and distributors). The trade buyers included most major chain restaurants and stores, chefs, and my master sommelier colleagues, among others. I also recruit tasters through my restaurant guests, my students at The French Culinary Institute, and of course the friends and family network, including family members I didn't even know I had until I found them on the e-mail trail. I originally thought consumers would be less keen than trade to share their wine opinions, but I was wrong. As noted previously, consumers account for more than seventy percent of the responses. Although I don't purposely exclude anyone, I do review every survey returned for signs of ballot stuffing from winery companies and eliminate all suspicious responses (there were literally just a couple).

Why Do These Tasters' Opinions Matter?

Clearly, this guide for everyone takes an utterly populist perspective that's different from every other wine publication on the market—and that is exactly what I intend. I think the honest assessments and perspective of consumers who have to pay their own money for wine (while wine journalists rarely do), and the restaurateurs and retailers who serve them, are extremely important and helpful—because they're the real world. (With so little of that perspective in the marketplace, can it be any wonder that wine is barely a blip on Americans' cultural radar screen?) I am not dismissing the value of, and expertise behind, the leading critics' scoring reports. But I do think they often further the notion that there are haves and have-nots in the wine world: the 90+-rated "good stuff" that none of us can afford; and the rest—the wines we see every day whose lower scores seem bad by comparison. That perspective is perhaps valuable to a tiny, elite group of luxury wine buyers. But for what I call the OTC (other than collectors) market, which comprises the bulk of the nation's buyers (including just about everyone I know), this dichotomy leaves us feeling utterly insecure about our own taste and budget, skeptical about the quality of the selection at the stores and restaurants we frequent, and self-conscious about our (legitimate) desire for value for the money—in the vernacular, good, cheap wine. If I've achieved my goal, this guide's real-world information will give you a renewed sense of confidence in your own taste and some great word-of-mouth guidance on new wines to try that are actually available where you shop and dine. Enjoy!

MY GUEST INSIDERS' VIEW OF WINE MARKET TRENDS

By Tylor Field III

DIRECTOR OF BEVERAGE OPERATIONS,
MORTON'S OF CHICAGO, INC.

Morton's, The Steakhouse is the world's leading fine-dining steakhouse restaurant company, with 66 restaurants in 27 states, and in Hong Kong, Singapore, and Canada. We currently serve our guests more than 750,000 bottles of wine yearly. As I sit in the trenches tasting and selecting wine for our guests to enjoy, I am seeing two very dramatic shifts—new global flavor trends from importers and the rapidly expanding domestic "value sector."

As recently as five years ago French, Italian, and American vintners were focused on the luxury wine sector—hoping to join the ranks of so-called "cult wines" courtesy of a high score from such magazines as *Wine Spectator* and Robert M. Parker, Jr.'s *Wine Advocate*. Everybody wanted to be the Lamborghini of his or her sector and the boom economy seemed to be able to support this. It was a very simple business model: sell one bottle for $200 rather than four bottles for $50.00. People will think it's better (because of the higher price) and we can make a higher profit and not make as much wine. At the same time, wine producers from Australia, New Zealand, Chile, Argentina, and South Africa were operating on a different plane—focusing on the value sector. They were putting wine on the shelf equal to the quality of their American and European counterparts, but at lower prices. Then two years ago, the economy stumbled during the most prolific time ever in American wine production. We are now in a glut situation that has forced wine makers to cut their prices—I'm seeing "fire sale" prices on great domestic wines, as well as ever-better deals in the value categories. Here are some specific ways you can take advantage of this phenomenon:

1. If buying U.S. red wines on a wine list, look for the 1998 vintage, whose lukewarm press was over-blown, but hard to overcome. As a result, there are lots of good wines out there at "fire sale" prices. Try the Franciscan Meritage, J. Lohr "Hilltop" Cabernet, Miner Cabernet, or the Rodney Strong Alexander's Crown Cabernet.

2. Australian Shiraz is, to me, what Merlot was in the 1980's—"the hot new thing." While Merlot was driven primarily as an easy-drinking, versatile alternative to Cabernet, I think people now crave more flavors, and Shiraz's spiciness fits the bill. The sales of Shiraz from Australia in Morton's have shown double-digit growth over the past three years. The values out of Australia are still outstanding. Rosemount, Greg Norman, Penfolds, and Wolf-Blass all still are impressive for their value.

3. Tempranillo and Grenache from Spain and Carmenere from Chile are being re-discovered as alternatives for the Cabernet/Merlot drinker. With taste preferences in the U.S. becoming more adventurous, these dry reds, which are full of flavor for the money, are becoming popular. Good value brands are Solaz (Tempranillo) from Osborne and Casillero del Diablo (Carmenere) from Concha y Toro, Primus (Carmenere/Cab/Merlot) from Franciscan's Veramonte brand, and almost any red wine you can currently find out of the small viticultural area of Priorato, Spain. These mainly Grenache-based wines are huge. Try finding a value brand called Onix by Vinicola del Priorato. Other great producers are Alvaro Palacios and Mas Martinet.

In closing, it has always been my dream to help increase the passion for wine of the average American. If we continue to make it an expensive and exclusive endeavor we'll see declining consumption trends. I have had a great time sharing these values with Morton's guests and I urge you to branch out and start trying some of these gems, too.

Best wishes!

By Greg Duppler
SENIOR VICE PRESIDENT, TARGET CORPORATION

The interest level in wine and food pairings is a growing trend across all generations. Gen X, Y, and Baby Boomers have become much more passionate about understanding how wine and food complement each other. In the past people considered wine choice as an independent decision, but as wine is becoming increasingly popular among the younger generations, this concept has changed. No longer are we tied to enjoying wine exclusively with elite gourmet meals, but rather with pizza, backyard grilling, snacks, and fruit. Wine pairing has truly gone casual—gatherings of friends at wine bars, or party hosts providing a multitude of inexpensive high quality wines to serve with easy appetizer fare are more popular than going off old set standards like "red wine with meat." Whether Riesling for the entire meal or a full bodied, oaky Chardonnay to complement a red meat dish—buyers are embracing the idea that their favorite varietals can provide enjoyment with all different types of foods.

In exploring the new wines available we have seen an explosion with Australian wines in the last 2-plus years. These have come on fast and furious as guests have recognized that the flavor is superior and the price point far lower than expected for the quality. These wines also provide the cachet of drinking imported wines. This import prominence is becoming more of a norm, with wines from Chile, Spain, and New Zealand as the next-up trends. This influence has added a whole new awareness in the guests' eyes of imported wines. Those once thought to be exclusive or high priced are now considered trendy and are often priced under $10/bottle. And even top bottles from these countries can be enjoyed in the $50–$80 range for special occasions—a relative value compared to the classic wine regions.

Our goal at Target has always been to be ahead of the trends and to provide this awareness to our guests with their shopping experience. As the wine industry adjusts to these new influences, you will see the top retail establishments and restaurants accommodating these needs through innovative merchandising and product offerings. And all wine lovers will be able to enjoy the rewards!

MOST POPULAR WINES—REFLECTING BOTH TASTE AND VALUE FOR THE MONEY

25 Most Popular Whites*
Based on Taste and Value

Name	Wtd. Avg. T/V Score**	Price Category
Robert Mondavi Fumé Blanc, Calif.	29	$$
Geyser Peak Chard., Calif.	29	$$
Gunderloch Riesling Jean Baptiste, Germany	29	$$
Au Bon Climat Chardonnay, Calif.	29	$$$
Chalone Central Coast Chard., Calif.	29	$$$
Domaine Carneros Brut, Calif.	29	$$$
Edna Valley Estate Chard., Calif.	28	$$
Benziger Chard., Calif.	27	$$
Fetzer Echo Ridge Riesling, Calif.	27	$
Buena Vista Sauv. Blanc, Calif.	27	$
Ferrari-Carano Fumé Blanc, Calif.	27	$$
Michel Redde Pouilly-Fumé, France	27	$$
Macrostie Chard., Calif.	27	$$$
Strub Niersteiner Paterberg Riesling Spätlese, Germany	27	$$
Charles Heidsieck Brut, France	27	$$$$
Roederer Estate Sparkling, Calif.	27	$$$
Château Ste. Michelle Riesling, Wash.	27	$

*To find the complete tasting notes for each wine, refer to the alphabetical winery index in the back of the book.

**Scores were rounded off. Wines are listed in order of actual score ranking. The number of wines in each "Most Popular" listing reflects the overall number of wines in the category. So our "Top Whites" list numbers 25, while the Top Rieslings ranking shows just five entries. It's also a fairly close reflection of each category's sales and prominence in the fine wine market overall.

Name	Wtd. Avg. T/V Score*	Price Category
Kendall-Jackson Vintner's Reserve Riesling, Calif.	26	$
Kenwood Sauv. Blanc, Calif.	26	$
Gallo of Sonoma Chardonnay, Calif.	26	$
Domaine Chandon Brut Classic, Sparkling, Calif.	26	$$
Hogue Fumé Blanc, Wash.	26	$
Robert Mondavi Private Selection Chard., Calif.	26	$
Penfolds Semillon/Chardonnay, Australia	26	$
Frog's Leap Sauv. Blanc, Calif.	26	$$

25 Most Popular Reds
Based on Taste and Value

Name	Wtd. Avg. T/V Score*	Price Category
Selvapiana Chianti Rufina, Italy	29	$$
Casa Lapostolle Classic Cab. Sauv., Chile	29	$
Los Vascos Cab. Sauv., Chile	29	$
Château Ste. Michelle Columbia Valley Merlot, Wash.	29	$$
Martinez, Faustino Rioja Crianza, Spain	28	$
Beringer Founders' Estate Pinot Noir, Calif.	27	$
Frescobaldi Chianti Rufina Riserva, Italy	27	$$$
La Vieille Ferme Côtes du Ventaux, France	27	$
St. Francis Sonoma Zin, Calif.	27	$$
Dry Creek Reserve Zin., Calif.	27	$$$
MacMurray Ranch Pinot Noir, Calif.	27	$$$
Rosemount G-S-M (Grenache-Syrah-Mourvedre), Aust.	27	$$
Kenwood Pinot Noir, Calif.	27	$$
Reynolds Shiraz, Aust.	27	$
Columbia Crest Cab. Sauv., Wash.	26	$
Cristom Pinot Noir, Oregon	26	$$$
Mt. Veeder Cab. Sauv., Calif.	26	$$$$
Stag's Leap Wine Cellars Napa Cab. Sauv., Calif.	26	$$$$
Au Bon Climat Pinot Noir, Calif.	26	$$$
Gallo of Sonoma Merlot, Calif.	26	$
Etude Pinot Noir, Calif.	26	$$$$

Name		
Rodney Strong Merlot, Calif.	26	$$
Château Larose-Trintaudon, Bordeaux, France	26	$$
Santa Rita 120 Cab. Sauv., Chile	26	$
Ridge Geyserville (Zin.), Calif.	26	$$$

Best of the Big 6 Grapes

Name	Wtd. Avg. T/V Score*	Price Category
5 Most Popular Rieslings		
Gunderloch Riesling Kabinett Jean Baptiste, Germany	29	$$
Fetzer Echo Ridge Riesling, Calif.	27	$
Strub Niersteiner Riesling Spätlese, Germany	27	$$
Château Ste. Michelle Riesling, Wash.	27	$
Kendall-Jackson Vintner's Reserve Riesling, Calif.	26	$
10 Most Popular Sauvignon/Fumé Blancs		
Robert Mondavi Fumé Blanc, Calif.	29	$$
Buena Vista Sauv. Blanc, Calif.	27	$
Ferrari-Carano Fumé Blanc, Calif.	27	$$
Michel Redde Pouilly-Fumé, France	27	$$
Kenwood Sauv. Blanc, Calif.	26	$
Hogue Fumé Blanc, Wash.	26	$
Frog's Leap Sauv. Blanc, Calif.	26	$$
Brancott Rsv. Sauv. Blanc., New Zealand	25	$$
Cloudy Bay Sauv. Blanc, New Zealand	25	$$$
Lucien Crochet Sancerre, France	25	$$
30 Most Popular Chardonnays		
Geyser Peak Chard., Calif.	29	$$
Au Bon Climat Chard., Calif.	29	$$$
Chalone Central Coast Chard., Calif.	29	$$$
Edna Valley Vineyard Chard., Calif.	28	$$
Benziger Chard., Calif.	28	$$
Macrostie Chard., Calif.	27	$$$
Gallo of Sonoma Chard., Calif.	26	$
Robert Mondavi Private Selection Chard., Calif.	26	$
Ferrari-Carano Sonoma Chard., Calif.	26	$$$
Grgich Hills Chard., Calif.	26	$$$$

*Scores were rounded off. Wines are listed in order of actual ranking.

Name	Wtd. Avg. T/V Score*	Price Category
J. Lohr Riverstone Chard., Calif.	26	$$
Robert Mondavi Napa Chard., Calif.	26	$$$
Cakebread Napa Chard., Calif.	25	$$$$
Louis Jadot Pouilly-Fuissé, France	25	$$
Estancia Pinnacles Chard., Calif.	25	$$
Hess Select Chard., Calif.	25	$
Meridian Chard., Calif.	25	$
La Crema Chard., Calif.	25	$$
Clos du Bois Chard., Calif.	24	$$
Columbia Crest Chard., Wash.	24	$
Joseph Drouhin Pouilly-Fuissé, France	24	$$
Kendall-Jackson Grand Reserve Chard., Calif.	24	$$
Macon-Lugny Les Charmes, France	24	$
Penfolds Koonunga Hill Chard., Australia	24	$
R. H. Phillips Dunnigan Hills Chard., Calif.	24	$
Sonoma-Cutrer Russian River Ranches Chard., Calif.	24	$$
St. Francis Sonoma Chard., Calif.	24	$
Louis Jadot Macon Blanc, France	23	$
R. H. Phillips Toasted Head Chard., Calif.	23	$$
Beringer Napa Chard., Calif.	23	$$

10 Most Popular Pinot Noirs

Name	Wtd. Avg. T/V Score*	Price Category
Beringer Founders' Estate Pinot Noir, Calif.	27	$
MacMurray Ranch Pinot Noir, Calif.	27	$$$
Kenwood Pinot Noir, Calif.	27	$$
Cristom Willamette Pinot Noir, Oregon	26	$$$
Au Bon Climat Pinot Noir, Calif.	26	$$$
Etude Pinot Noir, Calif.	26	$$$$
Frei Brothers Reserve Pinot Noir, Calif.	26	$$
Duck Pond Pinot Noir, Oregon	25	$
Cambria Pinot Noir, Calif.	24	$$$
Indigo Hills Pinot Noir, Calif.	24	$

20 Most Popular Merlots

Name	Wtd. Avg. T/V Score*	Price Category
Chât. Ste. Michelle Columbia Valley Merlot, Wash.	29	$$
Gallo of Sonoma Merlot, Calif.	26	$
Rodney Strong Merlot, Calif.	26	$$
Franciscan Oakville Estate Merlot, Calif.	25	$$$

Clos du Bois Sonoma Merlot, Calif.	25	$$
Fetzer Eagle Peak Merlot, Calif.	25	$
Bogle Merlot, Calif.	24	$$
Christian Moueix Merlot, France	24	$
Sutter Home Merlot, Calif.	24	$
Markham Merlot, Calif.	24	$$$
Trinchero Mario's Reserve Merlot, Calif.	24	$$
Casa Lapostolle Classic Merlot, Chile	23	$
Duckhorn Napa Merlot, Calif.	23	$$$$
St. Francis Sonoma Merlot, Calif.	23	$$$
Shafer Merlot, Calif.	23	$$$$
Beringer Founders' Estate Merlot, Calif.	23	$
Columbia Crest Merlot, Wash.	23	$
Frog's Leap Merlot, Calif.	23	$$$
Blackstone Merlot, Calif.	22	$$
Lindemans Bin 40 Merlot, Australia	22	$

30 Most Popular Cabernet Sauvignons and Blends

Casa Lapostolle Cab. Sauv., Chile	29	$
Los Vascos Cab. Sauv., Chile	29	$
Columbia Crest Cab. Sauv., Wash.	26	$
Mt. Veeder Napa Cab. Sauv., Calif.	26	$$$$
Stag's Leap Wine Cellars Napa Cab. Sauv., Calif.	26	$$$$
Château Larose-Trintaudon Bordeaux, France	26	$$
Santa Rita 120 Cab. Sauv., Chile	26	$
Black Opal Cab. Sauv., Australia	25	$
Gallo of Sonoma Cab. Sauv., Calif.	25	$
Escudo Rojo, Chile	25	$$
Joseph Phelps Napa Cab. Sauv., Calif.	25	$$$$
Chât. Ste. Michelle Columbia Valley Cab. Sauv., Wash.	25	$$
Robert Mondavi Napa Cab. Sauv., Calif.	24	$$$
Penfolds Bin 389 Cabernet/Shiraz, Australia	24	$$$
Château Gloria Bordeaux, France	24	$$$$
Raymond Napa Cab. Sauv., Calif.	24	$$
Rosemount Diamond Label Cab. Sauv./ Merlot, Australia	24	$
Simi Sonoma Cab. Sauv., Calif.	24	$$
Dynamite Cab. Sauv., Calif.	24	$$$
Château St. Jean Cinq Cepages, Calif.	24	$$$$
Beringer Knights Valley Cab. Sauv., Calif.	24	$$$

*Scores were rounded off. Wines are listed in order of actual ranking.

Name	Wtd. Avg. T/V Score*	Price Cate- gory
Sterling Vineyards Napa Cab. Sauv., Calif.	24	$$$
Rosemount Diamond Label Cab. Sauv., Australia	24	$
Rodney Strong Cab. Sauv., Calif.	23	$$
Estancia Cab. Sauv., Calif.	23	$$
Château Gruaud-Larose Bordeaux, France	23	$$$$
Arrowood Cab. Sauv., Calif.	23	$$$$
Franciscan Napa Cab. Sauv., Calif.	23	$$$
Greg Norman Cabernet/Merlot, Aust.	23	$$
Château Gruaud-Larose, Bordeaux, France	23	$$$$

Best of the Rest

Name	Wtd. Avg. T/V Score*	Price Cate- gory
10 Most Popular Champagnes and Sparkling Wines		
Domaine Carneros Brut, Calif.	29	$$$
Charles Heidsieck Brut Champ., France	27	$$$$
Roederer Estate Sparkling, Calif.	27	$$$
Domaine Chandon Brut Classic Spklg., Calif.	26	$$
Domaine Ste. Michelle Cuveé Brut Spklg., Wash.	26	$$
Taittinger Brut La Francaise NV Champ., France	25	$$$$
Iron Horse Wedding Cuvée Brut Spklg., Calif.	25	$$$
Mumm Cuvée Napa Brut Prestige Sparkling, Calif.	25	$$
Bollinger Special Cuveé Brut Champ., France	24	$$$$
Mionetto Prosecco Spklg., Italy	24	$$
5 Most Popular Pinot Grigio/Gris		
Alois Lageder Pinot Grigio, Italy	24	$$
Trimbach Pinot Gris, Alsace, France	23	$$
Bella Sera Pinot Grigio, Italy	22	$
Woodbridge (Robert Mondavi) Pinot Grigio, California	21	$
King Estate Pinot Gris, Oregon	21	$$

5 Most Popular Other Whites

Penfolds Semillon/Chardonnay, Australia	26	$
Pepperwood Grove Viognier, Calif.	26	$
Fetzer Echo Ridge Gewürztraminer, Calif.	25	$
Columbia Crest Semillon/Chard., Wash.	24	$
Hugel Gewürztraminer, Alsace, France	23	$$

10 Most Popular Italian and Spanish Reds

Selvapiana Chianti Rufina, Italy	29	$$
Martinez, Faustino Rioja Crianza, Spain	28	$
Frescobaldi Chianti Rufina Riserva, Italy	27	$$$
Alvaro Palacios Les Terrasses Priorat, Spain	25	$$$
Banfi Brunello di Montalcino, Italy	25	$$$$
Falesco Vitiano, Italy	25	$
Montecillo Rioja Crianza, Spain	24	$
Santa Cristina Sangiovese, Antinori, Italy	24	$
Ruffino Chianti, Italy	24	$
Montecillo Rioja Reserva, Spain	24	$$

10 Most Popular Shiraz/Syrahs and Rhône-Style Reds

La Vieille Ferme Côtes du Ventoux, France	27	$
Rosemount G-S-M, Aust.	27	$$
Reynolds Shiraz, Aust.	27	$
Hill of Content Grenache/Shiraz, Aust.	26	$
Rosemount Diamond Label Shiraz, Aust.	25	$
Rosemount Diamond Label Shiraz/ Cab. Sauv., Aust.	25	$
Château La Nerthe Chât.-du-Pape, France	24	$$$$
E&M Guigal Côtes du Rhone, France	24	$$
Fetzer Valley Oaks Syrah, Calif.	24	$
Chât. de Beaucastel Chât.-du-Pape, France	23	$$$$

10 Most Popular Red Zinfandels

St. Francis Sonoma Zin., Calif.	27	$$
Dry Creek Reserve Zin., Calif.	27	$$$
Ridge Geyserville (Zin.), Calif.	26	$$$
Seghesio Sonoma Zin., Calif.	25	$$
Beaulieu Vineyard (BV) Coastal Zin., Calif.	24	$
Grgich Hills Sonoma Zin., Calif.	24	$$$
Monteviña Amador Zin., Calif.	24	$
Robert Mondavi Private Selection Zin., Calif.	24	$
Gallo of Sonoma Frei Ranch Zin., Calif.	24	$$
Ravenswood Vintners Blend Zin., Calif.	23	$

*Scores were rounded off. Wines are listed in order of actual ranking.

TOP TASTE RANKINGS

Top 30 White Wines by Taste

Name	Taste Score*	Price Category
Robert Mondavi Napa Fumé Blanc, Calif.	29	$$
Chalone Central Coast Chard., Calif.	29	$$$
Geyser Peak Chard., Calif.	29	$$
Grgich Hills Chard., Calif.	29	$$$$
Bollinger Special Cuveé Brut Champagne, France	29	$$$$
Domaine Carneros Brut Sparkling, Calif.	29	$$$
Gunderloch Riesling Kabinett Jean Baptiste, Germany	29	$$
Au Bon Climat Chardonnay, Calif.	29	$$$
Macrostie Chard., Calif.	29	$$$
Cakebread Napa Chard., Calif.	28	$$$$
Edna Valley Chard., Calif.	28	$$
Taittinger Brut La Française Champagne, France	27	$$$$
Fetzer Echo Ridge Riesling, Calif.	27	$
Cloudy Bay Sauv. Blanc, New Zealand	27	$$$
Ferrari-Carano Fumé Blanc, Calif.	27	$$
Benziger Chard., Calif.	27	$$
Ferrari-Carano Sonoma Chard., Calif.	27	$$$
Robert Mondavi Napa Chard., Calif.	27	$$$
Pol Roger Blanc de Chardonnay Champ., France	27	$$$$
Strub Niersteiner Riesling Spätlese, Germany	27	$$
Cakebread Sauv. Blanc, Calif.	27	$$$
Gallo of Sonoma Chard., Calif.	27	$
Perrier-Joüet Grand Brut Champ. France	26	$$$$
Château Ste. Michelle Riesling, Wash.	26	$
Louis Jadot Pouilly-Fuissé, France	26	$$
Roederer Estate Sparkling, Calif.	26	$$$
Domaine Chandon Brut Classic Sparkling Calif.	26	$$

Hogue Fumé Blanc, Wash.	26	$
Lucien Crochet Sancerre, France	26	$$
Robert Mondavi Private Selection Chard., Calif.	26	$

Top 30 Red Wines by Taste

Name	Taste Score*	Price Category
Cristom Pinot Noir, Oregon	29	$$$
Selvapiana Chianti Rufina, Italy	29	$$
Los Vascos Cab. Sauv., Chile	29	$
Château La Nerthe Chât.-du-Pape, France	29	$$$
Dry Creek Reserve Zin., Calif.	29	$$
Au Bon Climat Pinot Noir, Calif.	29	$$$
MacMurray Ranch Pinot Noir, Calif.	29	$$$
Château St. Jean Cinq Cepages, Calif.	29	$$$$
Château Ste. Michelle Columbia Valley Merlot, Wash.	29	$$
Ridge Geyserville (Zin.), Calif.	29	$$$
Etude Pinot Noir, Calif.	28	$$$$
Franciscan Merlot, Calif.	28	$$$
Heitz Napa Cab. Sauv., Calif.	28	$$$$
Mt. Veeder Napa Cab. Sauv., Calif.	28	$$$$
Stag's Leap Wine Cellars Napa Cab. Sauv., Calif.	28	$$$$
Shafer Merlot, Calif.	28	$$$$
St. Francis Sonoma Zin., Calif.	28	$$
Banfi Brunello di Montalcino, Italy	27	$$$$
Joseph Phelps Napa Cab. Sauv., Calif.	27	$$$$
Casa Lapostolle Classic Cab. Sauv., Chile	27	$
Château Larose-Trintaudon Bordeaux, France	27	$$
Santa Rita 120 Cab. Sauv., Chile	27	$
Markham Merlot, Calif.	27	$$$
Far Niente Cab. Sauv., Calif.	27	$$$$
La Vieille Ferme Côtes du Ventoux, France	27	$
Elk Cove Pinot Noir, Oregon	26	$$
Archery Summit Arcus Estate Pinot Noir, Oregon	26	$$$$
St. Francis Sonoma Merlot, Calif.	26	$$

*Scores were rounded off. Wines are listed in order of actual ranking.

Name	Taste Score*	Price Category
Château Gruaud-Larose Bordeaux, France	26	$$$$
Alvaro Palacios Les Terrasses Priorat, Spain	26	$$$

Best of the Big 6 Grapes

Name	Taste Score*	Price Category
Top 10 Rieslings by Taste		
Gunderloch Riesling Kabinett Jean Baptiste, Germany	29	$$
Fetzer Echo Ridge Riesling, Calif.	27	$
Strub Niersteiner Paterberg Riesling Spätlese, Germany	27	$$
Château Ste. Michelle Riesling, Wash.	26	$
Kendall-Jackson Vintners Rsv. Riesling, Calif.	26	$
Trimbach Riesling, Alsace, France	24	$$
Beringer Riesling, Calif.	24	$
Columbia Winery Riesling, Wash.	24	$
Jekel Riesling, Calif.	24	$
Schmitt Soehne Riesling, Germany	24	$
Top 10 Sauvignon/Fumé Blancs by Taste		
Didier Dagueneau Silex Pouilly-Fumé, France	29	$$$
Michel Redde Pouilly-Fumé, France	29	$$
Robert Mondavi Napa Fumé Blanc, Calif.	29	$$
Cloudy Bay Sauv. Blanc., New Zealand	27	$$$
Ferrari-Carano Fumé Blanc, Calif.	27	$$
Cakebread Sauv. Blanc, Calif.	27	$$$
Hogue Fumé Blanc, Wash.	26	$
Lucien Crochet Sancerre, France	26	$$
Brancott Rsv. Sauv. Blanc., New Zealand	26	$$
Villa Maria Private Bin Sauv. Blanc, New Zealand	26	$
Top 30 Chardonnays by Taste		
Chalone Central Coast Chard., Calif.	29	$$$
Geyser Peak Chard., Calif.	29	$$
Grgich Hills Chard., Calif.	29	$$$$
Au Bon Climat Chard., Calif.	29	$$$
Macrostie Chard., Calif.	29	$$$
Cakebread Napa Chard., Calif.	28	$$$$

Edna Valley Vineyard Chard., Calif.	28	$$
Benziger Chard., Calif.	27	$$
Ferrari-Carano Sonoma Chard., Calif.	27	$$$
Robert Mondavi Napa Chard., Calif.	27	$$$
Gallo of Sonoma Chard., Calif.	27	$
Louis Jadot Pouilly-Fuissé, France	26	$$
Robert Mondavi Private Selection Chard., Calif.	26	$
La Crema Chard., Calif.	25	$$
Sonoma-Cutrer Russian River Ranches Chard., Calif.	25	$$
Beringer Napa Chard., Calif.	24	$$
Clos du Bois Sonoma Chard., Calif.	24	$$
Estancia Pinnacles Chard., Calif.	24	$$
Hess Select Chard., Calif.	24	$
J. Lohr Riverstone Chard., Calif.	24	$$
Jordan Chard., Calif.	24	$$$
Joseph Drouhin Pouilly-Fuissé, France	24	$$
Kendall-Jackson Grand Rsv. Chard., Calif.	24	$$
Kenwood Chard., Calif.	24	$$
Macon-Lugny Les Charmes, France	24	$
Penfolds Koonunga Hill Chard., Aust.	24	$
Rodney Strong Sonoma Chard., Calif.	24	$$
St. Francis Sonoma Chard., Calif.	24	$
Sterling Vineyards North Coast Chard., Calif.	24	$$
Talbott (Robert) Sleepy Hollow Vineyard Chard., Calif.	24	$$$$

Top 10 Pinot Noirs by Taste

Cristom Willamette Pinot Noir, Oregon	29	$$$
Au Bon Climat Pinot Noir, Calif.	29	$$$
MacMurray Ranch Pinot Noir, Calif.	29	$$$
Etude Pinot Noir, Calif.	28	$$$$
Frei Brothers Reserve Pinot Noir, Calif.	27	$$
Elk Cove Pinot Noir, Oregon	26	$$
Archery Summit Arcus Estate Pinot Noir, Oregon	26	$$$$
David Bruce Central Coast Pinot Noir, Calif.	25	$$$
Beringer Founders' Estate Pinot Noir, Calif.	24	$
Byron Santa Maria Valley Pinot Noir, Calif.	24	$$$

*Scores were rounded off. Wines are listed in order of actual ranking.

Name	Taste Score*	Price Category
Top 20 Merlots by Taste		
Chât. Ste. Michelle Columbia Valley Merlot, Wash.	29	$$
Franciscan Oakville Estate Merlot, Calif.	28	$$$
Shafer Merlot, Calif.	28	$$$$
Markham Merlot, Calif.	27	$$$
St. Francis Sonoma Merlot, Calif.	26	$$$
Rodney Strong Merlot, Calif.	26	$$
Duckhorn Napa Merlot, Calif.	25	$$$$
Bogle Merlot, Calif.	24	$$
Clos du Bois Sonoma Merlot, Calif.	24	$$
Frog's Leap Merlot, Calif.	24	$$$
Gallo of Sonoma Merlot, Calif.	24	$
Stag's Leap Wine Cellars Napa Merlot, Calif.	24	$$$$
Trinchero Mario's Reserve Merlot, Calif.	24	$$
Christian Moueix Merlot, France	23	$
Fetzer Eagle Peak Merlot, Calif.	23	$
Casa Lapostolle Classic Merlot, Chile	23	$
Sterling Vineyards Napa Merlot, Napa	23	$$$
Blackstone Merlot, Calif.	22	$
Lindemans Bin 40 Merlot, Aust.	22	$
Ravenswood Vintners Blend Merlot, Calif.	22	$$
Top 30 Cabernet Sauvignons and Blends by Taste		
Los Vascos Cab. Sauv., Chile	29	$
Château St. Jean Cinq Cepages, Calif.	29	$$$$
Heitz Napa Cab. Sauv., Calif.	28	$$$$
Mt. Veeder Napa Cab. Sauv., Calif.	28	$$$$
Stag's Leap Wine Cellars Napa Cab. Sauv., Calif.	28	$$$$
Joseph Phelps Napa Cab. Sauv., Calif.	27	$$$$
Casa Lapostolle Classic Cab. Sauv., Chile	27	$
Château Larose-Trintaudon Bordeaux, France	27	$$
Santa Rita 120 Cab. Sauv., Chile	27	$
Far Niente Cab. Sauv., Calif.	27	$$$$
Château Gruaud-Larose Bordeaux, France	26	$$$$
Arrowood Cab. Sauv., Calif.	25	$$$$
Penfolds Bin 389 Cabernet/Shiraz, Australia	25	$$$
Beringer Knights Valley Cab. Sauv., Calif.	25	$$$
Silver Oak Alexander Valley Cab. Sauv., Calif.	25	$$$$

Cakebread Napa Cab. Sauv., Calif.	25	$$$$
Sterling Vineyards Napa Cab. Sauv., Calif.	25	$$$
Gallo of Sonoma Cab. Sauv., Calif.	25	$
Robert Mondavi Napa Cab. Sauv., Calif.	25	$$$
Columbia Crest Cab. Sauv., Wash.	25	$
Black Opal Cab. Sauv., Australia	24	$
Cain Cuvée Bordeaux Style Red, Calif.	24	$$$
Dynamite Cab. Sauv., Calif.	24	$$$
Château Gloria, Bordeaux, France	24	$$$$
Franciscan Napa Cab. Sauv., Calif.	24	$$
Groth Napa Cab. Sauv., Calif.	24	$$$$
Raymond Napa Cab. Sauv., Calif.	24	$$
Rodney Strong Sonoma Cab. Sauv., Calif.	24	$$
Simi Sonoma Cab. Sauv., Calif.	24	$$
Escudo Rojo, Baron Philippe de Rothschild, Chile	24	$$

Best of the Rest

Name	Taste Score*	Price Category
Top 5 Champagnes and Sparkling Wines by Taste		
Bollinger Special Cuveé Brut Champ., France	29	$$$$
Domaine Carneros Brut Spklg., Calif.	29	$$$
Taittinger Brut La Francaise NV Champ., France	27	$$$$
Pol Roger Blanc de Chardonnay Champ., France	27	$$$$
Perrier-Jouët Grand Brut NV Champagne, France	26	$$$$
Top 5 Pinot Grigio/Gris by Taste		
Trimbach Pinot Gris, Alsace, France	25	$$
Alois Lageder Pinot Grigio, Italy	24	$$
Robert Mondavi Woodbridge Pinot Grigio, Calif.	24	$
Santa Margherita Pinot Grigio, Italy	22	$$$
Cavit Pinot Grigio, Italy	21	$
Top 5 Other Whites by Taste		
Fetzer Echo Ridge Gewürztraminer, Calif.	24	$
Hugel Gewürztraminer, Alsace, France	24	$$
Marqués de Riscal White Rueda, Spain	24	$

*Scores were rounded off. Wines are listed in order of actual ranking.

Name	Taste Score*	Price Category
Penfolds Semillon/Chardonnay, Australia	24	$
Pepperwood Grove Viognier, Calif.	24	$

Top 10 Italian and Spanish Reds by Taste

Name	Taste Score*	Price Category
Selvapiana Chianti Rufina, Italy	29	$$
Banfi Brunello di Montalcino, Italy	27	$$$$
Alvaro Palacios Les Terrasses Priorat, Spain	26	$$$
Pesquera Ribera del Duero, Spain	26	$$$
Martinez, Faustino Rioja Crianza, Spain	26	$
Antinori, Marchese Chianti Classico Riserva, Italy	25	$$$
Muga Rioja Reserva, Spain	25	$$$
Ruffino Chianti Classico Rsva. Ducale Gold Label, Italy	24	$$$$
Montecillo Rioja Crianza, Spain	24	$
Castello di Gabbiano Chianti Classico Risva., Italy	24	$$

Top 5 Shiraz/Syrahs and Rhône-Style Reds by Taste

Name	Taste Score*	Price Category
Château La Nerthe Chât.-du-Pape, France	28	$$$$
La Vieille Ferme Côtes du Ventoux, France	27	$
Rosemount G-S-M (Grenache-Shiraz-Mourvedre), Aust.	26	$$
Rosemount Diamond Label Shiraz, Australia	24	$
Chât. de Beaucastel Chât.-du-Pape, France	24	$$$$

Top 5 Red Zinfandels by Taste

Name	Taste Score*	Price Category
Dry Creek Reserve Zin., Calif.	29	$$$
Ridge Geyserville (Zin.), Calif.	29	$$$
St. Francis Sonoma Zin., Calif.	28	$$
Grgich Hills Sonoma Zin., Calif.	26	$$$
Seghesio Sonoma Zin., Calif.	26	$$

BEST OF THE BARGAIN-PRICED WINES

Top 20 Budget Whites

Name	Taste Score*
Fetzer Echo Ridge Riesling, Calif.	27
Gallo of Sonoma Chard., Calif.	27
Château Ste. Michelle Johannisberg Riesling, Wash.	26
Robert Mondavi Private Selection Chard., Calif.	26
Hogue Fumé Blanc, Wash.	26
Villa Maria Private Bin Sauvignon Blanc, New Zealand	26
Kendall-Jackson Vintners Rsv. Riesling, Calif.	26
Hess Select Chard., Calif.	24
Macon-Lugny Les Charmes, France	24
Penfolds Koonunga Hill Chard., Australia	24
St. Francis Sonoma Chard., Calif.	24
Meridian Chard., Calif.	24
Fetzer Echo Ridge Gewürztraminer, Calif.	24
Marqués de Riscal White Rueda, Spain	24
Penfolds Semillon/Chardonnay, Australia	24
Pepperwood Grove Viognier, Calif.	24
Weingartner Gruner-Veltliner, Austria	24
Robert Mondavi Woodbridge Pinot Grigio, Calif.	24
Columbia Winery Riesling, Wash.	24
Jekel Riesling, Calif.	24

Top 20 Budget Reds

Los Vascos Cab. Sauv., Chile	29
Casa Lapostolle Classic Cab. Sauv., Chile	27
Santa Rita 120 Cab. Sauv., Chile	27

*Scores were rounded off. Wines are listed in order of actual ranking.

Name	Taste Score*
La Vieille Ferme Côtes du Ventoux, France	27
Martinez, Faustino Rioja Crianza, Spain	26
Gallo of Sonoma Cab. Sauv., Calif.	25
Columbia Crest Cab. Sauv., Wash.	25
Rosemount Diamond Label Shiraz, Australia	24
Louis Jadot Beaujolais-Villages, France	24
Black Opal Cab. Sauv., Aust.	24
Ruffino Chianti, Italy	24
Falesco Vitiano, Italy	24
Gallo of Sonoma Merlot, Calif.	24
Navarro-Correas Malbec, Argentina	24
Beringer Founders' Estate Pinot Noir, Calif.	24
Indigo Hills Pinot Noir, Calif.	24
Beaulieu Vineyard (BV) Coastal Zin., Calif.	24
Monteviña Amador Zin., Calif.	24
Montecillo Rioja Crianza, Spain	24
Fetzer Valley Oaks Syrah, Calif.	24

Best of the Big 6 Grapes

Name	Taste Score*
Top 5 Budget Rieslings	
Fetzer Echo Ridge Riesling, Calif.	27
Château Ste. Michelle Johannisberg Riesling, Wash.	26
Kendall-Jackson Vintners Rsv. Riesling, Calif.	26
Columbia Winery Cellarmaster's Reserve Riesling, Wash.	24
Jekel Riesling, Calif.	24
Top 5 Budget Sauvignon Blancs	
Hogue Fumé Blanc, Wash.	26
Buena Vista Sauv. Blanc, Calif.	24
Kenwood Sauv. Blanc, Calif.	24
Canyon Road Sauv. Blanc, Calif.	24
Château Ste. Michelle Sauv. Blanc, Wash.	23
Top 10 Budget Chardonnays	
Gallo of Sonoma Chard., Calif.	27
Robert Mondavi Private Selection Chard., Calif.	26
Hess Select Chard., Calif.	24
Macon-Lugny Les Charmes, France	24
Penfolds Koonunga Hill Chard., Australia	24

St. Francis Sonoma Chard., Calif.	24
Meridian Chard., Calif.	24
Columbia Crest Chard., Washington	23
Beringer Founders' Estate Chard., Calif.	23
Louis Jadot Macon Blanc, France	23

Top 5 Budget Pinot Noirs

Beringer Founders' Estate Pinot Noir, Calif.	24
Indigo Hills Pinot Noir, Calif.	24
Duck Pond Pinot Noir, Oregon	22
Gallo of Sonoma Pinot Noir, Calif.	22
Lindemans Bin 99 Pinot Noir, Aust.	21

Top 10 Budget Merlots

Gallo of Sonoma Merlot, Calif.	24
Christian Moueix Merlot, France	23
Fetzer Eagle Peak Merlot, Calif.	23
Casa Lapostolle Classic Merlot, Chile	23
Lindemans Bin 40 Merlot, Australia	22
Columbia Crest Merlot, Wash.	21
Beringer Founders' Estate Merlot, Calif.	21
Sutter Home Merlot, Calif.	21
Beaulieu Vineyard (BV) Coastal Merlot, Calif.	21
Turning Leaf Merlot,Calif.	18

Top 10 Budget Cabernets and Blends

Los Vascos Cab. Sauv., Chile	29
Casa Lapostolle Classic Cab. Sauv., Chile	27
Santa Rita 120 Cabernet Sauv., Chile	27
Gallo of Sonoma Cab. Sauv., Calif.	25
Columbia Crest Cab. Sauv., Wash.	25
Black Opal Cab. Sauv., Australia	24
Rosemount Diamond Label Cab. Sauv./ Merlot, Australia	23
Beringer Founders' Estate Cab. Sauv., Calif.	22
Rosemount Diamond Label Cab. Sauv., Australia	22
Fetzer Valley Oaks Cab. Sauv., Calif.	21

*Scores were rounded off. Wines are listed in order of actual ranking.

Best of the Rest

Name	Taste Score*
Top 5 Budget Other Whites (budget Pinot Grigios were included in this taste ranking, but none made the top 5)	
Fetzer Echo Ridge Gewürztraminer, Calif.	24
Marqués de Riscal White Rueda, Spain	24
Penfolds Semillon/Chardonnay, Australia	24
Pepperwood Grove Viognier, Calif.	24
Weingartner Gruner-Veltliner, Austria	24
Top 5 Budget Italian and Spanish Reds	
Martinez, Faustino Rioja Crianza, Spain	26
Ruffino Chianti, Italy	24
Falesco Vitiano, Italy	24
Montecillo Rioja Crianza, Spain	24
Santa Cristina Sangiovese, Antinori, Italy	23
Top 5 Budget Shiraz/Syrahs and Rhône-Style Reds	
La Vieille Ferme Côtes du Ventoux, France	27
Rosemount Diamond Label Shiraz, Aust.	24
Fetzer Valley Oaks Syrah, Calif.	24
Hill of Content Grenache/Shiraz, Aust.	24
Reynolds Shiraz, Aust.	24
Top 5 Budget Red Zinfandels	
Beaulieu Vineyard (BV) Coastal Zin., Calif.	24
Monteviña Amador Zin., Calif.	24
Robert Mondavi Private Selection Zin., Calif.	24
Cline Zin., Calif.	23
Fetzer Valley Oaks Zin., Calif.	21

Top Values for the Money (Across All Prices)

Top 20 White Wine Values

Wine Name	Value Score*	Price Category
Buena Vista Sauv. Blanc, Calif.	29	$
Robert Mondavi Napa Fumé Blanc, Calif.	29	$$
Geyser Peak Chard., Calif.	29	$$
Columbia Crest Semillon/Chardonnay, Wash.	29	$
Gunderloch Riesling Kabinett Jean Baptiste, Germany	29	$$
Au Bon Climat Chardonnay, Calif.	29	$$$
Charles Heidsieck Brut Champ., France	29	$$$$
Kenwood Sauv. Blanc, Calif.	29	$
Benziger Chard., Calif.	28	$$
Edna Valley Vineyard Chard., Calif.	28	$$
Penfolds Semillon/Chardonnay, Australia	28	$
Roederer Estate Sparkling, Calif.	27	$$$
Fetzer Echo Ridge Riesling, Calif.	27	$
Kendall-Jackson Vintners Rsv. Riesling, Calif.	27	$
Ferrari-Carano Fumé Blanc, Calif.	27	$$
Frog's Leap Sauv. Blanc, Calif.	27	$$
Chalone Chard., Calif	27	$$$
J. Lohr Riverstone Chard., Calif.	27	$$
Domaine Carneros Brut Spklg., Calif.	27	$$$
Mionetto Prosecco Spklg., Italy	27	$$

*Scores were rounded off. Wines are listed in order of actual ranking.

Top 20 Red Wine Values

Wine Name	Value Score*	Price Cate-gory
Beringer Founders' Estate Pinot Noir, Calif.	29	$
Frescobaldi Chianti Rufina Riserva, Italy	29	$$$
Selvapiana Chianti Rufina, Italy	29	$$
Casa Lapostolle Classic Cab. Sauv., Chile	29	$
Martinez, Faustino Rioja Crianza, Spain	29	$
Kenwood Pinot Noir, Calif.	29	$$
Reynolds Shiraz, Aust.	29	$
Duck Pond Pinot Noir, Oregon	28	$
Rosemount G-S-M (Grenache-Shiraz-Mourvedre), Aust.	28	$$
Columbia Crest Cab. Sauv., Wash.	28	$
Gallo of Sonoma Merlot, Calif.	28	$
La Vieille Ferme Côtes du Ventoux, France	27	$
Sutter Home Merlot, Calif.	27	$
Los Vascos Cab. Sauv., Chile	27	$
Hill of Content Grenache/Shiraz, Aust.	27	$$
Château Ste. Michelle Columbia Valley Merlot, Wash.	27	$$
Rosemount Diamond Label Shiraz/Cab. Sauv., Aust.	27	$
Fetzer Eagle Peak Merlot, Calif.	26	$
St. Francis Sonoma Zin., Calif.	26	$$
Louis Jadot Beaujolais-Villages, France	26	$

Top 20 Chardonnay Values

Wine Name	Value Score*	Price Cate-gory
Geyser Peak Chard., Calif.	29	$$
Au Bon Climat Chard., Calif.	29	$$$
Benziger Chard., Calif.	28	$$
Edna Valley Vineyard Chard., Calif.	28	$$
Chalone Central Coast Chard., Calif.	27	$$$
J. Lohr Riverstone Chard., Calif.	27	$$
Estancia Pinnacles Chard., Calif.	26	$$
Hess Select Chard., Calif.	26	$
R. H. Phillips Dunnigan Hills Chard., Calif.	26	$
Robert Mondavi Private Selection Chard., Calif.	26	$

Wine	Value Score	Price Category
Gallo of Sonoma Chard., Calif.	26	$
Columbia Crest Chard., Washington	25	$
Beaulieu Vineyard (BV) Coastal Chard., Calif.	24	$
Beaulieu Vineyard (BV) Carneros Chard., Calif.	24	$$
Clos du Bois Sonoma Chard., Calif.	24	$$
Ferrari-Carano Chard., Calif.	24	$$$
Joseph Drouhin Pouilly-Fuissé, France	24	$$
Kendall-Jackson Grand Rsv. Chard, Calif.	24	$$
La Crema Chard., Calif.	24	$$
Louis Jadot Macon Blanc, France	24	$

Top 20 Cabernet Values

Wine Name	Value Score*	Price Category
Casa Lapostolle Classic Cab. Sauv., Chile	29	$
Columbia Crest Cab. Sauv., Wash.	28	$
Los Vascos Cab. Sauv., Chile	27	$
Black Opal Cab. Sauv., Australia	26	$
Rosemount Diamond Label Cab. Sauv./ Merlot, Australia	26	$
Château Ste. Michelle Columbia Valley Cab. Sauv., Wash.	26	$$
Escudo Rojo, Chile	26	$$
Gallo of Sonoma Cab. Sauv., Calif.	25	$
Rosemount Diamond Label Cab. Sauv., Australia	25	$
J. Lohr 7 Oaks Cab. Sauv., Calif.	24	$$
Caliterra Cab. Sauv., Chile	24	$
Château Gloria Bordeaux, France	24	$$$$
Château Larose-Trintaudon Bordeaux, France	24	$$
Estancia Cab. Sauv., Calif.	24	$$
Fetzer Valley Oaks Cab. Sauv., Calif.	24	$
Jacob's Creek Cab. Sauv., Australia	24	$
Mt. Veeder Napa Cab. Sauv., Calif.	24	$$$$
Raymond Napa Cab. Sauv., Calif.	24	$$
Robert Mondavi Napa Cab. Sauv., Calif.	24	$$$
Santa Rita 120 Cab. Sauv., Chile	24	$

*Scores were rounded off. Wines are listed in order of actual ranking.

THE REVIEWS

WHITE WINES

Sparkling/Champagne

Style Profile: Although all the world's bubblies are modeled on Champagne, only the genuine article from the Champagne *region* of France is properly called *Champagne*. *Sparkling wine* is the proper term for the other bubblies, some of which can be just as good as the real thing. Limited supply and high demand—plus a labor-intensive production process—make Champagne expensive compared to other sparklers but still an affordable luxury in comparison to other world-class wine categories, like top French Burgundy or California Cabernet estates. The other sparklers, especially Cava from Spain and Italian Prosecco (see the list of "Top 50 Wines You're Not Drinking" for my newest picks), are affordable for everyday drinking. *Brut* (rhymes with root) on the label means the wine is utterly dry, with no perceptible sweetness. But that *doesn't* mean they all taste the same. In fact, each French Champagne house is known for a signature style, which can range from delicate and elegant to rich, full, and toasty—meaning there's something for every taste and food partner.

Serve: Well chilled; young and fresh (only the rare luxury French Champagnes improve with age). Open with utmost care: flying corks can be dangerous.

When: Anytime! It's not just for special occasions, and it's great with meals.

With: Anything and anyone, but especially sushi and shellfish.

In: A narrow tulip- or flute-type glass; the narrow opening preserves the bubbles.

Kitchen Fridge Survival Tip for bubbly wine: Kitchenware shops and wine stores often sell "clamshell" stoppers specially designed to close Champagnes and sparkling wines if you don't finish the bottle. I've found that if you open the bottle carefully in the first place (avoid "popping" the cork, which is also the safest technique), a stoppered sparkling wine will keep its fizz for at least three days in the fridge, often longer. Having a hard time thinking of something else to toast? How about, "Here's to [insert day of week]." That's usually good enough for me!

| **Ballatore Gran Spumante NV** | PC | T | V |
| **California** | $ | 21 | 24 |

"Delightful with or without food, crisp and fun," say my tasters, who "feel we get more than we pay for." It's "nice and fruity" and "a little sweet—great for mimosas."

Kitchen Fridge Survivor™ Grade: A
Your notes:_____

| **Ballatore Red Spumante** | PC | T | V |
| **California** | $ | 18 | 18 |

The beautiful fuchsia color and gorgeous honeysuckle scent make this a festive choice. The "not overly sweet, subtle berry flavor" makes it "great for summer sipping."

Kitchen Fridge Survivor™ Grade: A
Your notes:_____

| **Bollinger (*BOLL-ehn-jur*) Special** | PC | T | V |
| **Cuvée Brut, France** | $$$$ | 29 | 18 |

My taster's "big, toasty, full bodied" description of this classic Champagne is right on. The complexity "really

Price Ranges: **$** = $12 or less; **$$** = 12.01–20; **$$$** = 20.01–35; **$$$$** => $35

Kitchen Fridge/Countertop Survivor™ Grades: *Avg.* = a "one-day wine," tastes noticeably less fresh the next day; *B* = holds its freshness for 2–3 days after opening; *B+* = holds *and gets better* over 2–3 days after opening; *A* = a 3- to 4-day "freshness window"; *A+* = holds *and gets better* over 3–4 days

captures your attention." No wonder it's James Bond's favorite.

Kitchen Fridge Survivor™ Grade: A

Your notes:_____

_____

Bouvet Brut (*boo-VAY broot*) NV   PC   T   V
Loire Valley, France $$ 18   24

This was the first *real* sparkling wine I ever tasted. My bubbly reference point up to then had been Cold Duck(!). Bouvet is affordable but also fantastic, with a very complex scent of wilted blossoms and sweet hay, a crisp apple-quince flavor, and creamy texture. If you, too, thought there was no such thing as worthy, well-priced bubbly, try this.

Kitchen Fridge Survivor™ Grade: B+

Your notes:_____

_____

Charles Heidsieck (*HIDE-sick*) Brut   PC   T   V
France $$$$ 24   29

This "well rounded and luxurious" bubbly in the full-bodied style is known for its creamy texture and toasted hazelnut scent. It's one of my favorites both for sipping, and to match with meals.

Kitchen Fridge Survivor™ Grade: A

Your notes:_____

_____

Charles Heidsieck (*HIDE-sick*) Brut   PC   T   V
Vintage Champ., France $$$$ 24   19

This "deep straw gold in color, full bodied" Champagne is one of my favorites for its nutty, croissant-bakery scent. My tasters note that "it mellows with bottle age."

Kitchen Fridge Survivor™ Grade: A

Your notes:_____

_____

Domaine Carneros Brut   PC   T   V
California $$$ 28   27

✓ This wine's definitely on my "short list" of favorite California sparklers. It has very ripe pineapple fruit, expertly balanced between generous juiciness and elegant restraint. It is one of my very favorite wines for food, because it enhances intricate flavors without competing.

Kitchen Fridge Survivor™ Grade: B

Your notes:_____

Domaine Chandon (*shahn-DOHN*)   PC   T   V
Blanc de Noirs, California $$$ 23   19

It's pronounced blahnk-duh-NWAHR, and it means this golden bubbly is made from black (Noir) grapes, which give it extra body and concentration.

Kitchen Fridge Survivor™ Grade: B

Your notes:_____

Domaine Chandon Extra Brut   PC   T   V
Classic Sparkling, California $$ 26   26

This American sparkler sibling of France's famous Moët & Chandon is a huge hit with my tasters, in part because it's one of the best bubblies for the price. It's got a yeasty, creamy style that's "classy, but affordable enough to drink often."

Kitchen Fridge Survivor™ Grade: B+

Your notes:_____

Domaine Ste. Michelle Cuvée Brut   PC   T   V
Sparkling, Washington $$ 24   27

Consumers and trade alike agree: "you can't beat the price" of this nicely balanced, fruity sparkler made in the Champagne method. I've been serving this wine for years by the glass and as my ultimate smooth-move wedding bubbly (brides can handle the taste and parents the price). DSM also makes Extra Dry and Blanc de Blancs styles—they're yummy, too.

Kitchen Fridge Survivor™ Grade: B

Your notes:_____

Price Ranges: **$** = $12 or less; **$$** = 12.01–20; **$$$** = 20.01–35; **$$$$** = > $35

Kitchen Fridge/Countertop Survivor™ Grades: *Avg.* = a "one-day wine," tastes noticeably less fresh the next day; *B* = holds its freshness for 2–3 days after opening; *B+* = holds *and gets better* over 2–3 days after opening; *A* = a 3- to 4-day "freshness window"; *A+* = holds *and gets better* over 3–4 days

Dom Pérignon Champagne   PC   T   V
France $$$$ 23   19

Though some say "you can do better for the price," you can't beat the pedigree "when you want to impress," and the "good fruit flavor" and "yeasty" scent are "always reliable."

Kitchen Fridge Survivor™ Grade: B

Your notes:_____

_____

Freixenet (*fresh-uh-NETT*) Brut   PC   T   V
de Noirs NV, Cava Rosé, Spain $ 19   19

Sometimes "yummy" is really the right word for a wine. This is one of those. It has a gorgeous pale watermelon color, a mouthwatering taste of tangy strawberries, and thirst-quenching juiciness that makes it great with fried foods, spicy foods . . . any foods. At this price, it's a gift. This actually held up for *weeks* in the fridge (I forgot it was in there).

Kitchen Fridge Survivor™ Grade: A+

Your notes:_____

_____

Freixenet NV Cordon Negro Brut   PC   T   V
Spain $$ 18   22

"Nice for the price" sums up the consensus among tasters who call this wine "simple and refreshing," and better "than most low-end California sparklers."

Kitchen Fridge Survivor™ Grade: Avg

Your notes:_____

_____

Gosset (*go-SAY*) Brut Rosé NV   PC   T   V
France $$$$ 24   24

Perhaps memories of those candy-sweet rosés we all drank in the seventies are to blame, but my experience is that when it comes to rosé Champagne, most people need convincing. This wine will do it. It's one of my favorite Champagnes, period. The scent and flavors, of dried cherries, exotic spices, and toasted nuts, would please any serious still wine drinker with their complexity and depth. Forget toasting and serve it with salmon, tuna, duck, or pork.

Kitchen Fridge Survivor™ Grade: A

Your notes:_____

_____

Gruet (*groo-AY*) Brut St. Vincent   PC   T   V
NV, New Mexico $ 19   19

"Who would believe New Mexico" as a source of
"great bubblies which are tasty and of good value."
And you don't have to go to New Mexico to get it—
the availability in major cities is pretty good.
Kitchen Fridge Survivor™ *Grade: B+*
Your notes:_____

_____

Iron Horse Wedding Cuvée   PC   T   V
(*coo-VAY*) Brut, California $$$ 26   24

Brides, of course, love the romantic name of this
vibrant bottling. It is my choice for receptions, having
inspired more "What was the name of that wine?"
reactions than any other in the history of my wine
career. Its breathtaking acidity and concentrated
tangerine and green apple flavors make it a great
choice for sushi, and I love it with egg dishes for
brunch.
Kitchen Fridge Survivor™ *Grade: B*
Your notes:_____

_____

J Vintage Brut   PC   T   V
California $$$ 26   22

"J produces wonderful sparkling wine … refreshing
and fun," say my tasters. It seems to get better and
better every year, and the package is gorgeous.
Kitchen Fridge Survivor™ *Grade: A*
Your notes:_____

_____

Korbel Brut Sparkling   PC   T   V
California $$ 20   19

This light, crisp sparkler is, quite possibly, used to
celebrate more weddings, anniversaries, and New
Year's countdowns than any other bubbly in America.

Price Ranges: **$** = $12 or less; **$$** = 12.01–20; **$$$** = 20.01–35;
$$$$ = > $35
Kitchen Fridge/Countertop Survivor™ Grades: *Avg.* = a "one-day
wine," tastes noticeably less fresh the next day; *B* = holds its fresh-
ness for 2–3 days after opening; *B+* = holds *and gets better* over 2–3
days after opening; *A* = a 3- to 4-day "freshness window"; *A+* =
holds *and gets better* over 3–4 days

That said, it's a tasty *sparkling wine* for the money. Korbel's use of the name "Champagne" on the label furthers consumer confusion over the term: true Champagne must come from that *region* in France.

Kitchen Fridge Survivor™ Grade: Avg

Your notes:_____

_____

	PC	T	V
Laurent-Perrier Cuvée Grand Siècle (*luh-RAHNT pear-ee-YAY coo-VAY grahnd see-YECK*)**, France**	$$$$	26	23

It's "delicious!!" and "worth every penny," say my tasters of Laurent-Perrier's top of the line bottling. The more delicate style makes it "great with food."

Kitchen Fridge Survivor™ Grade: A

Your notes:_____

_____

	PC	T	V
Mionetto DOC Prosecco (*me-oh-NETT-oh pro-SECK-oh*) **Veneto, Italy**	$$	21	27

Prosecco, once trendy, has gone mainstream, and for good reason: it's dry, refreshing, and sophisticated but also affordable. And its Italian pedigree confers instant chic. Prosecco is the grape name, and the wine can range from just lightly sparkling to fully *spumante* (the Italian word for "sparkling"). It's also the traditional bubbly mixed with peach puree to make the Bellini, Venice's signature cocktail.

Kitchen Fridge Survivor™ Grade: B

Your notes:_____

_____

	PC	T	V
Moët & Chandon (*MWETT eh shahn-DOHN*) **Imperial Brut NV France**	$$$$	25	26

This is one of the best Brut NVs on the market at the moment, with "medium body and more fruit flavor and acidity" than its sister bottling, Moët & Chandon White Star, making it "a real winner with oysters and sushi."

Kitchen Fridge Survivor™ Grade: B

Your notes:_____

_____

Moët & Chandon White Star	PC	T	V
Champagne, France	$$$$	23	19

Famous pedigree, flower and biscuit scents, and a peachy finish—what's not to love? Seriously, trade and consumer tasters alike tout this as "fantastic Champagne," and I agree. The "reliable, crowd-pleasing style" is owed to the dollop of sweetness used to round out the taste of the finished product. Great with spicy foods and sushi.

Kitchen Fridge Survivor™ Grade: A

Your notes:_____

_____

Mumm Cuvée Napa Brut	PC	T	V
Prestige Sparkling, California	$$	25	21

It's more popular then ever with my tasters, who rave about the "French style, for a great price."

Kitchen Fridge Survivor™ Grade: B

Your notes:_____

_____

Oudinot (*OOH-duh-know*) Brut	PC	T	V
Rose Champagne, France	$$$	X	X

✗ It was fun to see so many write-ins of small-grower Champagnes, such as this one, that's "a beautiful color, light and fun, with light fruit, a little yeasty, and yummy." The lesser-known name makes it "a great price for real rosé."

Kitchen Fridge Survivor™ Grade: B

Your notes:_____

_____

Perrier-Jouët (*PEAR-ee-ay JHWETT*)	PC	T	V
Grand Brut NV Champagne	$$$$	26	20
France			

"PJ" is definitely one of my favorites in the lighter-bodied Champagne style, offering a fresh and lively bouquet and subtle-but-complex flavors. It's a stellar

---

Price Ranges: **$** = $12 or less; **$$** = 12.01–20; **$$$** = 20.01–35; **$$$$** = > $35

Kitchen Fridge/Countertop Survivor™ Grades: *Avg.* = a "one-day wine," tastes noticeably less fresh the next day; *B* = holds its freshness for 2–3 days after opening; *B+* = holds *and gets better* over 2–3 days after opening; *A* = a 3- to 4-day "freshness window"; *A+* = holds *and gets better* over 3–4 days

survivor in the fridge, especially if you don't "pop" the cork when opening. Even when the bubbles do dissipate, it's delicious, more like complex white wine than like "flat Champagne."

Kitchen Fridge Survivor™ Grade: A+

Your notes:_____

_____

Piper-Heidsieck (*HIDE-sick*) Brut PC T V
Cuvée, France $$$$ 22 22

This "really dry brut style" has a tangy, snappy acidity that makes it great with salty and fatty flavors. The laser-crisp liveliness makes it "an absolute joy to drink."

Kitchen Fridge Survivor™ Grade: A

Your notes:_____

Piper-Sonoma Brut PC T V
California $$ 22 23

This California outpost of the French Champagne Piper-Heidsieck yields one of California's best bubblies. It's got a toasty quality that's wonderful on its own and with food. The leftovers hold up beautifully for days, too.

Kitchen Fridge Survivor™ Grade: A+

Your notes:_____

Pol Roger (*paul row-JHAY*) PC T V
Blanc de Chardonnay Champagne $$$$ 27 21
Brut, France

This wine has a toasted hazelnut scent that I'd normally associate with richer Champagne styles, yet the flavor has the tangy acidity and delicacy of blanc-de-blancs Champagnes (made solely from Chardonnay as opposed to the traditional blend that includes the red grapes Pinot Noir and Pinot Meunier).

Kitchen Fridge Survivor™ Grade: A

Your notes:_____

Pol Roger Brut Reserve NV PC T V
France $$$$ X X

X "Wonderful producer. Great product at this price point," noted my tasters. It is one of my favorite brut

Champagnes in the delicate, elegant style—a great choice with caviar or shellfish.

Kitchen Fridge Survivor™ Grade: A+

Your notes:_____

_____

Pommery (*POMM-er-ee*) Brut	PC	T	V
Royal, NV, France	$$$	24	22

Pommery, a major brand in France and one of the classic Champagne houses, is now well-known in the U.S. thanks to the trendy "Pops" mini-bottles. It's an elegant style with a creamy scent and subtle pear flavor.

Kitchen Fridge Survivor™ Grade: A

Your notes:_____

_____

Roederer Estate Sparkling	PC	T	V
California	$$$	26	27

Wine trade and consumers alike say this is about as close to Champagne as you can get without buying French, and I agree. The full, toasty style is right in keeping with the house style of its French parent (they make Cristal). Truly, this is the best of both worlds: although "reasonably priced," it offers the taste of "a special occasion wine."

Kitchen Fridge Survivor™ Grade: A

Your notes:_____

_____

Ruinart (*ROO-uh-nahr*) Brut NV	PC	T	V
France	$$$$	28	23

The taste is "delicate and refined," say my tasters. "The problem is just finding it in the U.S."

Kitchen Fridge Survivor™ Grade: A

Your notes:_____

_____

Price Ranges: **$** = $12 or less; **$$** = 12.01–20; **$$$** = 20.01–35; **$$$$** = > $35

Kitchen Fridge/Countertop Survivor™ Grades: *Avg.* = a "one-day wine," tastes noticeably less fresh the next day; *B* = holds its freshness for 2–3 days after opening; *B+* = holds *and gets better* over 2–3 days after opening; *A* = a 3- to 4-day "freshness window"; *A+* = holds *and gets better* over 3–4 days

Seaview Brut	PC	T	V
Australia	$	X	X

✗ "For $8.99 (in many markets), you can't miss!"
Indeed, this is "an excellent bubbly that has fooled
many 'experts' into thinking it was French! Best
value!"

Kitchen Fridge Survivor™ Grade: B

Your notes:_____

Segura Viudas (*seh-GUHR-uh*	PC	T	V
vee-YOU-duss) Aria Estate Extra	$$	18	24
Dry Cava, Spain			

For the money, this is one of the most unabashedly
delicious sparklers I have ever drunk. Although
Segura Viudas is Freixenet's upmarket cava brand, it
remains an awesome price for what you get—ripe,
vibrant pear fruit, creamy texture. If you like to
entertain, the beautiful bottle brings an elegant look
to the gathering.

Kitchen Fridge Survivor™ Grade: A

Your notes:_____

Taittinger (*TAIT-in-jur*) Brut La	PC	T	V
Française NV Champagne, France	$$$$	27	23

This is one of my favorites among the subtle, elegant
house-style Champagnes. The generous proportion of
Chardonnay in its blend lends finesse and delicacy.
My tasters wrote more poetically about this
Champagne, saying the refreshing acidity makes it
"simply dance across the tongue."

Kitchen Fridge Survivor™ Grade: A

Your notes:_____

Veuve Clicquot (*voov klee-COH*)	PC	T	V
Yellow Label NV Champagne	$$$$	22	20
France			

Both pro and consumer tasters were wishy-washy,
some saying "great, as always," and others saying "it's
gone down." I still love the full-bodied house style,
but judge for yourself.

Kitchen Fridge Survivor™ Grade: B+

Your notes:_____

Pinot Gris/Pinot Grigio

Grape Profile: Pinot Gris (*pee-no GREE*) is the French and Grigio (*GREE-jee-oh*) the Italian spelling for this crisp, delicate, very popular white wine grape. The French and American versions tend toward the luscious style, versus the Italians which are more tangy and crisp. To many of my trade tasters it's "the quintessential quaffing wine" and "a real winner by the glass" in restaurants. In the rising resistance to inflated wine prices, both my trade and consumer tasters lauded the fact that many of the cheapest Pinot Grigios were among the best. I couldn't put it better than the taster who wrote, "If it doesn't *taste* a lot better, why should I *pay* a lot more?" As the Italians would say, *Ecco!*

Serve: Well chilled; young and fresh (as one of my wine buying buddies says to the waiters *she* teaches: "The best vintage for Pinot Grigio? As close to yesterday as possible!").

When: Anytime, but ideal with cocktails, outdoor occasions, lunch, big gatherings (a crowd-pleaser).

With: Very versatile, but perfect with hors d'oeuvres, salads, salty foods, and fried foods.

In: An all-purpose wine stem is fine.

Alois Lageder (*la-GAY-der*; no one says the first part) Pinot Grigio, Italy	PC $$	T 24	V 24

✓ I join legions of fans of this "flowery" and "spicy" Pinot Grigio, which has a smoky finish and complexity that few expect from Pinot Grigio.

Kitchen Fridge Survivor™ Grade: B

Your notes:_____

_____

Price Ranges: **$** = $12 or less; **$$** = 12.01–20; **$$$** = 20.01–35; **$$$$** = > $35

Kitchen Fridge/Countertop Survivor™ Grades: *Avg.* = a "one-day wine," tastes noticeably less fresh the next day; *B* = holds its freshness for 2–3 days after opening; *B+* = holds *and gets better* over 2–3 days after opening; *A* = a 3- to 4-day "freshness window"; *A+* = holds *and gets better* over 3–4 days

Bella Sera Pinot Grigio	PC	T	V
Italy	$	20	24

My tasters laud this "easy to drink Pinot Grigio" as a "great inexpensive wine with nice flavor." It's crisp and pleasant for solo sipping, and a great food partner, too.

Kitchen Fridge Survivor™ Grade: B

Your notes:_____

_____

Bolla Pinot Grigio	PC	T	V
Italy	$	16	17

The Bolla name sells it, but it offers less flavor for the money than other PGs at the same price. Fans say it's a "refreshing, no-nonsense" wine, while detractors say it's thin-tasting.

Kitchen Fridge Survivor™ Grade: Avg

Your notes:_____

_____

CAVIT (*CAV-it;* rhymes with "have-it") Pinot Grigio , Italy	PC	T	V
	$	21	20

Fans say this wine's "a nice summertime sipper," and I think it's great by the glass in a restaurant, or for cocktail parties. It's light, crisp, and easy on the wallet, too.

Kitchen Fridge Survivor™ Grade: B

Your notes:_____

_____

Ecco Domani (*ECK-oh dough-MAH-nee*) Pinot Grigio, Italy	PC	T	V
	$	15	16

"Tastes clean and refreshing," say fans of Gallo's Italian offspring that tastes like spice and pear. Pros point out that it's "a great value for the money."

Kitchen Countertop Survivor™ Grade: B

Your notes:_____

_____

Folonari (*foe-luh-NAH-ree*) Pinot Grigio, Italy	PC	T	V
	$	20	20

Trade buyers call this PG an "underrated overachiever"—definitely worth a look when you're seeking Italian, white, value, or any combination of the three. It's crisp and mouthwatering.

Kitchen Fridge Survivor™ Grade: Avg

Your notes:_____

_____

King Estate Pinot Gris   **PC**   **T**   **V**
Oregon   **$$**   **21**   **21**

After a few years of inflation, this wine's price has returned to value territory—great value given the quality. Yay! Enjoy the "cornucopia of tropical fruit flavors" with sushi, spicy fare, you name it!

Kitchen Fridge Survivor™ Grade: A

Your notes:_____

Livio Felluga (*LIV-ee-oh fuh-LOO-*   **PC**   **T**   **V**
***guh*) Pinot Grigio, Italy**   **$$**   **22**   **21**

"Lean," "stylish," and "exciting" are words pros use to describe this standout Pinot Grigio with the cool map label. I like the pretty floral nose, ripe apricot flavors, and fruity richness.

Kitchen Fridge Survivor™ Grade: B

Your notes:_____

Meridian Pinot Grigio,   **PC**   **T**   **V**
California—Santa Barbara   **$**   **X**   **X**

✗ The Meridian stamp—luscious fruit flavor—comes through here as ripe pear and nectarine. It's delicious on its own, but also great with spicy food, tuna salad, and sushi.

Kitchen Fridge Survivor™ Grade: B+

Your notes:_____

MezzaCorona (*METT-suh*   **PC**   **T**   **V**
***coh-ROH-nuh*) Pinot Grigio**   **$**   **15**   **16**
Italy

"A nice staple" and "great everyday wine," say my pro tasters, who say it's a "mouthwatering" and "refresh-ing" crowd pleaser.

Kitchen Fridge Survivor™ Grade: B

Your notes:_____

Price Ranges: **$** = $12 or less; **$$** = 12.01–20; **$$$** = 20.01–35; **$$$$** = > $35

Kitchen Fridge/Countertop Survivor™ Grades: *Avg.* = a "one-day wine," tastes noticeably less fresh the next day; *B* = holds its fresh-ness for 2–3 days after opening; *B+* = holds *and gets better* over 2–3 days after opening; *A* = a 3- to 4-day "freshness window"; *A+* = holds *and gets better* over 3–4 days

Monteviña Pinot Grigio   PC   T   V
California $$ X   X

✗ This wine bursts with ripe pear fruit, while the crisp acidity keeps it flexible with a wide array of food partners, from spicy sausage pizza to hot and sour soup and garlic chicken.

Kitchen Fridge Survivor™ Grade: B

Your notes:_____

_____

Pighin (*PEE-ghin*) Pinot Grigio   PC   T   V
Italy $$ X   X

✗ "Mineral, stonefruit, and good acidity make this a very complete wine" and "one of the best Pinot Grigios on the market," according to my tasters, who suggest it's "a good bet on wine lists."

Kitchen Fridge Survivor™ Grade: B

Your notes:_____

_____

Puiatti (*poo-YAH-tee*) Pinot Grigio   PC   T   V
Italy $$ X   X

✗ "This is one of the great Pinot Grigios," and "worth the slight premium" compared to the major brands due to its "complex pear and spice character."

Kitchen Fridge Survivor™ Grade: B

Your notes:_____

_____

Rancho Zabaco Pinot Grigio   PC   T   V
California $$ 19   20

An exotic scent and flavor of honeydew and kiwi makes this lovely for sipping, and great with Asian or Mexican food, too.

Kitchen Fridge Survivor™ Grade: B

Your notes:_____

_____

Santa Margherita Pinot Grigio   PC   T   V
Italy $$$ 22   16

While some consumers echo the majority of trade tasters in appraising Santa Margherita as "way over-priced" for the quality, many tasters still say it's a "favorite" that will "impress your friends." And while retail sales have slipped a bit (perhaps due to the high price), it's still a "comfort zone" wine for many—a known name they'll pay up for.

Kitchen Fridge Survivor™ Grade: Avg

Your notes:_____

_____

Trimbach (*TRIM-bock*) Pinot Gris	PC	T	V
Alsace, France	$$	25	21

Here to join Italy and the U.S. is this world-class French Alsace version of PG. The silky body and tropical fruit, balanced with crisp acidity, make it versatile with food, from fiery to five-star.

Kitchen Fridge Survivor™ Grade: B+

Your notes:_____

_____

Turning Leaf Pinot Grigio	PC	T	V
California	$	13	15

The reviews are mixed on this light quaffing wine. While fans say it's "an inexpensive crowd pleaser," many pros expect more flavor oomph from the Gallo family.

Kitchen Fridge Survivor™ Grade: Avg

Your notes:_____

_____

Zemmer Pinot Grigio	PC	T	V
Italy	$	X	X

✗ This Pinot Grigio has "more concentration than most" in its price range, and "a great nose, great food compatibility."

Kitchen Fridge Survivor™ Grade: B

Your notes:_____

_____

Riesling

Grape Profile: Take note of two great things about the Riesling (*REES-ling*) category. The first is not a

Price Ranges: **$** = $12 or less; **$$** = 12.01–20; **$$$** = 20.01–35; **$$$$** = > $35

Kitchen Fridge/Countertop Survivor™ Grades: *Avg.* = a "one-day wine," tastes noticeably less fresh the next day; *B* = holds its freshness for 2–3 days after opening; *B+* = holds *and gets better* over 2–3 days after opening; *A* = a 3- to 4-day "freshness window"; *A+* = holds *and gets better* over 3–4 days

lot of dollar signs (so lots of value prices). Second, check out all the high survivor grades. Thanks to their tangy, crisp acidity, Riesling wines really hold up in the fridge. That makes them ideal for lots of everyday dining situations—you want a glass of white with your takeout sushi, but your dinner mate wants red with the beef teriyaki. At home I sometimes want to start with a glass of white while I'm cooking and then switch to red with the meal. It's nice to know that I can go back to the wine over several days, and every glass will taste as good as the first one.

Tasters for the first Guide who wondered "Where are the Germans?" will be pleased with their Cinderella story: a string of great vintages means we got lots of write-in wines. They're worth the search. No other region offers so many *world class* wines for under $20. Look for German Rieslings from the Mosel, Rheingau, Pfalz, and Nahe regions.

Prepare to be impressed. Rieslings are light-bodied but loaded with stunning fruit flavor, balanced with tangy acidity. It's my favorite white grape.

Serve: Lightly chilled is fine (the aromas really shine when it's not ice-cold); it's good young and fresh, but the French and German versions can evolve nicely for up to five years.

When: Every day (OK, my personal taste there); classy enough for "important" meals and occasions.

With: Outstanding with shrimp cocktail and other cold seafood, as well as ethnic foods with a "kick" (think Asian, sushi, Indian, Mexican). There's also an awesome rule-breaker match: braised meats!

In: An all-purpose wineglass.

		PC	T	V
Allan Scott Marlborough Riesling				
New Zealand		$$	X	X

✗ Wow—Allan Scott puts practically psychedelic flavor in the bottle with this exotic, zingy, peach and passion fruit Riesling that holds up for days in the fridge (but you probably won't have leftovers!).
Kitchen Fridge Survivor™ Grade: A+
Your notes:_____

_____

| **Beringer Johannisberg Riesling** | PC | T | V |
| **California** | $ | 24 | 24 |

The fruit-salad-in-a-glass flavor of this wine rocks. I think it's one of the best values in the Beringer lineup.

Kitchen Fridge Survivor™ Grade: B+

Your notes:_____

_____

| **Bonny Doon Pacific Rim Riesling** | PC | T | V |
| **USA/Germany** | $ | 23 | 25 |

This is one of the most written-about wines in the survey—scores of reviewers raved about the "yummy, juicy-fruity yet dry" flavor. "Pacific Rim" is the winery's shorthand for "Drink this with Asian foods"—in case you didn't already get it from the cute sushi morsels on the label.

Kitchen Fridge Survivor™ Grade: A

Your notes:_____

_____

| **Château Ste. Michelle Johannisberg** | PC | T | V |
| **Riesling, Washington** | $ | 26 | 27 |

Peach and apricot flavor and crisp, lively acidity give this wine the balance that is the hallmark of well-made Riesling. I often serve this to my wine students as an example of "textbook" Riesling.

Kitchen Fridge Survivor™ Grade: A

Your notes:_____

_____

| **Columbia Crest Johannisberg** | PC | T | V |
| **Riesling, Washington** | $ | 23 | 26 |

I completely agree with the taster who recommends this honeysuckle-peachy wine "with shucked oysters." At this price you can afford a whole mess of them.

Kitchen Fridge Survivor™ Grade: A

Your notes:_____

_____

Price Ranges: **$** = $12 or less; **$$** = 12.01–20; **$$$** = 20.01–35; **$$$$** = > $35

Kitchen Fridge/Countertop Survivor™ Grades: *Avg.* = a "one-day wine," tastes noticeably less fresh the next day; *B* = holds its freshness for 2–3 days after opening; *B+* = holds *and gets better* over 2–3 days after opening; *A* = a 3- to 4-day "freshness window"; *A+* = holds *and gets better* over 3–4 days

Columbia Winery Cellarmaster's | PC | T | V
Reserve Riesling, Washington | $ | 24 | 24

This wine is one of *the* great Rieslings made in North America, lush with ripe peach, apricot, and honey flavors, spiked with crisp acidity. It's a major bargain.

Kitchen Fridge Survivor™ Grade: A+

Your notes:_____

_____

Covey Run Riesling | PC | T | V
Washington | $ | 21 | 24

A pleasant aroma of nectarine and peaches and a nice balance between sweetness and acidity, all at a great price.

Kitchen Fridge Survivor™ Grade: B

Your notes:_____

_____

Eroica (*ee-ROY-cuh*) Riesling | PC | T | V
Washington | $$$ | X | X

✗ I've included this entire quote because my experience is the same: "What a phenomenal wine…so nice on hot days…seems to complement many foods…I served this to friends who drink primarily red wines & they couldn't believe how much they liked it!!!" It's a collaboration between Château Ste. Michelle and Dr. Ernst Loosen of the Mosel, which may explain why it's "as good as German Riesling."

Kitchen Fridge Survivor™ Grade: A+

Your notes:_____

_____

Fetzer Echo Ridge Johannisberg | PC | T | V
Riesling, California | $ | 27 | 27

My tasters call this a "bold" Riesling, with "huge pear fruit" and a hint of sweetness that's ideal for foods with a little bit of chile heat—Thai, Indian, and southwestern for example.

Kitchen Fridge Survivor™ Grade: B+

Your notes:_____

_____

Gunderloch Riesling Kabinett | PC | T | V
Jean Baptiste, Germany | $$ | 29 | 29

✓ This wine is a perfect example of what great German Riesling is about—so approachable, yet with amazing complexity of scent and flavor—flowers, chamomile tea, fresh cream, white peach. And it's magical with food.

Kitchen Fridge Survivor™ Grade: A

Your notes:_____

_____

Hogue Fruit Forward Johannisberg Riesling, Washington	**PC**	**T**	**V**
	$	22	22

Attention all white Zinfandel fans: here's a great alternative that's a little on the sweet side, with ripe, peachy fruit flavor and a candied orange finish.

Kitchen Fridge Survivor™ Grade: B

Your notes:_____

_____

Jekel Riesling California	**PC**	**T**	**V**
	$	24	18

I love this wine's floral nose and juicy peach flavor. The touch of sweetness makes it a perfect partner for spicy foods.

Kitchen Fridge Survivor™ Grade: B+

Your notes:_____

_____

J. Lohr Bay Mist White Riesling California	**PC**	**T**	**V**
	$	18	18

This wine's enticing floral scent and apple fruit, balanced by crisp acidity, make it a perfect aperitif.

Kitchen Fridge Survivor™ Grade: B+

Your notes:_____

_____

Kendall-Jackson Vintner's Reserve Riesling, California	**PC**	**T**	**V**
	$	26	27

For tasters new to Riesling, I often recommend this one, because it is a textbook "tasting lesson" for the

Price Ranges: **$** = $12 or less; **$$** = 12.01–20; **$$$** = 20.01–35; **$$$$** = > $35

Kitchen Fridge/Countertop Survivor™ Grades: *Avg.* = a "one-day wine," tastes noticeably less fresh the next day; *B* = holds its freshness for 2–3 days after opening; *B+* = holds *and gets better* over 2–3 days after opening; *A* = a 3- to 4-day "freshness window"; *A+* = holds *and gets better* over 3–4 days

Riesling style from a blue chip winery, with lush peach and tangerine flavors at a great price.

Kitchen Fridge Survivor™ Grade: A+

Your notes:_____

_____

Lengs & Cooter Riesling	PC	T	V
Australia	$$	X	X

✗ "This is one terrific bone-dry Riesling," with delicious lime and mineral flavors. Plus, it comes with a screw-cap on top of its beautifully shaped bottle—no doubt, "a sign of things to come" because "you can't beat the convenience."

Kitchen Fridge Survivor™ Grade: A

Your notes:_____

_____

Lingenfelder Bird Label Riesling	PC	T	V
Germany	$$	18	24

This pro's comments capture the consensus perfectly: "one of the gems of the 2001 vintage" in Germany. The amazing acidity, mineral character, and snappy apple flavor make it "perfect to sip on" but also great with food, from sushi to ceviche.

Kitchen Fridge Survivor™ Grade: A+

Your notes:_____

_____

Pierre Sparr Carte D'Or Riesling	PC	T	V
Alsace, France	$	24	24

"When you're sick of oak, take this for the cure," say my tasters of this sleek, tangy, mouthwatering Riesling with the scent of honey and Asian pears. Yum!

Kitchen Fridge Survivor™ Grade: A+

Your notes:_____

_____

Pikes Riesling	PC	T	V
Australia	$$	18	24

This bone dry, tongue-tingling Riesling is packed with pineapple and green apple fruit, "like a Jolly Rancher" on steroids. The screwcap is convenient to open and to keep the leftovers, which last seemingly forever.

Kitchen Fridge Survivor™ Grade: A+

Your notes:_____

_____

Schmitt Söhne (*SHMITT ZOHN-uh*;	PC	T	V
Söhne is German for "sons")	$	24	24
Riesling Kabinett, Germany			

This "solid bet for the money" has tart, Granny Smith apple flavors and a crisp and lively texture. The light body and low alcohol make it a good summertime/picnic quaff.

Kitchen Fridge Survivor™ Grade: A

Your notes:_____

_____

Strub Niersteiner Paterberg	PC	T	V
Riesling Spätlese, Germany	$$	27	27

"What a great QPR" (quality price ratio), say my tasters. And I agree, it's "one of the best Rieslings from the region" (Germany's Pfalz district). The creamy texture and lively acidity remind me of lemon custard.

Kitchen Fridge Survivor™ Grade: A+

Your notes:_____

_____

"TJ" Riesling Selbach-Oster	PC	T	V
(*ZELL-bock OH-stir*), Germany	$	24	24

This wine has neither a tongue-twister name nor a flabby-sweet taste. It *does* have classic German Riesling character: delicate peaches-and-cream scent, fruit flavors of tangerine and apricot, and endless finish.

Kitchen Fridge Survivor™ Grade: A

Your notes:_____

_____

Trimbach Riesling	PC	T	V
Alsace, France	$$	23	21

The fan club grows and grows for this classically Alsace Riesling. It's bone dry, with an amazing balance of delicate yet deep fruit flavor and mouthwatering

Price Ranges: **$** = $12 or less; **$$** = 12.01–20; **$$$** = 20.01–35; **$$$$** = > $35

Kitchen Fridge/Countertop Survivor™ Grades: *Avg.* = a "one-day wine," tastes noticeably less fresh the next day; *B* = holds its freshness for 2–3 days after opening; *B+* = holds *and gets better* over 2–3 days after opening; *A* = a 3- to 4-day "freshness window"; *A+* = holds *and gets better* over 3–4 days

acidity, which gives it amazing survivor potential. Could there *be* a bad food match? Maybe M&Ms.

Kitchen Fridge Survivor™ Grade: A+

Your notes:_____

_____

Weingut Louis Guntrum (*VINE-gut LOO-ee GUN-trum*) 'Royal Blue' Riesling, Germany	PC $	T X	V X

✗ The "awesome acidity" makes it "mouthwatering." And the "nice bottle and price" and food versatility make it "a great go-to choice for Riesling lovers."

Kitchen Fridge Survivor™ Grade: A

Your notes:_____

_____

Wente (*WEN-tee*) Riesling California	PC $	T 21	V 22

This is one of the few California Rieslings with the aromatic character we Riesling fanatics look for: "petrol," which sounds negative but is awesome! It totally tames briny, fishy flavors, but you don't have to eat such extreme food to love it. It will go with anything, and for the price you can afford to drink it often.

Kitchen Fridge Survivor™ Grade: A

Your notes:_____

_____

Sauvignon Blanc/Fumé Blanc

Grape Profile: Sauvignon Blanc (*soh-veen-yoan BLAHNK*) is one of my favorite everyday white wine grapes. Truly great ones are still available for under $10, which is something you can't say about many wine categories these days. Depending on whether it's grown in cool, moderate, or warm conditions, the exotically pungent scent and taste range from zesty and herbaceous to tangy lime-grapefruit to juicy peach and melon. All of the styles share vibrant acidity and growing admiration in the marketplace, as my tasters' comments and assessments made clear. The grape's home base is France's Loire Valley and Bordeaux regions. California and Washington state make excellent versions, sometimes labeled Fumé Blanc (*FOO-may BLAHNK*). In the Southern Hemisphere, Chile makes tasty examples, but it's the New Zealand Sauvignon Blanc category that continues to earn pro and consumer raves. Another of Sauvignon Blanc's major virtues is its food versatility: it goes so well with the foods many people eat regularly (especially those following a less-red-meat regimen), like chicken and turkey, salads, sushi, Mexican, and vegetarian.

> **THANKS, KIWIS!** Many NZ SBs are now bottled in screw cap for your convenience, and to ensure you get fresh wine without "corkiness" (see the glossary for a definition). Hooray!

Serve: Chilled but not ice-cold.

When: An amazing food partner, but the following notes spotlight specific styles that are good on their own, as an aperitif.

With: As noted, great with most everyday eats, as well as popular ethnic tastes like Mexican food.

In: An all-purpose wineglass.

	PC	T	V
Allan Scott Marlborough			
'Vineyard Select' Sauvignon Blanc	$$	X	X
New Zealand			

✗ Another "wow" from Allan Scott, and a perfect rendition of NZ SB: grassy, with gooseberry, grapefruit, and passion fruit that just jumps out of the glass and does somersaults on your tongue. Awesome.
Kitchen Fridge Survivor™ Grade: A+
Your notes:_____
_____

Price Ranges: **$** = $12 or less; **$$** = 12.01–20; **$$$** = 20.01–35; **$$$$** = > $35
Kitchen Fridge/Countertop Survivor™ Grades: *Avg.* = a "one-day wine," tastes noticeably less fresh the next day; *B* = holds its freshness for 2–3 days after opening; *B+* = holds *and gets better* over 2–3 days after opening; *A* = a 3- to 4-day "freshness window"; *A+* = holds *and gets better* over 3–4 days

Babich Marlborough Sauvignon Blanc, New Zealand	PC	T	V
	$$	X	X

✗ This "light, crisp, and pretty" bottling "gets less attention than NZ SBs like Brancott but is just as good." It's "a great value and a great food wine."

Kitchen Fridge Survivor™ Grade: B+

Your notes:_____

_____

Barnard Griffin Fumé Blanc Washington	PC	T	V
	$	20	18

This is classic Columbia Valley Fumé, balancing up-front flavors of pear, apple, and tropical fruit, steely, flinty notes, and a distinct grassiness that's typical of the grape—in short, lots of flavor and character for the price.

Kitchen Fridge Survivor™ Grade: B

Your notes:_____

_____

Beaulieu Vineyard (BV) Coastal Sauvignon Blanc, California	PC	T	V
	$	20	20

The fruity, crisp citrus flavors balanced with a zestiness that some call herbal and others "spicy jalapeño" make this wine a great choice for appetizers and spicy food.

Kitchen Fridge Survivor™ Grade: B

Your notes:_____

_____

Benziger Sauvignon Blanc California	PC	T	V
	$$	24	25

A "great wine list buy," say fans, citing the bright citrus, apple, and melon aromas and clean, crisp acidity that make it extremely versatile with a wide range of foods.

Kitchen Fridge Survivor™ Grade: B+

Your notes:_____

_____

Beringer Founders' Estate Sauvignon Blanc, California	PC	T	V
	$	20	20

I was blown away by the flavor depth and true-to-the-grape character of this wine—melon and grapefruit in luscious profusion, but not at all heavy. The "can't go

> **COASTAL: WORTH THE COST?:** In the 1990s, most major California wineries added a "coastal" family of wines to their lineup, meaning the grapes are sourced in California's prime coastal vineyard zones (roughly, Mendocino to Santa Barbara and everything in between), rather than the Central Valley, where a lot of bulk wines and low-priced varietal wines are grown. Presumably, the better grapes should yield a better wine that's worthy of the premium prices often charged (around $12–14 suggested retail). But in tasting after tasting, the quality of the "coastals" is disappointing, with a few exceptions (as noted in these reviews)—a sentiment echoed by my trade colleagues across the country. Ugh! The good news is that a grape glut means prices should improve a bit. Here's hoping quality does, too.

wrong price" is a gift, and the open bottle stays fresh for days.

Kitchen Fridge Survivor™ Grade: A+

Your notes:_____

Beringer Napa Sauvignon Blanc	PC	T	V
California	$$	18	24

The less-expensive Founders' gets better taste marks, perhaps because this bottling's very ripe fruit and oakiness taste like it's "trying to be Chardonnay." But to fans, that's a plus.

Kitchen Fridge Survivor™ Grade: B

Your notes:_____

Brancott Reserve Sauvignon Blanc	PC	T	V
New Zealand	$$	26	24

More gushing praise from trade and consumers for this SB, "one of New Zealand's best." The "uniquely

Price Ranges: **$** = $12 or less; **$$** = 12.01–20; **$$$** = 20.01–35; **$$$$** = > $35

Kitchen Fridge/Countertop Survivor™ Grades: *Avg.* = a "one-day wine," tastes noticeably less fresh the next day; *B* = holds its freshness for 2–3 days after opening; *B+* = holds *and gets better* over 2–3 days after opening; *A* = a 3- to 4-day "freshness window"; *A+* = holds *and gets better* over 3–4 days

Kiwi SB flavors" of lime, crushed herbs, and passion fruit are irresistible. Holds up great in the fridge or by the glass.

Kitchen Fridge Survivor™ Grade: A+

Your notes:_____

_____

Buena Vista Sauvignon Blanc	PC	T	V
California	$	24	29

What a great "house wine" candidate. The juicy nectarine and lime flavors sing with food or for just sipping, and the price is super.

Kitchen Fridge Survivor™ Grade: A

Your notes:_____

_____

Cakebread Sauvignon Blanc	PC	T	V
California	$$$	27	17

Fans of Cakebread's Chardonnay should try this Sauvignon Blanc. You get intense grapefruit aromas, with a hint of fig and vanilla, and much better bang for the buck.

Kitchen Fridge Survivor™ Grade: A

Your notes:_____

_____

Canyon Road Sauvignon Blanc	PC	T	V
California	$	24	24

A great Sauvignon Blanc that shows the true character of the grape: a hint of grassiness and grapefruit pungency, with lots of melon and peach fruit.

Kitchen Fridge Survivor™ Grade: A

Your notes:_____

_____

Casa Lapostolle (*lah-poh-STOLE*)	PC	T	V
Sauvignon Blanc, Chile	$	22	24

This bottling has so much more than I expect from a one-dollar-sign wine: vivid honeydew and kiwi flavors with a kiss of lime, and a long finish.

Kitchen Fridge Survivor™ Grade: A

Your notes:_____

_____

Chât. Ste. Michelle Columbia Valley	PC	T	V
Sauvignon Blanc, Washington	$	23	24

Three cheers: tasty, affordable, consistent. Okay, four—exotic: a scent of grapefruit zest and lemongrass tea, a hint of ginger flavor, and a creamy texture.

Kitchen Fridge Survivor™ Grade: B

Your notes:_____

Château St. Jean Fumé Blanc	PC	T	V
California	$$	23	20

This wine is aged, in part, in oak barrels, which give a creamy vanilla scent. That richness is balanced by fruit flavors of grapefruit, melon, and fig, plus a spark of tangy acidity. Yum!

Kitchen Fridge Survivor™ Grade: B+

Your notes:_____

Clos du Bois (*Cloh-dew-BWAH*)	PC	T	V
Sonoma Sauvignon Blanc, California	$	18	18

Scores have dipped a little, but it's still got a blue chip name and oaky richness, balanced with a crisp grapefruit character. I still think it is well priced for the quality.

Kitchen Fridge Survivor™ Grade: B

Your notes:_____

Cloudy Bay Sauvignon Blanc	PC	T	V
New Zealand	$$$	27	23

This delicious wine put the now-famous kiwi-lime character of NZ SB on the map in the 1980s. The consensus now is that it's "hard to find outside restaurants" and "expensive."

Kitchen Fridge Survivor™ Grade: A

Your notes:_____

Price Ranges: **$** = $12 or less; **$$** = 12.01–20; **$$$** = 20.01–35; **$$$$** = > $35

Kitchen Fridge/Countertop Survivor™ Grades: *Avg.* = a "one-day wine," tastes noticeably less fresh the next day; *B* = holds its freshness for 2–3 days after opening; *B+* = holds *and gets better* over 2–3 days after opening; *A* = a 3- to 4-day "freshness window"; *A+* = holds *and gets better* over 3–4 days

Columbia Crest Sauvignon Blanc	PC	T	V
Washington	$	20	20

Pros laud this round, crisp wine for its no-nonsense, classic Washington SB profile of melon, herbs, and flintiness. Super-versatile with food; great price.

Kitchen Fridge Survivor™ Grade: A

Your notes:_____

_____

Concha y Toro Casillero del Diablo	PC	T	V
(*cah-see-YAIR-oh dell dee-AH-blo*)	$	19	19
Sauvignon Blanc, Chile			

A perfect example of what Chile can achieve, for cheap, with Sauvignon Blanc: lots of ripe kiwi and honeydew fruit flavor, and that signature tangy zestiness. A real "wow" wine for the money.

Kitchen Fridge Survivor™ Grade: B

Your notes:_____

_____

Corbett Canyon Sauvignon Blanc	PC	T	V
California	$	13	13

Retail pros describe this wine as "plain and simple," though there's an interesting twist in that it's blended with Viognier and Colombard grapes. Although they give it an unusual green tea and gooseberry aroma, I wish more came through in the flavor, which is light.

Kitchen Fridge Survivor™ Grade: Avg

Your notes:_____

_____

Covey Run Fumé Blanc	PC	T	V
Washington	$	18	18

A super example of how Washington Fumé can balance a clean and crisp taste profile without being light. The lovely lemongrass and pink grapefruit character is "bracing enough for oysters but has enough substance to handle a big halibut steak."

Kitchen Fridge Survivor™ Grade: Avg

Your notes:_____

_____

Didier Dagueneau Silex Pouilly Fumé	PC	T	V
(*DID-ee-yay DAG-uh-no poo-YEE*	$$$	29	15
foo-MAY), France			

While lamenting the high price, buyers love this wine anyway. I, too, find the "bewitching" earthy, exotic, tropical, and herbal notes, all in one bottle, to be truly unique and delicious and, thus, worth the money.

Kitchen Fridge Survivor™ Grade: A+

Your notes:_____

_____

Domaine Thomas Sancerre	PC	T	V
Clos de la Crele (*cloe duh la KRELL*)	$$	X	X
France			

✗ Tasters love the "wonderful peach and lime flavors," the fact that it's "a reliable favorite every year," and often a "great bet on wine lists."

Kitchen Fridge Survivor™ Grade: A

Your notes:_____

_____

Dry Creek Fumé Blanc	PC	T	V
California	$$	25	24

Although the price has nudged up a bit, tasters still laud the flavor bang for the buck. You get "jam-packed, tangy" tangerine and peach flavors that get better and better over several days in the fridge. Magic with Tex-Mex.

Kitchen Fridge Survivor™ Grade: A+

Your notes:_____

_____

Duckhorn Sauvignon Blanc	PC	T	V
California	$$$	24	21

The "high price" reflects a premium for the Duckhorn name, made justly famous by its benchmark Merlot. I think the tangerine fruit, nice balance, and good length are worth it when you want to impress.

Kitchen Fridge Survivor™ Grade: A

Your notes:_____

_____

Price Ranges: **$** = $12 or less; **$$** = 12.01–20; **$$$** = 20.01–35; **$$$$** = > $35

Kitchen Fridge/Countertop Survivor™ Grades: *Avg.* = a "one-day wine," tastes noticeably less fresh the next day; *B* = holds its freshness for 2–3 days after opening; *B+* = holds *and gets better* over 2–3 days after opening; *A* = a 3- to 4-day "freshness window"; *A+* = holds *and gets better* over 3–4 days

Ernest & Julio Gallo Twin Valley   PC   T   V
Sauvignon Blanc, California $ 17   18

Pros are quick to point out the Gallo winery's split personality. On the one hand it's proven it can make serious, world-class wines. In addition, its "enormous portfolio" features plenty of "no-frills" wines like this Twin Valley Sauvignon Blanc. It's light and soft, for pleasant everyday drinking on a budget.

Kitchen Fridge Survivor™ Grade: Avg

Your notes:_____

_____

Ferrari-Carano Fumé Blanc   PC   T   V
California $$ 27   27

This is one of California's benchmark Fumés, balancing crisp tanginess with melony fig fruit and an extra layer of richness due to the oak barrel aging. Delish!

Kitchen Fridge Survivor™ Grade: B+

Your notes:_____

_____

Fetzer Echo Ridge Sauvignon Blanc   PC   T   V
California $ 18   18

The praise for offering a lot of varietal character for the money is well deserved. The pretty aromas and flavors of apples, grass, and citrus are lively, easy to drink, and great with so many foods.

Kitchen Fridge Survivor™ Grade: B

Your notes:_____

_____

Frog's Leap Sauvignon Blanc   PC   T   V
California $$ 24   27

This has been a fine dining wine list "regular" for years, whose name recognition pushed it into the "pricey" zone for a few years. But happily, I'm seeing better deals for it, so check it out. The 100 percent Sauvignon Blanc character of gooseberries, white grapefruit, and flinty, penetrating citrus flavors is delicious.

Kitchen Fridge Survivor™ Grade: A

Your notes:_____

_____

Geyser Peak Sauvignon Blanc	PC	T	V
California	$$	24	26

Although the price has jumped, this remains a lovely, classic California Sauvignon Blanc, combining the crisp tang of citrus with the juicier taste of kiwi.

Kitchen Fridge Survivor™ Grade: B+

Your notes:_____

Glen Ellen Proprietor's Reserve	PC	T	V
Sauvignon Blanc, California	$	14	15

Pro buyers recommend this wine if you're having an intimate gathering of, say, a few hundred people, as it's "OK for a big party on a small budget." Other varietals in the Glen Ellen line fare better than this Sauvignon Blanc (check the Chardonnay, for example), which to me tastes pretty plain. Even at this price, there are Sauvignon Blancs with more flavor.

Kitchen Fridge Survivor™ Grade: Avg.

Your notes:_____

Goldwater Estate Dog Point	PC	T	V
"Cork Free" Sauvignon Blanc,	$$	X	X
New Zealand			

✗ Another fearless adopter of the screw-top, which doesn't phase its fans who "love the lime-passion-grapefruit scent" enough to "buy it by the case."

Kitchen Fridge Survivor™ Grade: A

Your notes:_____

Grgich (*GER-gich;* both are hard	PC	T	V
"g" like "girl") Hills Fumé Blanc	$$$	24	18
California			

I'm happy that Grgich Hills keeps true to its distinct style: crisp, with scents of fresh herbs and citrus and flavors of tangy grapefruit and melon. Quality's

Price Ranges: **$** = $12 or less; **$$** = 12.01–20; **$$$** = 20.01–35; **$$$$** = > $35

Kitchen Fridge/Countertop Survivor™ Grades: *Avg.* = a "one-day wine," tastes noticeably less fresh the next day; *B* = holds its freshness for 2–3 days after opening; *B+* = holds *and gets better* over 2–3 days after opening; *A* = a 3- to 4-day "freshness window"; *A+* = holds *and gets better* over 3–4 days

high, but the blue chip name commands a premium price.

Kitchen Fridge Survivor™ Grade: B

Your notes:_____

_____

Guenoc Sauvignon Blanc   PC   T   V
California $ 19   18

This wine's got impeccable balance and complex flavors—vanilla, orange, peaches, and lime. A lot of stylish flavor for the price.

Kitchen Fridge Survivor™ Grade: B

Your notes:_____

_____

Henri Bourgeois (*ahn-REE buh-*   PC   T   V
***JWAH*) Pouilly Fumé, France** $$ 22   20

This Loire Valley classicist winemaker is considered "one of the best" by pros. Indeed the wine offers excellent balance and classic French subtlety and complexity, with floral and smoky scents, bracing acidity, and an elegant tanginess that's true to the Sauvignon Blanc grape.

Kitchen Fridge Survivor™ Grade: B+

Your notes:_____

_____

Hogue Fumé Blanc   PC   T   V
Washington $ 26   26

"A very good wine at a very good price," say trade buyers, and I agree. It is rare to find this level of complexity—fresh ginger spice, crushed herbs, citrus peel, plus a juicy mouthfeel, in an under-ten-dollars wine.

Kitchen Fridge Survivor™ Grade: A+

Your notes:_____

_____

Honig Sauvignon Blanc   PC   T   V
California $$ 21   21

One of the few California Sauvignon Blancs in a classic Loire Valley style. That means flinty, grassy, and balanced with delicate herb and spice notes.

Kitchen Fridge Survivor™ Grade: B+

Your notes:_____

_____

Jolivet (Pascal) Sancerre	PC	T	V
(*jhoe-lee-VAY sahn-SAIR*), France	$$	21	21

"Oh, Sancerre!" That taster's enthusiasm reflects the consensus of my tasters (and me), especially for this producer, a Loire star. This wine's elegant, well-balanced, and utterly "alive" taste and scent (lemon-grass, lime cream, and even a hint of honey) are great for the price. A great survivor, too.

Kitchen Fridge Survivor™ Grade: A+

Your notes:_____

_____

Joseph Phelps Sauvignon Blanc	PC	T	V
California	$$	X	X

✗ "Lots of ZING and ZANG" for the money, including "grapefruit and citrus flavors" and "softer fruit flavors" like peach and melon, and "an impress-your-guests winery name."

Kitchen Fridge Survivor™ Grade: B+

Your notes:_____

_____

Kendall-Jackson Vintner's Reserve	PC	T	V
Sauvignon Blanc, California	$	18	15

My tasters like the "bang for the buck" you get buying this cousin to the Chardonnay on which K-J stakes its reputation, because this wine offers comparable quality but at a cheaper price. Although it's Sauvignon Blanc in the richer style, it is still true to the melon, kiwi, and tangerine flavors of the grape. A good bet for people who prefer a white that's less heavy than Chardonnay.

Kitchen Fridge Survivor™ Grade: B+

Your notes:_____

_____

Kenwood Sauvignon Blanc	PC	T	V
California	$	24	29

The taste of this gorgeous Sauvignon reminds me of a summer melon salad with lime, honey, and mint. It

Price Ranges: **$** = $12 or less; **$$** = 12.01–20; **$$$** = 20.01–35; **$$$$** = > $35

Kitchen Fridge/Countertop Survivor™ Grades: *Avg.* = a "one-day wine," tastes noticeably less fresh the next day; *B* = holds its freshness for 2–3 days after opening; *B+* = holds *and gets better* over 2–3 days after opening; *A* = a 3- to 4-day "freshness window"; *A+* = holds *and gets better* over 3–4 days

has amazing kitchen countertop staying power, to boot, and a huge following: it was one of the most-rated wines in this year's survey.

Kitchen Fridge Survivor™ Grade: A+

Your notes:_____

_____

Lucien Crochet (*loo-SYEN crow-SHAY*) Sancerre, France	PC	T	V
	$$	26	24

"Definitive Sauvignon Blanc" captures the consensus from tasters on this top-scoring wine. The gorgeous, floral-herbaceous nose, creamy-but-not-heavy texture, crisp citrus and lemon pie flavor, and overall finesse were also cited as "a huge relief for the oak-weary." I'll drink to that!

Kitchen Fridge Survivor™ Grade: B+

Your notes:_____

_____

Mason Sauvignon Blanc California	PC	T	V
	$$	X	X

✗ My wine students love this kiwi and passion fruit–scented Sauvignon Blanc that's "like New Zealand SB without the grassiness." A great wine for savory or spicy food.

Kitchen Fridge Survivor™ Grade: B

Your notes:_____

_____

Matua (*muh-TOO-uh*) Sauvignon Blanc, New Zealand	PC	T	V
	$	18	18

This wine's "nice grapefruit taste" and lively herbal-kiwi scent are textbook NZ Sauvignon, and the "nice price" means you can enjoy it often—a great match for Mexican food.

Kitchen Fridge Survivor™ Grade: B

Your notes:_____

_____

Meridian Sauvignon Blanc California	PC	T	V
	$	21	18

For the money, I've always found this wine high on the yum factor. Just juicy, forward honeydew melon flavor, a kiss of subtle oak that gives it roundness, and a whiff of just-cut grass in the scent.

Kitchen Fridge Survivor™ Grade: B

Your notes:_____

_____

Michel Redde Pouilly Fumé	**PC**	**T**	**V**
France	**$$**	**29**	**24**

Trade buyers call this Loire Valley classic "a winner" and "a great value." It's textbook Pouilly-Fumé with smoky gunflint and herbal scents, elegant structure, and clean-as-a-whistle acidity. Try it with fresh goat cheese for a classic combination.

Kitchen Fridge Survivor™ Grade: B

Your notes:_____

_____

Murphy-Goode Fumé Blanc	**PC**	**T**	**V**
California	**$$**	**22**	**24**

While some call it "too Chardonnay-like," many tasters were thumbs-up on the less herbaceous, passion fruit and tropical flavor profile that some consumers said "tastes more expensive than it is."

Kitchen Fridge Survivor™ Grade: Avg

Your notes:_____

_____

R.H. Phillips Dunnigan Hills	**PC**	**T**	**V**
Sauvignon Blanc, California	**$**	**18**	**18**

The taste of this wine is like ripe tropical fruits—think mango, guava, and papaya—with a squeeze of lime. Delicious for the price.

Kitchen Fridge Survivor™ Grade: B+

Your notes:_____

_____

Robert Mondavi Private Selection	**PC**	**T**	**V**
Sauvignon Blanc, California	**$**	**18**	**24**

The bottle-to-bottle variation continues for this wine (which I've tasted more than a dozen times since the last edition of the *Guide*)—with some bottles seeming

Price Ranges: **$** = $12 or less; **$$** = 12.01–20; **$$$** = 20.01–35; **$$$$** => $35

Kitchen Fridge/Countertop Survivor™ Grades: *Avg.* = a "one-day wine," tastes noticeably less fresh the next day; *B* = holds its freshness for 2–3 days after opening; *B+* = holds *and gets better* over 2–3 days after opening; *A* = a 3- to 4-day "freshness window"; *A+* = holds *and gets better* over 3–4 days

fine and others tasting a bit off. At its best, there's easy-drinking green apple fruit.

Kitchen Fridge Survivor™ Grade: B

Your notes:_____

_____

Robert Mondavi Napa Fumé Blanc	PC	T	V
California	$$	29	29

✓ Robert Mondavi pioneered the use of the name Fumé Blanc for SB, and this is one of the winery's best offerings, as the stellar reviews show. It's layered with fruit, spice, and lemongrass and crisp, vivid citrus notes, all coming together in a richly textured and well-balanced whole. The complexity of flavor makes it very food-versatile and thus a good wine list choice when the table's ordering a diverse range of dishes and you don't know what will match them all.

Kitchen Fridge Survivor™ Grade: Avg.

Your notes:_____

_____

Rodney Strong Charlotte's Home	PC	T	V
Sauvignon Blanc, California	$$	24	24

For oak fans, this Sauvignon Blanc delivers plenty, plus loads of tropical fruit, banana, and apricot flavor, and a very full-bodied, creamy mouthfeel. It might overpower delicate flavors such as shellfish but would match up to bolder dishes and even meat.

Kitchen Fridge Survivor™ Grade: Avg.

Your notes:_____

_____

Silverado Sauvignon Blanc	PC	T	V
California	$$	24	24

On California's oak-lavished landscape, Silverado's stainless-steel style offers an alternative: clean, crisp apple and grapefruit character and medium body. The style is great with raw bar, fresh salads, and the like.

Kitchen Fridge Survivor™ Grade: B

Your notes:_____

_____

Simi Sauvignon Blanc	PC	T	V
California	$$	24	24

While many California wineries with blue chip reps and great track records have ridden a wave of rising prices, Simi has kept the magic combination—high quality yet still fair prices. This Sauvignon Blanc in the rich style, given creamy roundness by a dose of Semillon, and well-integrated oak, has nice tangy-apple flavors to balance it.

Kitchen Fridge Survivor™ Grade: B+

Your notes:_____

Sterling Vineyards North Coast Sauvignon Blanc, California

	PC	T	V
	$$	20	20

Yes, it's gotten slightly pricey as some tasters pointed out, but now the quality has leapt up, too. It's a vibrant style, with grapefruit, nectarines, and even Key lime flavors and scents.

Kitchen Fridge Survivor™ Grade: B

Your notes:_____

St. Supery Sauvignon Blanc, California (*saint SUPER-ee*)

	PC	T	V
	$$	26	23

The raves poured in for what many, including me, consider "one of the best" California SBs, "bright, crisp and amazingly complex for the price" and "great with goat cheese salad." I love this wine.

Kitchen Fridge Survivor™ Grade: A+

Your notes:_____

Sutter Home Sauvignon Blanc California

	PC	T	V
	$	16	16

Sutter Home wines are, across the board, some of the best at this easy-does-it price point. This is easy drinking, with light, fresh grapefruit, lime, and apple flavors that go very well with Tex-Mex and other spicy dishes. Holds well in the fridge after opening, too.

Kitchen Fridge Survivor™ Grade: B

Your notes:_____

Price Ranges: **$** = $12 or less; **$$** = 12.01–20; **$$$** = 20.01–35; **$$$$** = > $35

Kitchen Fridge/Countertop Survivor™ Grades: *Avg.* = a "one-day wine," tastes noticeably less fresh the next day; *B* = holds its freshness for 2–3 days after opening; *B+* = holds *and gets better* over 2–3 days after opening; *A* = a 3- to 4-day "freshness window"; *A+* = holds *and gets better* over 3–4 days

Villa Maria Private Bin Sauvignon Blanc, New Zealand	PC $$	T 26	V 24

This wine continues to rank, with my tasters, as one of the great New Zealand Sauvignon Blancs for the money (one of the first to offer the convenience of screw cap, too!). It's a nice balance between the grassy/herbal style in the scent but passion fruit-melon in the taste, with a green-apple tanginess that I love.

Kitchen Fridge Survivor™ Grade: B+

Your notes:_____

_____

Woodbridge (Robert Mondavi) Sauvignon Blanc, California	PC $	T 15	V 15

Among my favorites in the Woodbridge family of wines. Lively citrus character that's refreshing, crisp, and enjoyable, especially for the price.

Kitchen Fridge Survivor™ Grade: B

Your notes:_____

_____

Chardonnay

Grape Profile: Chardonnay is the top-selling white varietal wine in this country, and the fullest-bodied of the major white grapes. That rich body, along with Chardonnay's signature fruit intensity, could explain its extraordinary popularity with Americans, although in truth this grape's style is pretty chameleonlike. It can yield wines of legendary quality, ranging from crisp and austere to soft and juicy to utterly lush and exotic (and very often oaky), depending on whether it's grown in a cool, moderate, or warm climate. I am pleased to say that, as these notes indicate, buyers find all of these styles worthy, perhaps offering some hope to pros who bemoan a noticeable "sameness" to many of the brand names. All Chardonnays are modeled on white Burgundy wines from France. The world-class versions are known for complexity, and often oakiness; the very best are age-worthy. The rest, in the $ and $$ price categories, are pleasant styles meant for current drinking. California Chardonnays by far dominate store and restaurant sales, but the quality and value of both Washington State's and Australia's are just as good. Although no New Zealand or Oregon offerings made the survey due to limited production, they're worth sampling. Chile's popular-priced Chardonnays sell a lot, but in my opinion there are still few quality stand-outs (they do better with Sauvignon Blanc for whites, and with reds like Merlot and Cabernet).

Serve: Chilled; however, extreme cold mutes the complexity of the top bottlings. Pull them off the ice if they get too cold.

When: There's no occasion where Chardonnay *isn't* welcomed by the majority of wine lovers; the grape's abundant fruit makes it great on its own, as an aperitif or a cocktail alternative.

With: Some sommeliers carp that Chardonnay "doesn't go well with food," but I don't think most consumers agree. Maybe they have a point that it "overpowers" some delicate culinary creations in luxury restaurants, but for those of us doing most of our eating and drinking in less-rarefied circumstances, it's a great partner for all kinds of food. The decadent, oaky/buttery styles that are California's calling card can even handle steak.

In: An all-purpose wineglass.

	PC	T	V
Acacia Chardonnay			
California	**$$**	21	21

I've been serving this elegant Chardonnay to my restaurant guests for more than ten years. It's a perfect, silky style to serve when you want to the food to star—especially seafood, roasted poultry, or mushroom dishes.

Kitchen Fridge Survivor™ Grade: B

Your notes:_____

_____

Price Ranges: **$** = $12 or less; **$$** = 12.01–20; **$$$** = 20.01–35; **$$$$** = > $35

Kitchen Fridge/Countertop Survivor™ Grades: *Avg.* = a "one-day wine," tastes noticeably less fresh the next day; *B* = holds its freshness for 2–3 days after opening; *B+* = holds *and gets better* over 2–3 days after opening; *A* = a 3- to 4-day "freshness window"; *A+* = holds *and gets better* over 3–4 days

Almaden Chardonnay	PC	T	V
California	$	9	11

"Only half the party," jokes one sommelier, referring to Almaden's "Party in a Box," which contains two bags in the box, one this "tutti-frutti" Chardonnay, the other a white Zinfandel. It's light and simple, but as box Chardonnays go, one of the better ones.

Kitchen Fridge Survivor™ Grade: NA—bag-in-box package

Your notes:_____

_____

Artesa Carneros Estate Chardonnay	PC	T	V
California	$$$	24	24

This wine is plush with rich pear and pineapple fruit, but the acidity keeps it lively and inviting, so your palate doesn't feel numb after a few sips. The oak is sweet and toasty but supports the fruit rather than overwhelming it.

Kitchen Fridge Survivor™ Grade: A+

Your notes:_____

_____

Au Bon Climat Santa Barbara	PC	T	V
Chardonnay, California	$$$	29	29

The "wow complexity" and "elegant tropical fruit" make this wine a major favorite of wine pros. It gets high marks for value, too, because, as the tasters noted, "it's twice the wine at half the price" compared to many big-name California Chardonnays.

Kitchen Fridge Survivor™ Grade: A

Your notes:_____

_____

Beaulieu Vineyard (BV) Carneros	PC	T	V
Chardonnay, California	$$	18	24

If you want to taste "buttery" Chardonnay done right, this is it. Not at all heavy, and beautifully balanced, with both "lemony crisp" and apple notes balancing the richness. The price is right, too, and the quality consistency over the last few years exemplary.

Kitchen Fridge Survivor™ Grade: B+

Your notes:_____

_____

Beaulieu Vineyard (BV) Coastal   PC   T   V
Chardonnay, California $ 18   24

Like the entire BV Coastal line, this Chardonnay is a solid performer, with consistently good feedback from the entire range of tasters—novice to collector. It's textbook apple-pear Chardonnay in the not-too-heavy style. It gets extra points from me for being among the best of all the "coastal" Chardonnays, yet one of the cheapest.

Kitchen Fridge Survivor™ Grade: Avg

Your notes:_____

_____

Benziger Chardonnay   PC   T   V
California $$ 27   28

My tasters give top marks to this wine, which features prominent oak, tropical fruit, and buttery vanilla scents.

Kitchen Fridge Survivor™ Grade: Avg.

Your notes:_____

_____

Beringer Founders' Estate   PC   T   V
Chardonnay, California $ 23   23

Citrus/tropical fruit, a whiff of vanilla-scented oak, and a juicy mouthfeel put this in the top budget Chardonnay ranks with my tasters. A lot of pleasure for the price.

Kitchen Fridge Survivor™ Grade: A

Your notes:_____

_____

Beringer Napa Chardonnay   PC   T   V
California $$ 24   22

I consider this wine to be benchmark Napa Valley Chardonnay—rich baked apple fruit, creamy texture, toasty oak. The dead-on consistency of quality and style is also amazing, as is the value for money in a

Price Ranges: **$** = $12 or less; **$$** = 12.01–20; **$$$** = 20.01–35; **$$$$** = > $35

Kitchen Fridge/Countertop Survivor™ Grades: *Avg.* = a "one-day wine," tastes noticeably less fresh the next day; *B* = holds its freshness for 2–3 days after opening; *B+* = holds *and gets better* over 2–3 days after opening; *A* = a 3- to 4-day "freshness window"; *A+* = holds *and gets better* over 3–4 days

California marketplace where so many well-known wineries raise prices willy-nilly.
Kitchen Fridge Survivor™ Grade: Avg.
Your notes:_____

_____

Bernardus Chardonnay	PC	T	V
California	$$$	21	18

This Chardonnay has great complexity-for-the-money: enticing layers of flavor, including pear, pineapple, fig, honey, even butterscotch, enveloped in a creamy texture.
Kitchen Fridge Survivor™ Grade: B
Your notes:_____

_____

Buena Vista Chardonnay,	PC	T	V
California	$	19	20

Buena Vista "puts a lot of flavor in the bottle for a good price" with this Chardonnay, which is lush with soft baked apple fruit. It's also buttery in the scent, so check it out if you want to experience "buttery" Chardonnay.
Kitchen Fridge Survivor™ Grade: B
Your notes:_____

_____

Burgess Chardonnay	PC	T	V
California	$$$	22	22

This wine is the antithesis of the fruit- and oak-bomb style of California Chardonnay. Yes, there is fruit. But it is subtle and touched with a toasty nuttiness and soft oakiness that's similar to French Meursault.
Kitchen Fridge Survivor™ Grade: A+
Your notes:_____

_____

Cakebread Napa Chardonnay	PC	T	V
California	$$$$	28	22

This longtime favorite Napa Chardonnay is a classic in the category. I've noticed more prominent oakness along with the ripe pear and green apple fruit. The high demand keeps its availability limited largely to fine restaurants and boutique shops.

Kitchen Fridge Survivor™ Grade: B

Your notes:_____

_____

Caliterra Chardonnay   PC   T   V
Chile $ 18   19

"Always a favorite," say fans of this medium-bodied, great-with-anything Chilean charmer, especially at this price. Considering the pretty layers of vanilla and spice notes, I'd have to agree with them.

Kitchen Fridge Survivor™ Grade: Avg

Your notes:_____

_____

Callaway Coastal Chardonnay   PC   T   V
California $ 17   17

This wine's mouthwatering citrus, pear, and apple fruit and crisp acidity make it a delicious quaff on its own, but also a great food partner—particularly for Asian flavors, fresh vegetables, and seafood.

Kitchen Fridge Survivor™ Grade: B

Your notes:_____

_____

Cambria Katherine's Vineyard   PC   T   V
Chardonnay, California $$ 21   20

In both stores and restaurants this wine is a "big seller," and it's no wonder: you get the big oaky California Chardonnay style that's popular with many consumers, for under $20 retail in most markets. It's rich and plump with tropical fruit, a whiff of buttery scent, and the signature toasty oakiness. Nice.

Kitchen Fridge Survivor™ Grade: Avg

Your notes:_____

_____

Price Ranges: **$** = $12 or less; **$$** = 12.01–20; **$$$** = 20.01–35; **$$$$** = > $35

Kitchen Fridge/Countertop Survivor™ Grades: *Avg.* = a "one-day wine," tastes noticeably less fresh the next day; *B* = holds its freshness for 2–3 days after opening; *B+* = holds *and gets better* over 2–3 days after opening; *A* = a 3- to 4-day "freshness window"; *A+* = holds *and gets better* over 3–4 days

Camelot Chardonnay   PC   T   V
California $ 23   19

As pros note, this Chardonnay from the Kendall-Jackson family is "just darn good for the price." K-J fans flock to it for its crowd-pleaser buttery aromas and flavors, and creamy finish.

Kitchen Fridge Survivor™ Grade: Avg

Your notes:_____

_____

Casa Lapostolle Chardonnay   PC   T   V
Chile $ 22   23

Another excellent value from Lapostolle's basic line, this Chard's rich with pineapple fruit, yet not at all heavy, so it's great for budget sipping.

Kitchen Fridge Survivor™ Grade: B

Your notes:_____

_____

Casa Lapostolle Cuvée Alexandre   PC   T   V
Chardonnay, Chile $$ 23   20

I serve this Chardonnay to my wine students as a benchmark Chardonnay in the "oaky" style—it's toasty, cinnamon-spicy, and vanilla-scented, with soft and rich tropical fruit.

Kitchen Fridge Survivor™ Grade: B

Your notes:_____

_____

Chalk Hill Chardonnay   PC   T   V
California $$$$ 20   17

This classy Chardonnay's rich oak and luscious tropical fruit flavor gives it enough body to pair it even with steak. My tasters point out that it's gotten "pricey," but it's a quality leader whose price still is reasonable compared to the overall category of luxury California Chardonnays. I often recommend it as an impress-the-client wine.

Kitchen Fridge Survivor™ Grade: B

Your notes:_____

_____

Chalone Central Coast Chardonnay   PC   T   V
California $$$ 29   27

Since the early days of my career, this pioneering Central Coast Chardonnay has been a favorite of wine lovers—a bit "pricey," but "worth it." Pros cite its "unique mineral quality," as well as the elegant style and "beautiful stone fruit" flavor of peaches and apricots. It gains in complexity with bottle age, if you've got the patience to wait.

Kitchen Fridge Survivor™ Grade: B+

Your notes:_____

| Château Montelena Chardonnay | PC | T | V |
| California | $$$$ | 24 | 20 |

"Worth every penny," say both pros and consumers of Montelena's restrained, understated, and elegant Chardonnay that features flinty-spicy aromas, firm, crisp apple fruit, and a subtle, long finish. It gains extraordinary complexity with age.

Kitchen Fridge Survivor™ Grade: A

Your notes:_____

| Château Ste. Michelle Columbia | PC | T | V |
| Valley Chardonnay, Washington | $$ | 21 | 23 |

This Columbia Valley Chardonnay offers amazingly consistent quality. The style has grown more buttery, forsaking the clean citrus notes of old.

Kitchen Fridge Survivor™ Grade: B

Your notes:_____

| Château St. Jean Sonoma | PC | T | V |
| Chardonnay, California | $$ | 21 | 23 |

Pros laud the "tremendous quality for the price," a consistent virtue of St. Jean Chardonnay since at least the 1980s. The name recognition sells this wine, and then the taste delivers. It is creamy and complex, rich with tropical fruit and ripe pear and an elegant, restrained touch of oak.

Kitchen Fridge Survivor™ Grade: B

Your notes:_____

Price Ranges: **$** = $12 or less; **$$** = 12.01–20; **$$$** = 20.01–35; **$$$$** = > $35

Kitchen Fridge/Countertop Survivor™ Grades: *Avg.* = a "one-day wine," tastes noticeably less fresh the next day; *B* = holds its freshness for 2–3 days after opening; *B+* = holds *and gets better* over 2–3 days after opening; *A* = a 3- to 4-day "freshness window"; *A+* = holds *and gets better* over 3–4 days

CK Mondavi Chardonnay	PC	T	V
California	$	16	17

Some confuse the name with Robert Mondavi, but it's a different winery (his brother's). Regardless, it's a solid crowd pleaser, with soft fruit and a "bargain price."

Kitchen Fridge Survivor™ Grade: Avg

Your notes:_____

Clos du Bois Sonoma Chardonnay	PC	T	V
California	$$	24	24

This wine rocks the house with balance and quality in a category—California Chardonnay—where in the 1990s so many big names slipped in quality while prices climbed. Not here, where there's real excitement in the bottle: lots of citrus, peach, and melon fruit, subtly framed in oak, at a great price. The open bottle lasts and lasts, getting better and better, in the fridge.

Kitchen Fridge Survivor™ Grade: A+

Your notes:_____

Columbia Crest Grand Estates	PC	T	V
Chardonnay, Washington	$	23	25

"Great value" is the consensus among buyers of Columbia Crest varietals across the board. This wine's got precisely what Chardonnay drinkers look for: sweet spices, baked apple fruit, and a hint of butter in the taste and scent; all in balance and not too heavy.

Kitchen Fridge Survivor™ Grade: B+

Your notes:_____

Concha y Toro Sunrise Chardonnay	PC	T	V
Chile	$	16	18

This "bargain-priced" Chilean Chardonnay has plumped up of late, toward a medium-bodied—and more oaky— wine. But tasters note that it's still "light enough to be your house white" and easy to pair with food.

Fridge Survivor Grade: Avg

Your notes:_____

Cuvaison (*KOO-veh-sahn*) Napa Valley Chardonnay, California

	PC	T	V
	$$	23	21

This is a "wow" wine for the price, with a luscious tropical richness that's wonderful on its own and with food, especially curried dishes.

Fridge Survivor Grade: Avg

Your notes:_____

_____

DeLoach Chardonnay California

	PC	T	V
	$$	24	18

I, like several sommelier respondents, have served this "classy, good-value" Chard, which is redolent with peach and melon flavors, to my restaurant guests for years. Always a big thumbs-up.

Kitchen Fridge Survivor™ Grade: A

Your notes:_____

_____

Edna Valley Vineyard Chardonnay California

	PC	T	V
	$$	28	28

Although "outstanding quality and taste" and "nice price" reflect the consensus among tasters of every stripe, they don't do the wine justice. It has an amazing balance between Burgundian subtlety and complexity in the scent—cream, pear, toasted nuts, and smoke—and vibrant fruit in the taste. It ages well, too.

Kitchen Countertop Survivor™ Grade: A

Your notes:_____

_____

Ernest & Julio Gallo Twin Valley Chardonnay, California

	PC	T	V
	$	18	18

I agree with tasters who say this wine delivers well-made, soft, and easy Chardonnay at the budget price point.

Kitchen Fridge Survivor™ Grade: Avg

Your notes:_____

_____

Price Ranges: **$** = $12 or less; **$$** = 12.01–20; **$$$** = 20.01–35; **$$$$** = > $35

Kitchen Fridge/Countertop Survivor™ Grades: *Avg.* = a "one-day wine," tastes noticeably less fresh the next day; *B* = holds its freshness for 2–3 days after opening; *B+* = holds *and gets better* over 2–3 days after opening; *A* = a 3- to 4-day "freshness window"; *A+* = holds *and gets better* over 3–4 days

Estancia Pinnacles Chardonnay	PC	T	V
California	$$	24	26

Although the price is inching up, this Chardonnay remains nice for the money. The vibrant acidity makes it great with food, while the soft tropical fruit tastes delicious on its own.

Kitchen Fridge Survivor™ Grade: A

Your notes:_____

Ferrari-Carano Sonoma Chardonnay	PC	T	V
California	$$$	27	24

"Excellent value if you can afford it" is how one taster summed up the fact that in the luxury Chardonnay category this wine is among the most accessible. I think its quality easily matches that of many others at higher prices. With its spicy fruit and oak, and luscious citrus and honey flavors, this splurge is totally worth it.

Kitchen Fridge Survivor™ Grade: B

Your notes:_____

Fetzer Barrel Select Chardonnay	PC	T	V
California	$$	18	19

This wine, a pioneer in the category of big-fruit Chardonnay at everyday prices, remains a classic, offering a lot of consistency and juicy drinkability for the money.

Kitchen Fridge Survivor™ Grade: B

Your notes:_____

Fetzer Sundial Chardonnay	PC	T	V
California	$	22	22

A great sipping wine that's always dependable. The cheap price and enticing aromas and flavors of fresh pears and apples make it a fail-safe crowd pleaser.

Kitchen Fridge Survivor™ Grade: B

Your notes:_____

Forest Glen Chardonnay	PC	T	V
California	$	21	21

"Lots of oak" and "lots of toast and butter" dominate the scent, but there's pleasant apple fruit, too.

Kitchen Fridge Survivor™ Grade: Avg

Your notes:_____

Franciscan Oakville Chardonnay   PC   T   V
California $$ 22   20

"A very nice bottle of Chardonnay" with "the same characteristics" of the monster Chards—toasty oak and ripe pineapple/mango fruit, but "not over blown." A "great bet at steakhouses if you want a white."

Kitchen Fridge Survivor™ Grade: Avg

Your notes:_____

_____

Franzia Chardonnay   PC   T   V
California $ 10   11

Franzia is one of the best-selling wines in America. Obviously this no-nonsense, supercheap, no-corkscrew-needed white fills the bill for a lot of buyers.

Kitchen Fridge Survivor™ Grade: NA

Your notes:_____

_____

Gallo of Sonoma Chardonnay   PC   T   V
California $ 27   26

I keep waiting for this Chard, which my pro tasters call "outstanding for the price," to get expensive, or over-oaked. It's neither, offering ripe, intense flavors of pineapples, pears, and apples, and nice balance. Some buyers say the Gallo jug stigma affects consumer acceptance, but the sales stats say otherwise. People know a good thing when they taste it.

Kitchen Fridge Survivor™ Grade: A

Your notes:_____

_____

Geyser Peak Chardonnay   PC   T   V
California $$ 29   29

✓ This fresh, complex wine exhibits a perfect balance of apple, pear, and melon fruit, augmented by well-

---

Price Ranges: **$** = $12 or less; **$$** = 12.01–20; **$$$** = 20.01–35; **$$$$** = > $35

Kitchen Fridge/Countertop Survivor™ Grades: *Avg.* = a "one-day wine," tastes noticeably less fresh the next day; *B* = holds its freshness for 2–3 days after opening; *B+* = holds *and gets better* over 2–3 days after opening; *A* = a 3- to 4-day "freshness window"; *A+* = holds *and gets better* over 3–4 days

balanced nuances of smoky oak and a soft, creamy finish. As you can see, the tasters noticed!

Kitchen Fridge Survivor™ Grade: B

Your notes:_____

_____

Glen Ellen Proprietor's Reserve Chardonnay, California	PC	T	V
	$	14	14

I taste 'em all, and this is the best cheap Chard on the market, with juicy apple flavor and a great Survivor grade.

Kitchen Fridge Survivor™ Grade: B+

Your notes:_____

_____

Grgich Hills Chardonnay California	PC	T	V
	$$$$	29	21

Though many reviewers asked how to pronounce the producer's name (it's "GER-gich"), none seemed to have trouble praising this Napa Chard as one of the best. It's made in a complex, focused style that's packed with fruit yet balanced with elegance.

Kitchen Fridge Survivor™ Grade: A

Your notes:_____

_____

Hess Select Chardonnay California	PC	T	V
	$	24	26

Consumers and trade alike agree that this crisp, clean Chard is a "great value for the money"; layered with a full spectrum of fruits, from pineapple and mango to banana, pear, and lemon.

Kitchen Fridge Survivor™ Grade: B

Your notes:_____

_____

Inglenook Chardonnay California	PC	T	V
	$	11	12

Like all leading names in the formerly dominant jug market, Inglenook joined the varietal business, and its Chardonnay is a big seller with consumers because it gets decent taste marks for the price.

Kitchen Fridge Survivor™ Grade: Avg

Your notes:_____

_____

Jacob's Creek Chardonnay   PC   T   V
Australia $ 16   22

Both trade and consumers rate this a value star. I give
it extra credit for consistency and for the bright citrus
and peach flavor.

Kitchen Fridge Survivor™ Grade: Avg.

Your notes:_____

_____

J. Lohr Riverstone Chardonnay   PC   T   V
California $$ 24   27

This Chardonnay is a great value for the price, made
in the big buttery style, with flavors and scents of
lime, peaches, and minerals, complemented by
vanilla, and toasted oak scents.

Kitchen Fridge Survivor™ Grade: B

Your notes:_____

_____

Jordan Chardonnay   PC   T   V
California $$$ 24   18

Jordan's Chardonnay has come into its own after
some so-so early vintages. New fruit sources have
contributed a crisp vibrancy and length; the creamy
citrus flavors and gentle toastiness are subtle, classy,
and built for food.

Kitchen Fridge Survivor™ Grade: B

Your notes:_____

_____

Joseph Drouhin Pouilly-Fuissé   PC   T   V
(*poo-YEE fwee-SAY*), France $$ 24   24

This wine offers classic, understated Pouilly-Fuissé
character, with creamy apple and fresh almond
scents, plus steely dryness and a long finish.

Kitchen Fridge Survivor™ Grade: A

Your notes:_____

_____

Price Ranges: **$** = $12 or less; **$$** = 12.01–20; **$$$** = 20.01–35;
$$$$ = > $35

Kitchen Fridge/Countertop Survivor™ Grades: *Avg.* = a "one-day
wine," tastes noticeably less fresh the next day; *B* = holds its fresh-
ness for 2–3 days after opening; *B+* = holds *and gets better* over 2–3
days after opening; *A* = a 3- to 4-day "freshness window"; *A+* =
holds *and gets better* over 3–4 days

Kendall-Jackson Grand Reserve Chardonnay, California

PC	T	V
$$	24	24

K-J's trade-up Chardonnay is fuller-bodied and more intense than the Vintner's Reserve, with more prominent oak and lots of tropical fruit flavor. Some trade buyers say it should be "a measuring stick for others" in the luxury Chardonnay category, due to the high quality for the price.

Kitchen Fridge Survivor™ Grade: Avg

Your notes:_____

_____

Kendall-Jackson Vintner's Reserve Chardonnay, California

PC	T	V
$$	22	22

This wine seems to trap snobby sommeliers in a catch-22—torn by the fact that this is the top-selling wine on the market. The snobbery centers on the signature style—a whisper of sweetness to kick up the juicy fruit—that's widely imitated. And why not? What consumers have figured out is that sweetness doesn't always taste sugary. Like oak and ripe fruit, it often just tastes yummy. So enjoy but also know this: there are many similar Chardonnays out there at or below this price level. So you may want to experiment (and a good sommelier or shop will be happy to help you do just that).

Kitchen Fridge Survivor™ Grade: A

Your notes:_____

_____

Kenwood Chardonnay California

PC	T	V
$$	24	18

This Chardonnay gets good taste marks, thanks to the clean, refreshing citrus and apple fruit, the bright acidity, and the fact that it's not overly oaky.

Kitchen Fridge Survivor™ Grade: Avg

Your notes:_____

_____

Labouré-Roi Puligny-Montrachet (*lah-boo-ray WAH poo-leen-YEE mohn-rah-SHAY*), France

PC	T	V
$$$$	21	19

The subtle apple and mineral complexity of this wine garners good marks for taste, but the value assessment shows that at that price most buyers want more. Buyers should remember that Burgundy is pretty vintage-sensitive. Look for years with good harvest season weather to get this wine at its best.

Kitchen Fridge Survivor™ Grade: B

Your notes:_____

_____

La Crema Chardonnay	PC	T	V
California	$$	25	24

"Balanced and yummy" is one consumer's tasting note for this wine, whose value rating shows that many tasters appreciate that style for the price. I'd describe it as classically California—vividly ripe peach and tropical fruit, plus refreshing acidity, framed with toasty-sweet oak.

Kitchen Fridge Survivor™ Grade: Avg

Your notes:_____

_____

Landmark Vineyards Overlook	PC	T	V
Chardonnay, California	$$$	X	X

✗ This is classic "California tropical" Chardonnay, with "huge body, heavy-duty oak, and smooooth" rich texture

Kitchen Fridge Survivor™ Grade: Avg

Your notes:_____

_____

Leflaive (*luh-FLEV*) (Domaine)	PC	T	V
Puligny-Montrachet	$$$$	26	21
France			

Fans of Domaine Leflaive white Burgundies laud their "delicious," "finessed" Chardonnays that sing with style, complexity, and layers of baked apple and peach fruit—even in so-so vintages. Although such quality is pricey, the consistency and remarkable ageability earn this wine points for value for the money.

Kitchen Fridge Survivor™ Grade: B+

Your notes:_____

_____

Price Ranges: **$** = $12 or less; **$$** = 12.01–20; **$$$** = 20.01–35; **$$$$** = > $35

Kitchen Fridge/Countertop Survivor™ Grades: *Avg.* = a "one-day wine," tastes noticeably less fresh the next day; *B* = holds its freshness for 2–3 days after opening; *B+* = holds *and gets better* over 2–3 days after opening; *A* = a 3- to 4-day "freshness window"; *A+* = holds *and gets better* over 3–4 days

Leflaive (Olivier) (*luh-FLEV,*
***oh-LIV-ee-ay*) Puligny-Montrachet**
France

	PC	T	V
	$$$$	24	21

Because Olivier Leflaive blends wines from many growers, availability of this brand and sometimes prices can be better than the wines of Domaine Leflaive (the families are related). Though not quite on a par with the Domaine's, Olivier's Puligny is a worthy example. The refined citrus and pear fruit, and hints of mineral and toasty oak on the scent, gain complexity with a few years' bottle age.

Kitchen Fridge Survivor™ Grade: B

Your notes:_____

_____

Lindemans Bin 65 Chardonnay
Australia

	PC	T	V
	$	22	23

This wine encores as one of the top Chardonnay values with my tasters. The rich style—fragrant vanilla scent and tropical fruit—is balanced with lovely, bright acidity. The consistency of quality and style from year to year is impressive.

Kitchen Fridge Survivor™ Grade: B+

Your notes:_____

_____

Livingston Cellars Chardonnay
California

	PC	T	V
	$	16	14

Any Chardonnay at this price that actually tastes like Chardonnay deserves kudos. This is lemon-appley, soft, and perfectly pleasant.

Kitchen Fridge Survivor™ Grade: Avg

Your notes:_____

_____

Louis Jadot Mâcon-Villages
(*LOO-ee jhah-DOUGH mah-COHN*
***vill-AHJH*) Chardonnay, France**

	PC	T	V
	$	23	24

The clean, refreshing green apple and citrus fruit, sparked with vivid acidity and free of oak heaviness, is wonderful by itself and with food. It also holds nicely in the fridge, so you can enjoy it with Tuesday's takeout sushi and Thursday's tacos.

Kitchen Fridge Survivor™ Grade: B+

Your notes:_____

_____

Louis Jadot Pouilly-Fuissé	PC	T	V
(*poo-YEE fwee-SAY*), France	$$$	24	26

With my tasters, there's much to love in this wine: classic Pouilly-Fuissé elegance with fresh, unoaked Chardonnay fruit flavor, a touch of mineral, and good length. It's consistent from year to year. Finally, it's available and reasonable, sometimes at the two-dollar-sign level, thanks to favorable exchange rates at the time of importation.

Kitchen Fridge Survivor™ *Grade: A*

Your notes:_____

_____

Luna di Luna Chardonnay/	PC	T	V
Pinot Grigio, Italy	$	15	16

I respect savvy marketing, and I also love a good package as much as the next person. But I have tasted this wine repeatedly and cannot recommend it, in light of the many other worthy wines in this price point.

Kitchen Fridge Survivor™ *Grade: Avg.*

Your notes:_____

_____

Mâcon-Lugny "Les Charmes"	PC	T	V
France	$	24	24

This wine's shown amazing quality consistency throughout my career. It's true to the Mâcon style— soft and elegant, with a little snap of green apple acidity and good fridge staying power.

Kitchen Fridge Survivor™ *Grade: B*

Your notes:_____

_____

Macrostie Chardonnay	PC	T	V
California	$$$	29	24

My tasters call this "a 'splurge' wine" that's "worth it." I love the baked apple crisp scent and flavor, and the balance—lots of fruit, soft oak, nothing over the top.

Kitchen Fridge Survivor™ *Grade: Avg*

Your notes:_____

_____

Price Ranges: **$** = $12 or less; **$$** = 12.01–20; **$$$** = 20.01–35; **$$$$** = > $35

Kitchen Fridge/Countertop Survivor™ Grades: *Avg.* = a "one-day wine," tastes noticeably less fresh the next day; *B* = holds its freshness for 2–3 days after opening; *B+* = holds *and gets better* over 2–3 days after opening; *A* = a 3- to 4-day "freshness window"; *A+* = holds *and gets better* over 3–4 days

Meridian Chardonnay | PC | T | V
California | $ | 24 | 24

Meridian is ripe with pineapple fruit, lush in texture, and inexpensive for the flavor and quality. Thanks to its acidity, it's also versatile with food.

Kitchen Fridge Survivor™ Grade: B

Your notes:_____

_____

Merryvale Starmont Chardonnay | PC | T | V
California | $$$ | X | X

X "An excellent Chardonnay" with "ripe, tropical fruit flavors" and a "dose of toasty oak."

Kitchen Fridge Survivor™ Grade: Avg

Your notes:_____

_____

Michel Laroche Chablis St. Martin | PC | T | V
Burgundy, France | $$$ | 23 | 19

This is a rare find: French white Burgundy that's relatively available and affordable. It's a great one: true, classic Chablis, with elegant, piercingly pure apple and citrus fruit, a scent tinged with chamomile and a bit of mineral (like the smell of wet rocks), and amazing fridge staying power. Awesome!

Kitchen Fridge Survivor™ Grade: A+

Your notes:_____

_____

Nathanson Creek Chardonnay | PC | T | V
California | $ | 15 | 15

I find that this wine's value-for-money ratio has declined since it first hit the market in the early nineties. There are better choices for the money.

Kitchen Fridge Survivor™ Grade: Avg

Your notes:_____

_____

Penfolds Koonunga Hill | PC | T | V
Chardonnay, Australia | $ | 24 | 24

Sommeliers say that this Chard practically sells itself, because the boatload of tropical fruit and creamy butterscotch character offer great bang for the buck.

Kitchen Countertop Survivor™ Grade: B

Your notes:_____

_____

Penfolds Rawson's Retreat
Chardonnay, Australia

	PC	T	V
	$	20	23

This new Chardonnay from Penfolds offers lipsmacking apple and tangerine flavor that's clean, refreshing, not heavy—"so easy-drinking," as my tasters note.

Kitchen Fridge Survivor™ Grade: Avg
Your notes:_____

_____

Raymond Estates Napa Chardonnay
California

	PC	T	V
	$$	21	20

I'm a bigger fan of Raymond's red wines, but my tasters find this Napa Chard to be faithful, dependable, and consistent—delivering the requisite apple and pear flavors and toasty oak finish.

Kitchen Fridge Survivor™ Grade: Avg
Your notes:_____

_____

R.H. Phillips Dunnigan Hills
Chardonnay, California

	PC	T	V
	$	22	26

This wine's shown consistent quality and value for many years. It's got vivid citrus and nectarine fruit, with a nice kiss of oak that's not too heavy.

Kitchen Fridge Survivor™ Grade: A
Your notes:_____

_____

R.H. Phillips Toasted Head
Chardonnay, California

	PC	T	V
	$$	23	23

"Toasted Head" refers to more oakiness—they toast not only the inside of the barrel staves for flavor but the "head" (end piece) of the barrel, too. The result is very oaky, toasty, rich, butterscotch-scented Chardonnay. And the cool fire-breathing-bear label has earned practically cult status.

Kitchen Fridge Survivor™ Grade: Avg
Your notes:_____

_____

Price Ranges: **$** = $12 or less; **$$** = 12.01–20; **$$$** = 20.01–35; **$$$$** = > $35

Kitchen Fridge/Countertop Survivor™ Grades: *Avg.* = a "one-day wine," tastes noticeably less fresh the next day; *B* = holds its freshness for 2–3 days after opening; *B+* = holds *and gets better* over 2–3 days after opening; *A* = a 3- to 4-day "freshness window"; *A+* = holds *and gets better* over 3–4 days

Robert Mondavi Private Selection (formerly Coastal) Chardonnay California

	PC	T	V
	$	26	26

The raves out-cheer the few so-so reactions to this wine, which most of my tasters consider "rock-solid" and "always yummy." I like the harmony and complexity of the citrus and oak flavors.

Kitchen Fridge Survivor™ Grade: B

Your notes:_____

_____

Robert Mondavi Napa Chardonnay California

	PC	T	V
	$$$	27	24

"You pay more for the name," my tasters noted. But it delivers the baked apple and toasty-spice flavor of benchmark Napa Chardonnay.

Kitchen Fridge Survivor™ Grade: Avg

Your notes:_____

_____

Rodney Strong Chalk Hill Estate Bottled Chardonnay, California

	PC	T	V
	$$	23	22

The Chalk Hill sub-region of Sonoma yields the grapes for this rich, luscious Chardonnay. "Wow," say my tasters of this "mouthful of a wine" with "yummy" fruit and toasty oak.

Kitchen Fridge Survivor™ Grade: Avg

Your notes:_____

_____

Rodney Strong Sonoma Chardonnay California

	PC	T	V
	$$	24	22

This wine's a huge seller. The coconut-sweet scent from oak and the ripe apple fruit are classic Sonoma.

Kitchen Fridge Survivor™ Grade: Avg

Your notes:_____

_____

Rombauer Chardonnay California

	PC	T	V
	$$$	24	18

"Buttery and lightly toasty" is Napa's signature Chardonnay style, and it's perfectly rendered here. Tastes a lot more expensive than it is, too!

Kitchen Fridge Survivor™ Grade: B

Your notes:_____

_____

Rosemount Diamond Label	PC	T	V
Chardonnay, Australia	$	22	24

This "great for the money" wine's got a remarkably fresh aroma of melons, peaches, and citrus fruits, a little bit of oak richness, and a clean finish—all of which make it delicious and flexible with food.

Kitchen Fridge Survivor™ Grade: B+

Your notes:_____

_____

Sonoma-Cutrer Russian River	PC	T	V
Ranches Chardonnay, California	$$	25	23

This "quintessential California Chardonnay" has been a wine list stalwart for years. In contrast to the "monster Chardonnay genre," it holds out for elegance, complexity, and crispness. I have to caution that I have experienced some bottle-to-bottle inconsistency of late. Look out for SC's newest luxury bottling—in screw cap!

Kitchen Fridge Survivor™ Grade: Avg.

Your notes:_____

_____

St. Francis Sonoma Chardonnay	PC	T	V
California	$	24	24

I don't think you can find this much real Sonoma Chardonnay character at a better price. That means ripe pear and tropical fruit, soft vanilla oak, buttery scent, and a nice acid balance. It's a major fridge survivor, too.

Kitchen Fridge Survivor™ Grade: A+

Your notes:_____

_____

Sterling Vineyards North Coast	PC	T	V
Chardonnay, California	$$	24	21

This wine has made a jump in price but also in quality in the last few vintages. It's actually quite subtly

Price Ranges: **$** = $12 or less; **$$** = 12.01–20; **$$$** = 20.01–35; **$$$$** = > $35

Kitchen Fridge/Countertop Survivor™ Grades: *Avg.* = a "one-day wine," tastes noticeably less fresh the next day; *B* = holds its freshness for 2–3 days after opening; *B+* = holds *and gets better* over 2–3 days after opening; *A* = a 3- to 4-day "freshness window"; *A+* = holds *and gets better* over 3–4 days

exotic, with a vanilla, brown sugar, and nutmeg scent, and vibrant peach fruit on the palate.

Kitchen Fridge Survivor™ Grade: A

Your notes:_____

_____

Sutter Home Chardonnay	PC	T	V
California	$	21	21

My consumer tasters give credit where it's due, saying this wine's "pretty good for the price," with nice tangerine fruit flavor that's food-versatile and pleasant.

Kitchen Fridge Survivor™ Grade: Avg

Your notes:_____

_____

Talbott (Robert) Sleepy Hollow	PC	T	V
Vineyard Chardonnay, California	$$$$	24	21

Every guest I've ever served this wine adored the exotic marzipan, toasted nut, and tart pear flavors of this "restaurant" wine (rarely found in stores). As the price has risen, perceived value has suffered. However, among California's big-ticket Chardonnays it remains among the most reasonable for the quality.

Kitchen Fridge Survivor™ Grade: B

Your notes:_____

_____

Talus Chardonnay	PC	T	V
California	$	14	14

Major marketing has gotten this wine in front of many tasters, but reactions are lackluster. The advertising-driven brand awareness ensures it sells well, but there are many better choices for the money.

Kitchen Fridge Survivor™ Grade: Avg

Your notes:_____

_____

Turning Leaf Chardonnay	PC	T	V
California	$	14	14

I have always found Chardonnay to be the Turning Leaf brand's best foot forward—soft, clean, and citrusy, not heavy and very food-versatile. You'll have to decide for yourself!

Kitchen Fridge Survivor™ Grade: Avg

Your notes:_____

_____

Veramonte Chardonnay | PC | T | V
Chile | $ | 18 | 22

This Chilean Chardonnay gives you lovely tropical fruit flavor, without being too heavy. It's wonderful on its own, with salads, mac and cheese, you name it.

Kitchen Fridge Survivor™ Grade: Avg

Your notes:_____

_____

Woodbridge (Robert Mondavi) | PC | T | V
Chardonnay, California | $ | 12 | 12

Mixed reviews for this "sweet and oaky" Chardonnay whose name recognition keeps it wildly popular. In the final tally, it's not a taste and value leader in its price category, but on balance I find it pleasant.

Kitchen Fridge Survivor™ Grade: Avg

Your notes:_____

_____

Yangarra Park Chardonnay | PC | T | V
Australia | $ | 18 | 29

One taster called it, "very much in the same style as K-J," which makes sense since Kendall-Jackson does own this winery offering "tasty, juicy" Chardonnay for a "nice price."

Kitchen Fridge Survivor™ Grade: Avg

Your notes:_____

_____

Yellowtail Chardonnay | PC | T | V
Australia | $ | 21 | 23

Can you say "on fire"? In the wine trade this is considered one of the most successful new wine launches, ever. And no wonder: the "unbelievable price" makes it affordable to try, and the "most delicious, easy-drinking" taste keeps buyers coming back.

Kitchen Fridge Survivor™ Grade: Avg

Your notes:_____

_____

Price Ranges: **$** = $12 or less; **$$** = 12.01–20; **$$$** = 20.01–35; **$$$$** = > $35

Kitchen Fridge/Countertop Survivor™ Grades: *Avg.* = a "one-day wine," tastes noticeably less fresh the next day; *B* = holds its freshness for 2–3 days after opening; *B+* = holds *and gets better* over 2–3 days after opening; *A* = a 3- to 4-day "freshness window"; *A+* = holds *and gets better* over 3–4 days

Other Whites

Category Profile: A label of "other" for wines that don't fit neatly into a major category means some do not get the respect they deserve. The group does include a wildly diverse collection of wine types, from generic wines to uncommon grapes and regions to unique blends and proprietary branded wines—all of them commercially valid. Here is some background on each:

Generics—I include a few bag-in-box and jug wines in this survey because, although the category is losing ground to premium wines in a big way, the top brands are still big sellers. They are typically commercial blends of unspecified grapes. What riles wine pros and purists is the generic naming, which uses classic regional names like Chablis, Burgundy, and Rhine, even though the wines aren't from the named region and bear no resemblance to their quality level.

Uncommon Grapes and Regions—This category includes the grapes Albariño (from Spain), Pinot Blanc, Gewürztraminer, and Viognier, all meriting high marks from tasters and definitely worth your attention. The other–than–Pinot Grigio Italian whites are also here. (See the Wine List Decoder for more on these.)

Unique Blends—Although untraditional, blends of the white grapes Semillon and Chardonnay are proving successful, mainly in Australia and Washington state.

Proprietary Brands—These used to dominate the wine market in the seventies, and a few like Blue Nun have retained significant market presence.

Serve: Well chilled.

When: The uncommon grapes (like Gewürztraminer) and unique blends are wonderful when you want to surprise guests with a different flavor experience; see the notes that follow for ideas with the generic wines, but most tasters think of them when cost is a major consideration because ounce for ounce they're the least expensive wines in this book.

With: In my opinion, Gewürztraminer, Albariño, and the Semillon-Chardonnay blends are some of the most exciting food partners out there. My Best Bets indexes are full of specific food recommendations.

In: An all-purpose wineglass.

Alice White Semillon-Chardonnay	PC	T	V
Australia	$	19	20

Australia's blends of the Semillon and Chardonnay grapes are always fun, and this relative newcomer keeps the streak going with juicy peach flavor streaked with a zingy lime tanginess. Yum!

Kitchen Fridge Survivor™ Grade: Avg

Your notes:_____

_____

Almaden Mountain Chablis	PC	T	V
USA	$	7	10

Proof that bag-in-box wines are here to stay, this perennially popular "oldie but goodie" has been abandoned by the average buyer in favor of cork-finished varietal wines. It is still perfectly OK but decidedly after its time in many markets.

Kitchen Fridge Survivor™ Grade: NA

Your notes:_____

_____

Blue Nun Liebfraumilch	PC	T	V
(*LEEB-frow-milk*), Germany	$	12	12

"This one's proof of our sweet-tooth past," said one sommelier, referring to America's love of off-off-dry wines back in the 1970s. If you liked this then, you'll like it now. It's light, fresh, and soft like a fruit salad. Pair with spicy foods to tone down the heat.

Kitchen Fridge Survivor™ Grade: B

Your notes:_____

_____

Price Ranges: **$** = $12 or less; **$$** = 12.01–20; **$$$** = 20.01–35; **$$$$** = > $35

Kitchen Fridge/Countertop Survivor™ Grades: *Avg.* = a "one-day wine," tastes noticeably less fresh the next day; *B* = holds its freshness for 2–3 days after opening; *B+* = holds *and gets better* over 2–3 days after opening; *A* = a 3- to 4-day "freshness window"; *A+* = holds *and gets better* over 3–4 days

Bolla Soave (*BOWL-uh SWAH-vay*)
Italy

	PC	T	V
	$	21	20

This Soave is soft and simple, and still popular for everyday drinking.

Kitchen Fridge Survivor™ *Grade: Avg*

Your notes:_____

_____

Burgans Albariño (*boor-GAHNS all-buh-REEN-yoh*), Bodegas Vilarino-Cambados, Spain

	PC	T	V
	$	X	X

✗ "A wonderful alternative to Chardonnay; great with shellfish" say my tasters, who note that this peachy, aromatic white specialty from Spain "won't stay a secret for long."

Kitchen Fridge Survivor™ *Grade: B+*

Your notes:_____

_____

Ca' del Solo Big House White
California

	PC	T	V
	$	X	X

✗ This "great blend of ABCs" (a who's who of **A**nything **B**ut **C**hardonnay white grapes) was one of the first California wines to go screwcap with its entire production. The "bargain price" and "totally refreshing" flavors make it "a wonderful summer wine." It keeps fresh-tasting for weeks in the fridge, too.

Kitchen Fridge Survivor™ *Grade: A+*

Your notes:_____

_____

Carlo Rossi Chablis
USA

	PC	T	V
	$	8	10

Pros decry the use of the classic Burgundy name "Chablis" on a generic wine like this. But in the category of generic white wines, this is among the best.

Kitchen Fridge Survivor™ *Grade: B*

Your notes:_____

_____

Carlo Rossi Rhine
USA

	PC	T	V
	$	8	10

As another generic use of a classic wine region name, Rhine (as in Germany), this wine irritates pros. But it's soft and a little sweet, making it "OK for spritzers."

Kitchen Fridge Survivor™ Grade: Avg

Your notes:_____

Columbia Crest Semillon | PC | T | V
(*sem-ee-YOHN*)/Chardonnay | $ | 18 | 29
Washington

Blending the Semillon grape (which is typically partnered with Sauvignon Blanc) into Chardonnay gives a tantalizing bite of acidity and earthiness to the ripe Chardonnay fruit, and adds intriguing layers to the scent—honey, chamomile, and lime. It's a value star.

Kitchen Fridge Survivor™ Grade: B

Your notes:_____

Fetzer Echo Ridge Gewürztraminer | PC | T | V
(*guh-VERTZ-trah-mee-ner* or | $ | 24 | 25
simply *guh-VERTZ* as it's known
in the trade), California

My tasters praise this wine's luscious floral and apricot aromas and flavors. If you haven't tried Gewürz, you should, and this wine makes it affordable to do so. It's amazing with Thai and Chinese food.

Kitchen Fridge Survivor™ Grade: B

Your notes:_____

Franzia Chablis | PC | T | V
USA | $ | 8 | 9

Another huge generic seller primarily for package— no corkscrew, no wasted leftovers—and price.

Kitchen Fridge Survivor™ Grade: NA

Your notes:_____

Price Ranges: **$** = $12 or less; **$$** = 12.01–20; **$$$** = 20.01–35; **$$$$** = > $35

Kitchen Fridge/Countertop Survivor™ Grades: *Avg.* = a "one-day wine," tastes noticeably less fresh the next day; *B* = holds its freshness for 2–3 days after opening; *B+* = holds *and gets better* over 2–3 days after opening; *A* = a 3- to 4-day "freshness window"; *A+* = holds *and gets better* over 3–4 days

Hildago La Gitana (*ee-DAHL-go la hee-TAH-nuh*) Manzanilla Sherry, Spain	PC $$	T X	V X

✗ Hooray! My tasters wrote-in this "lovely" sherry that's a darling of restaurateurs, "especially with tapas-type and Mediterranean food." The "nutty," "clean" flavor is such a treat with salty fare and fried foods, too.

Kitchen Fridge Survivor™ Grade: A

Your notes:_____

Hugel (*hew-GELL*) Gewürztraminer France	PC $$	T 22	V 23

This wine was a runaway success with my tasters, who laud the character-for-the-money. The beautiful floral and sweet spice scent, and lychee-nut/apricot flavor, deliver nearly cultlike seduction. Sommeliers recommend it with Asian food and curry.

Kitchen Fridge Survivor™ Grade: A

Your notes:_____

Hugel Pinot Blanc France	PC $	T 21	V 18

Riesling is Alsace's calling card, but Pinot Blanc is its value grape. The concentrated apple-pear flavor, mineral complexity, and liveliness of this Pinot Blanc are great for the price.

Kitchen Fridge Survivor™ Grade: B

Your notes:_____

Knoll Gruner Veltliner (*kuh-NOLL GROO-ner Velt-LEEN-er*) Federspiel Trocken Wachau, Austria	PC $$	T X	V X

✗ "The retail price (in most markets) is about $15 and the taste is about $50!" said one taster, and I have to agree. Sommeliers "love this wine" because the "zippy, grapefruit-spice character" is "magic with food."

Kitchen Fridge Survivor™ Grade: A

Your notes:_____

La Scolca Black Label Gavi   PC T V
Italy   **$$$$** 19 19

As with many Italian whites, it's a perfectly "nice, appley" food wine. But the prices these days for wines from the Gavi region (it's the Cortese grape) are quite high, due to supply and demand. Pinot Grigio generally offers the same quality, for less.

Kitchen Fridge Survivor™ Grade: B

Your notes:_____

Livingston Cellars Chablis PC T V
USA   **$** 10 11

A simple, fruity generic wine that's a huge seller and good in its category.

Kitchen Fridge Survivor™ Grade: Avg

Your notes:_____

Marqués de Riscal Rueda (*mar-KESS PC T V
***deh ree-SCAHL roo-AY-duh*), Spain** **$** 24 18

My pro tasters always cite this wine's great value. It's fresh, sleek, and vibrant, tasting of Key lime and kiwi, without oak flavor and delish with all manner of foods, from sandwiches to sushi.

Kitchen Fridge Survivor™ Grade: B+

Your notes:_____

Martin Codax Albariño   PC T V
(*all-buh-REEN-yo*), Spain **$$** 22 18

This is "magic with food," say my tasters. It's a gorgeous wine: floral and citrus scents, passion fruit and pear on the palate, all on an ultralight, oak-free frame.

Kitchen Fridge Survivor™ Grade: B+

Your notes:_____

Price Ranges: **$** = $12 or less; **$$** = 12.01–20; **$$$** = 20.01–35; **$$$$** = > $35

Kitchen Fridge/Countertop Survivor™ Grades: *Avg.* = a "one-day wine," tastes noticeably less fresh the next day; *B* = holds its freshness for 2–3 days after opening; *B+* = holds *and gets better* over 2–3 days after opening; *A* = a 3- to 4-day "freshness window"; *A+* = holds *and gets better* over 3–4 days

Miguel Torres Viña Sol   PC   T   V
Spain $ 18   18

I love this wine—a fine bargain from one of Spain's top wineries. It's dry and fresh, with crisp apple flavor and a crisp finish.

Kitchen Fridge Survivor™ Grade: B+

Your notes:_____

Penfolds Semillon/Chardonnay   PC   T   V
Australia $ 24   28

✓ My tasters call this a "delicious sleeper of a wine." Its provocative pear aromas and citrus flavors make for a mouthwatering wine that's great alone or with food.

Kitchen Fridge Survivor™ Grade: B+

Your notes:_____

Pepperwood Grove Viognier   PC   T   V
(*vee-own-YAY*), California $ 24   27

The Viognier grape is often pricey because it's rare and tough to grow. This is an exception. It has real Viognier character—exotic honeysuckle, lavender, and ripe pineapple scents and flavors—at an afford-able price. Try it with Asian, Latin, and southwestern foods.

Kitchen Fridge Survivor™ Grade: Avg

Your notes:_____

Pierre Sparr Alsace-One   PC   T   V
France $ X   X

✗ One reviewer called it "a bizarre blend of Riesling, Pinot Blanc, Muscat, Gewürztraminer & Pinot Gris" but actually that's a classic trick in Alsace: blend all the local grapes to make a "delicate, pleasant" bottling with lots of peach and pear fruit that's "great with food, great price."

Kitchen Fridge Survivor™ Grade: B

Your notes:_____

Pierre Sparr Pinot Blanc   PC   T   V
France $ 20   20

As is traditional in Alsace, there's no oak or high alcohol here to get your attention. This wine screams character through its lip-smacking pear and quince fruit, with a whisper of mineral scent, all on a sleek, light-bodied frame. Yum.

Kitchen Fridge Survivor™ Grade: B

Your notes:_____

_____

Rosemount Chardonnay/Semillon	PC	T	V
Australia	$	21	24

The "ultimate seafood wine," say fans of this juicy citrus-styled blend, featuring gorgeous tangerine fruit, a creamy texture, and bright spiciness that makes it perfect with shellfish or just on its own.

Kitchen Fridge Survivor™ Grade: A

Your notes:_____

_____

Ruffino Orvieto	PC	T	V
Italy	$	19	21

This wine is a favorite of tasters for its crisp, refreshing acidity, clean melon fruit, and nutty qualities. It's what everyday Italian white wine should be, in both style and price: a light-bodied wine that makes a perfect *aperitivo*.

Kitchen Fridge Survivor™ Grade: B

Your notes:_____

_____

Schmitt Söhne (*SHMITT ZOHN-uh;*	PC	T	V
Söhne is German for "sons")	$	14	14
Liebfraumilch, Germany			

"Definitely on the sweet side," says a pro of this off-off-dry wine that's still popular with Americans who like a little spritz in their wine.

Kitchen Fridge Survivor™ Grade: Avg

Your notes:_____

_____

Price Ranges: **$** = $12 or less; **$$** = 12.01–20; **$$$** = 20.01–35; **$$$$** = > $35

Kitchen Fridge/Countertop Survivor™ Grades: *Avg.* = a "one-day wine," tastes noticeably less fresh the next day; *B* = holds its freshness for 2–3 days after opening; *B+* = holds *and gets better* over 2–3 days after opening; *A* = a 3- to 4-day "freshness window"; *A+* = holds *and gets better* over 3–4 days

Sokol Blosser Evolution   PC   T   V
Oregon $ 21   20

The way-cool label will impress your friends, and the taste will delight them. It is a blend of a whole bunch of aromatic white grapes, and that's exactly what it tastes like. The scent and juicy flavor are like an aromatherapy treatment—honeysuckle, peach, apricot, pear, and more—but a lot cheaper!

Kitchen Fridge Survivor™ Grade: B

Your notes:_____

_____

Sutter Home Gewürztraminer   PC   T   V
California $ 21   23

Guh-VURTS-truh-meen-er has to be one of the funnest grapes around. The flavor: fruit-salad-in-a-glass; the awesome matches: Tex-Mex, barbecued chicken, tuna salad with grapes.

Kitchen Fridge Survivor™ Grade: B

Your notes:_____

_____

Walter Glatzer Gruner Veltliner   PC   T   V
Kabinett, Austria $ X   X

✗ Another sommelier favorite, so "look for it on fancy wine lists," say my tasters, and "you'll find a steal." The "tangy, mouthwatering lemongrass and spice" character "works perfectly with vegetable first courses," as well as shellfish and exotic foods like Thai, Japanese, or Indian

Kitchen Fridge Survivor™ Grade: A

Your notes:_____

_____

Weingärtner (*WINE-gart-ner*)   PC   T   V
Gruner Veltliner Federspiel, Austria $ 24   18

The easy price of this wine makes it a good intro to the amazing character of Austria's signature white grape, which the vintners call Gru-V (as in groovy) for short. And that it is—ginger, grapefruit, and cardamom scents; apple, peach, and lemon zest flavors, great acidity, great food compatibility. Go for it!

Kitchen Fridge Survivor™ Grade: A

Your notes:_____

_____

BLUSH/PINK/ROSÉ WINES

Category Profile: Although many buyers are snobby about the blush category, the truth is that for most of us white Zinfandel was probably the first wine we drank that had a cork. It's a juicy, uncomplicated style that makes a lot of buyers, and their wallets, very happy. Now for the gear switch—rosé. The only thing true rosés have in common with the blush category is appearance. Rosé wines are classic to many world-class European wine regions. They are absolutely dry, tangy, crisp, and amazingly interesting wines for the money. I often say that with their spice and complexity they have red wine flavor, but the lightness of body and chillability gives them white wine style. They are *great* food wines. Don't miss the chance to try my recommendations or those of your favorite shop or restaurant. You will love them.

Serve: The colder the better.

When: The refreshing touch of sweetness in blush styles makes them great as an aperitif. (Some wine drinkers are snobby about the slight sweetness in popular wines, but actually their style is right in sync with the other popular drinks out there—sodas and sweet cocktails like the cosmopolitan and the margarita.)

With: A touch of sweetness in wine can tone down heat, so spicy foods are an especially good partner for blush wine. Dry rosés go with everything.

In: An all-purpose wineglass.

Beringer White Zinfandel	PC	T	V
California	$	18	19

The standard-bearer in the WZ category, and for good reason. It's got lots of fresh strawberry, sweet

Price Ranges: **$** = $12 or less; **$$** = 12.01–20; **$$$** = 20.01–35; **$$$$** = > $35
Kitchen Fridge/Countertop Survivor™ Grades: *Avg.* = a "one-day wine," tastes noticeably less fresh the next day; *B* = holds its freshness for 2–3 days after opening; *B+* = holds *and gets better* over 2–3 days after opening; *A* = a 3- to 4-day "freshness window"; *A+* = holds *and gets better* over 3–4 days

raspberry, and lively citrus aromas and flavors and a juicy texture.

Kitchen Fridge Survivor™ Grade: B

Your notes:_____

_____

| Bonny Doon Vin Gris de Cigare | PC | T | V |
| Pink Wine, California | $$ | 24 | 29 |

Randall Grahm of Bonny Doon doesn't do anything halfway, including this quaffer that's all about bone-dry, tangy, spicy refreshment. Nor does he trifle with self-conscious window dressing. This is *pink wine*—if there's an image problem with that, it's in your head.

Kitchen Fridge Survivor™ Grade: B

Your notes:_____

_____

| Buehler White Zinfandel | PC | T | V |
| California | $ | 18 | 20 |

A favorite of restaurant buyers because it's not as sweet as its peers and has some nice berry flavors.

Kitchen Fridge Survivor™ Grade: B

Your notes:_____

_____

| Ernest & Julio Gallo Twin Valley | PC | T | V |
| White Zinfandel, California | $ | 13 | 17 |

Quite light in the category. A summer staple for many, thanks to the refreshing watermelon flavor.

Kitchen Fridge Survivor™ Grade: Avg

Your notes:_____

_____

| Franzia Blush | PC | T | V |
| USA | $ | 8 | 12 |

A huge bag-in-box seller, among the most obviously sweet of the bunch.

Kitchen Fridge Survivor™ Grade: NA

Your notes:_____

_____

Franzia White Zinfandel   PC   T   V

California $ 9   12

For white Zin drinkers, a mega-budget choice that's decent.

Kitchen Fridge Survivor™ Grade: NA

Your notes:_____

_____

Inglenook White Zinfandel   PC   T   V

California $ 12   18

Experienced buyers note that as far as white Zins go, this one is nice for the price.

Kitchen Fridge Survivor™ Grade: Avg

Your notes:_____

_____

Lang & Reed Wild Hare Rosé   PC   T   V

Cabernet Franc, California $$ X   X

✗ This is "hard to find but worth the search" say my tasters, who "see it mostly on hip wine lists." It's got "great strawberries on the nose and a nice mouthfeel." A "great, totally dry" rosé bottling that's "perfect for summer."

Kitchen Fridge Survivor™ Grade: B+

Your notes:_____

_____

Marqués de Cáceres Rioja Rosado   PC   T   V

Spain $ 24   24

If your store doesn't stock this wine, ask them to order it. The tangy strawberry-watermelon-spice flavor is delish! You can invite *any* food to this party.

Kitchen Fridge Survivor™ Grade: Avg

Your notes:_____

_____

Price Ranges: **$** = $12 or less; **$$** = 12.01–20; **$$$** = 20.01–35; **$$$$** = > $35

Kitchen Fridge/Countertop Survivor™ Grades: *Avg.* = a "one-day wine," tastes noticeably less fresh the next day; *B* = holds its freshness for 2–3 days after opening; *B+* = holds *and gets better* over 2–3 days after opening; *A* = a 3- to 4-day "freshness window"; *A+* = holds *and gets better* over 3–4 days

McDowell Grenache Rosé   PC   T   V
California $ 20   20

Lively strawberry and pomegranate flavor, tangy
acidity and spice, clean as a whistle, great with food.

Kitchen Fridge Survivor™ Grade: B

Your notes:_____

Regaleali Rosato, Tasca D'Almerita   PC   T   V
Italy $ 21   20

Proof that Italians put all their *passione* into reds
(the hot-weather version of which are rosatos like
this one). If you don't like white, you can have this
spicy, mouthwatering, bone-dry rosé to cool you down
and complement your summertime or seaside fare.

Kitchen Fridge Survivor™ Grade: B

Your notes:_____

Sutter Home White Zinfandel   PC   T   V
California $ 15   18

Purportedly invented out of necessity in the 1980s
(the winery had lots of red grapes planted, but taste
trends had shifted to favor white wines), Sutter
Home's trailblazing WZ is still one of the best. It's
juicy and pleasing.

Kitchen Fridge Survivor™ Grade: B

Your notes:_____

Vendange White Zinfandel   PC   T   V
California $ 10   12

Great package, simple and fruity style, and widely
available—but not a taste leader in the WZ category.

Kitchen Countertop Survivor™ Grade: Avg

Your notes:_____

RED WINES

Beaujolais/Gamay

Category Profile: Beaujolais Nouveau (*bow-jhoe-LAY*), the new wine of the vintage that each year is shipped from France on the third Thursday in November (just in time for Thanksgiving), dominates sales in this category. (It also inspires scores of nouveau imitators riding its cash-cow coattails.) You can have fun with nouveau, but don't skip the real stuff—particularly Beaujolais-Villages (*vill-AHJH*) and Beaujolais Cru (named for the town where they're grown, e.g., Morgon, Brouilly, Moulin-à-Vent, etc.). These Beaujolais categories are a wine world rarity, in that they offer real character at a low price. The signature style of Beaujolais is a juicy, grapey fruit flavor and succulent texture with, in the crus, an added layer of earthy spiciness. All red Beaujolais is made from the Gamay grape.

Serve: Lightly chilled, to enhance the vibrant fruit.

When: Great as an aperitif and for alfresco occasions such as picnics and barbecues.

With: Many tasters said they swear by it for Thanksgiving. It's so soft, smooth, and juicy I think it goes with everything, from the simplest of sandwich meals to brunch, lunch, and beyond. It's often a great buy on restaurant wine lists and versatile for those really tough matching situations where you've ordered everything from oysters to osso bucco but you want one wine.

In: An all-purpose wineglass.

	PC	T	V
Barton & Guestier (B&G) Beaujolais	**$**	**18**	**18**
France			

Here's a good-value, food-friendly wine that's great for parties, because it won't break your bank. What more could you ask for?" (FYI: Insiders call it "B&G" for short.)
Kitchen Countertop Survivor™ Grade: Avg
Your notes:_____

_____

Price Ranges: **$** = $12 or less; **$$** = 12.01–20; **$$$** = 20.01–35; **$$$$** = > $35
Kitchen Fridge/Countertop Survivor™ Grades: *Avg.* = a "one-day wine," tastes noticeably less fresh the next day; *B* = holds its freshness for 2–3 days after opening; *B+* = holds *and gets better* over 2–3 days after opening; *A* = a 3- to 4-day "freshness window"; *A+* = holds *and gets better* over 3–4 days

Duboeuf (*Duh-BUFF*) (Georges)   PC   T   V
Beaujolais Nouveau, France $ 18   20

Although nouveau remains a hugely popular seasonal French wine, pros have seen consumers cool a bit to the hype. Duboeuf's nouveau is always a festive, juicy crowd-pleaser that consumers find "drinkable with or without food," great with Thanksgiving dinner, and bargain-priced.

Kitchen Countertop Survivor™ *Grade: Avg*

Your notes:_____

_____

Duboeuf (Georges) Beaujolais-   PC   T   V
Villages, France $ 20   23

I agree with trade colleagues that it's "hard not to love" this widely available bottling from the King of Beaujolais. Its plump berry flavor is great with a wide variety of foods and a good wine to offer those who don't normally drink red.

Kitchen Countertop Survivor™ *Grade: B*

Your notes:_____

_____

Duboeuf (Georges) Moulin-A-Vent   PC   T   V
France $ X   X

✗ "A great intro to the Beaujolais crus," the single-vineyards with more concentration and character than straight Beaujolais. Like other Georges Duboeuf wines, this is "great for the money" with lots of "spice, smooth berry fruit" and "more complexity than you'd expect."

Kitchen Countertop Survivor™ *Grade: B*

Your notes:_____

_____

Louis Jadot Beaujolais-Villages   PC   T   V
France $ 24   26

I've tasted—and sold in restaurants—*every* vintage of this wine for the last ten years, and my guests' upbeat reaction is as consistent as the wine: delish! The light body and berry fruit make it "the perfect sipping wine." It's food versatile too, with everything from "roasted chicken and salad" to "sushi if you want a red," and Chinese food.

Kitchen Countertop Survivor™ Grade: B

Your notes:_____

Pinot Noir

Category Profile: Pinot Noir is my favorite of the major classic red grape varieties, because I love its smoky-ripe scent, pure fruit flavor, and, most of all, silken texture. It also offers red wine intensity and complexity, without being heavy. Although Pinot Noir's home turf is the Burgundy region of France, few of those wines make the list of top sellers in the U.S., because production is tiny. The coolest parts of coastal California (especially the Russian River Valley, Carneros, Monterey, Sonoma Coast, and Santa Barbara County) specialize in Pinot Noir, as does Oregon's Willamette (*will-AM-ett*) Valley. New Zealand is also becoming an important Pinot source. Pinot Noir from all the major regions is typically oak aged, but as with other grapes the amount of oakiness is matched to the intensity of the fruit. Generally the budget bottlings are the least oaky.

Serve: *Cool* room temperature; don't hesitate to chill the bottle briefly if needed.

When: Although the silky texture makes Pinot Noir quite bewitching on its own, it is also the ultimate "food wine." It is my choice to take to dinner parties and to order in restaurants, because I know it will probably delight both white and red wine drinkers and will go with most any food.

With: Pinot's versatility is legendary, but it is *the* wine for mushroom dishes, salmon, rare tuna, and any bird (especially duck).

Price Ranges: **$** = $12 or less; **$$** = 12.01–20; **$$$** = 20.01–35; **$$$$** = > $35

Kitchen Fridge/Countertop Survivor™ Grades: *Avg.* = a "one-day wine," tastes noticeably less fresh the next day; *B* = holds its freshness for 2–3 days after opening; *B+* = holds *and gets better* over 2–3 days after opening; *A* = a 3- to 4-day "freshness window"; *A+* = holds *and gets better* over 3–4 days

In: An all-purpose wineglass. Or try a larger balloon stem; the extra air space enhances the wine's aroma.

Acacia Carneros Pinot Noir	PC	T	V
California	$$$	X	X

✗ This "smooth as silk Pinot" has a "lovely berry flavor" and "spice and earth" scent. One reviewer pointed out it "ages nicely for a few years" and this was indeed our experience at Windows on the World.
Kitchen Countertop Survivor™ Grade: B+
Your notes:_____

_____

Anapamu Pinot Noir	PC	T	V
California	$$	18	19

It's pronounced *ah-nuh-PAH-moo*. Pros laud the classic Pinot Noir character that's often hard to find at this price point: "elegant and supple" texture, "juicy cherry" fruit.
Kitchen Countertop Survivor™ Grade: B
Your notes:_____

_____

Archery Summit Arcus Estate	PC	T	V
Pinot Noir, Oregon	$$$$	26	18

The "intense and opulent" black cherry fruit and layers of flavor have lots of fans, but some pros find it "over-oaked for the amount of fruit." It needs aeration to soften up.
Kitchen Countertop Survivor™ Grade: B
Your notes:_____

_____

Au Bon Climat Pinot Noir Santa	PC	T	V
Barbara, California	$$$	29	22

Oh-bohn-clee-MAHT has a cult following and a nickname—"ABC." It's among the truly great American Pinots, with vivid black cherry fruit, structural components (the oak, body, and tannin) in perfect balance, and a slightly animal note in the scent that to me marks the ABC style.
Kitchen Countertop Survivor™ Grade: B+
Your notes:_____

_____

Beaulieu Vineyards (BV) Carneros Pinot Noir, California

PC	T	V
$$	21	18

This wine displays "classic Carneros Pinot" character—silky cherry fruit, spicy, and soft. The reasonable price and blue chip name make it a great wine for business or casual entertaining.

Kitchen Countertop Survivor™ Grade: B

Your notes:_____

_____

Beringer Founders' Estate Pinot Noir California

PC	T	V
$	24	29

✓ Inexpensive Pinot Noir can fall short on flavor, but this one's an exception: it's a taste and value star. Its soft berry flavors and silky texture, without heavy alcohol, are probably what people looking for the smoothness credited to Merlot actually want.

Kitchen Countertop Survivor™ Grade: B

Your notes:_____

_____

Brancott Vineyards Marlborough Reserve Pinot Noir, New Zealand

PC	T	V
$$	X	X

✗ Pinot lovers have a lot to look forward to as New Zealand steps up production of this grape, with wonderful versions like this wine. The cherry cola scent and cinnamon-black cherry flavors are lush, but the structure is incredibly balanced and sleek. Great stuff.

Kitchen Countertop Survivor™ Grade: A

Your notes:_____

_____

Buena Vista Carneros Pinot Noir California

PC	T	V
$$	18	24

Real Pinot Noir character for well under $20. It's got classic Carneros elegance, with aromas of potpourri

Price Ranges: **$** = $12 or less; **$$** = 12.01–20; **$$$** = 20.01–35; **$$$$** = > $35

Kitchen Fridge/Countertop Survivor™ Grades: *Avg.* = a "one-day wine," tastes noticeably less fresh the next day; *B* = holds its freshness for 2–3 days after opening; *B+* = holds *and gets better* over 2–3 days after opening; *A* = a 3- to 4-day "freshness window"; *A+* = holds *and gets better* over 3–4 days

and exotic tea leaves and flavors of dried fruit and spices. A triumph, especially for the money.

Kitchen Countertop Survivor™ Grade: B

Your notes:_____

_____

| **Byron Santa Maria Valley Pinot Noir** | PC | T | V |
| **California** | $$$ | 24 | 19 |

This Pinot's complexity, ripe dark cherry fruit, and silky texture are consistently good, but my tasters were rueful over the rising price.

Kitchen Countertop Survivor™ Grade: B+

Your notes:_____

_____

| **Calera Central Coast Pinot Noir** | PC | T | V |
| **California** | $$$ | 19 | 20 |

Calera Pinot Noirs deliver a rare and great combination: a blue chip track record in hand-crafted but available quantities. Year in and year out, the "supple, earthy" style, redolent of "dried cherry fruit," comes through—a house style I've loved since at least the late eighties. Look also for the delicious single-vineyard Calera Pinots.

Kitchen Countertop Survivor™ Grade: B+

Your notes:_____

_____

| **Cambria (*CAME-bree-uh*) Julia's** | PC | T | V |
| **Vineyard Pinot Noir, California** | $$$ | 24 | 24 |

This wine's signature style—savory earth and spice character alongside chunky, concentrated plum flavor and a tug of tannin in the mouth get top taste marks.

Kitchen Countertop Survivor™ Grade: B

Your notes:_____

_____

| **Carneros Creek Los Carneros** | PC | T | V |
| **Pinot Noir, California** | $$ | X | X |

✗ This "great Pinot" has a "smooth" texture, and great food compatibility, with deep raspberry and spice flavors and a "great finish."

Kitchen Countertop Survivor™ Grade: B+

Your notes:_____

_____

Clos du Bois Sonoma County Pinot Noir, California

	PC	T	V
	$$	23	23

Good availability and great price are things you rarely find in the world of Pinot, but this one's dead-on: strawberry-rhubarb and smoky scent, "great bing cherry flavors and the perfect amount of acid." The open bottle holds up beautifully, too.

Kitchen Countertop Survivor™ Grade: A

Your notes:_____

Coldstream Hills Pinot Noir, Australia

	PC	T	V
	$$	X	X

✗ This Aussie offering has a knack for getting Burgundian smokiness and complexity in the bottle, as well as the ripe black cherry fruit you'd expect from sunny Australia. At this price, it's a gift to Pinot lovers.

Kitchen Countertop Survivor™ Grade: B

Your notes:_____

Cristom Willamette Pinot Noir Oregon

	PC	T	V
	$$$	29	22

A "Pinot to write home about," says a trade taster. I couldn't agree more. I have been bewitched by the smoky/cocoa scent of this wine since its debut. The deep cherry fruit and satiny texture are amazing.

Kitchen Countertop Survivor™ Grade: B+

Your notes:_____

David Bruce Central Coast Pinot Noir, California

	PC	T	V
	$$$	25	22

This characterful, vibrant Pinot laced with savory spice, earth, and raspberry fruit, is a sleeper favorite of Pinot fans, who laud the quality for the price.

Kitchen Countertop Survivor™ Grade: B

Your notes:_____

Price Ranges: **$** = $12 or less; **$$** = 12.01–20; **$$$** = 20.01–35; **$$$$** = > $35

Kitchen Fridge/Countertop Survivor™ Grades: *Avg.* = a "one-day wine," tastes noticeably less fresh the next day; *B* = holds its freshness for 2–3 days after opening; *B+* = holds *and gets better* over 2–3 days after opening; *A* = a 3- to 4-day "freshness window"; *A+* = holds *and gets better* over 3–4 days

Domaine Carneros Pinot Noir	PC	T	V
California	$$$	X	X

✗ There were so many raves from tasters for this wine, and I agree with every one. This wine's been great since the first vintage and, incredibly, still seems to get better every year. It's got a "sophisticated" scent, subtle oakiness and long finish "like GREAT red Burgundy," yet with the "bold fruit" of its California home base.

Kitchen Countertop Survivor™ Grade: A

Your notes:_____

_____

Domaine Drouhin (*droo-AHN*)	PC	T	V
Willamette Valley Pinot Noir	$$$$	24	21
Oregon			

This wine has "exuberant raspberry and cherry fruit," and intense oak, which dominates when the wine is young. Sommeliers point out that "it needs at least 2 years' bottle age to show its classy complexity."

Kitchen Countertop Survivor™ Grade: Avg

Your notes:_____

_____

Duck Pond Pinot Noir	PC	T	V
Oregon	$	22	22

Look for this "light on the wallet" Pinot on wine lists when you want to impress. It has strawberry aromas and ripe raspberry flavors and great food compatibility, for a great price.

Kitchen Countertop Survivor™ Grade: B

Your notes:_____

_____

Echelon Central Coast Pinot Noir	PC	T	V
California	$	X	X

✗ "Burgundy meets California" is how my tasters put it. The smoky, wild raspberry scent and flavor and silky texture are Pinot perfection—an amazing find for the price. The open bottle holds up nicely for days, too.

Kitchen Countertop Survivor™ Grade: B+

Your notes:_____

_____

Elk Cove Pinot Noir	PC	T	V
Oregon	$$	26	24

This is a nice Oregon Pinot Noir in the lighter-bodied style, whose savory spice and dried cherry character make it really versatile with food.

Kitchen Countertop Survivor™ Grade: Avg

Your notes:_____

_____

Estancia Pinnacles Pinot Noir	PC	T	V
California	$$	21	23

With its distinct herbal, strawberry compote, and smoky character this is a great Pinot Noir for the money.

Kitchen Countertop Survivor™ Grade: B+

Your notes:_____

_____

Etude Carneros Pinot Noir	PC	T	V
California	$$$$	28	23

My enthusiasm is just a drop in the bucket of tasting panel raves for this "blissful Pinot Noir" with "great structure" and elegance. The delicately fragrant, softly spicy scent, mouthwatering cherry-cranberry fruit and long finish have been style signatures since the first vintage. A truly special wine.

Kitchen Countertop Survivor™ Grade: A

Your notes:_____

_____

Firesteed Pinot Noir	PC	T	V
Oregon	$	20	20

The delicious cranberry and dried cherry fruit and nice kick of acid make this wine a great food partner. The "great price" makes it a favorite among restaurant buyers.

Kitchen Countertop Survivor™ Grade: B

Your notes:_____

_____

Price Ranges: **$** = $12 or less; **$$** = 12.01–20; **$$$** = 20.01–35; **$$$$** = > $35

Kitchen Fridge/Countertop Survivor™ Grades: *Avg.* = a "one-day wine," tastes noticeably less fresh the next day; *B* = holds its freshness for 2–3 days after opening; *B+* = holds *and gets better* over 2–3 days after opening; *A* = a 3- to 4-day "freshness window"; *A+* = holds *and gets better* over 3–4 days

Frei Brothers Reserve Pinot Noir	PC	T	V
California	$$	27	24

This is quite a special wine, scented with cherry and cinnamon on the nose, and silky-rich on the palate. One taster's comment, "Gallo owns it, and the wine is very good," explains its edge: the Gallos own some of the best vineyards in Sonoma County.

Kitchen Countertop Survivor™ Grade: B+

Your notes:_____

_____

Gallo of Sonoma Pinot Noir	PC	T	V
California	$	22	25

Both trade and consumer tasters lauded this Pinot's classic character—pure "raspberry and cherry" fruit, a soft vanilla-cream oakiness, and supple-but-lively texture—especially for the price.

Kitchen Countertop Survivor™ Grade: B+

Your notes:_____

_____

Indigo Hills Pinot Noir	PC	T	V
California	$	24	24

Light-bodied and tangy, with sour cherry and savory spice notes. Another Gallo brand offering good Pinot Noir character at a value price.

Kitchen Countertop Survivor™ Grade: Avg

Your notes:_____

_____

Joseph Drouhin Chorey Les Beaune	PC	T	V
(*shore-ay lay BONE*), France	$$$	23	20

Mixed reviews: To some tasters the "pretty, delicate" style equates to "more aroma than flavor," with scents of raspberries and red currant, but "not much body." Some like the subtlety; to others, it's "too light."

Kitchen Countertop Survivor™ Grade: Avg

Your notes:_____

_____

J Wine Company Russian River	PC	T	V
Pinot Noir, California	$$$	X	X

✗ "So incredibly jammy and rich, it drinks like a Cabernet," said one taster, but I do think it maintains the balance and silken mouthfeel Pinot lovers look for. The scent of sweet spices from oak frames a lovely ripe, black cherry flavor.

Kitchen Countertop Survivor™ Grade: B

Your notes:_____

_____

Kendall-Jackson Vintner's Reserve   PC   T   V
Pinot Noir, California $$ 18   20

This is a good introductory Pinot, with classic cherry and spice character at an affordable price.

Kitchen Countertop Survivor™ Grade: A

Your notes:_____

_____

King Estate Pinot Noir   PC   T   V
Oregon $$ 23   20

This is one of the most consistent and widely available of the Oregon Pinots, and it follows the Burgundy model: medium bodied and elegant, with soft cherry fruit.

Kitchen Countertop Survivor™ Grade: B

Your notes:_____

_____

La Crema Pinot Noir   PC   T   V
California $$ 23   24

Here's a controversial wine that's a "favorite Pinot" for some, and to others, "heavy on the oak and tannin." It has deep cherry-cola flavor, and a toasty scent.

Kitchen Countertop Survivor™ Grade: Avg

Your notes:_____

_____

Lindemans Bin 99 Pinot Noir   PC   T   V
Australia $ 21   26

My tasters say you "can't beat the value" of this light, approachable wine. It's got supple cherry fruit and a silky texture.

Kitchen Countertop Survivor™ Grade: Avg

Your notes:_____

_____

Price Ranges: **$** = $12 or less; **$$** = 12.01–20; **$$$** = 20.01–35; **$$$$** = > $35

Kitchen Fridge/Countertop Survivor™ Grades: *Avg.* = a "one-day wine," tastes noticeably less fresh the next day; *B* = holds its freshness for 2–3 days after opening; *B+* = holds *and gets better* over 2–3 days after opening; *A* = a 3- to 4-day "freshness window"; *A+* = holds *and gets better* over 3–4 days

Louis Jadot Bourgogne (*boor-GUHN-yuh*) **Pinot Noir, France**

PC	T	V
$$	X	X

✗ This wine showcases, at an affordable price, the "classic Bourgogne" character: "light on tannins and oak," with "flavors of tart cherries and cranberries."

Kitchen Countertop Survivor™ Grade: B

Your notes:_____

_____

Louis Latour Nuits-St.-Georges (*nwee-saint-GEORGE*), **France**

PC	T	V
$$$$	24	18

This wine is "not one to share with friends," "considering it costs a small fortune," say some. This French Pinot Noir has a beautifully perfumed berry nose punctuated with hints of violets and a supple tannic structure. A vintage-sensitive bottling, so ask your merchant for a recommendation.

Kitchen Countertop Survivor™ Grade: B

Your notes:_____

_____

MacMurray Ranch Sonoma Coast Pinot Noir, California

PC	T	V
$$$	29	24

Fred (as in *My Three Sons*) bought this ranch years ago. His daughter works with the Gallo family to farm and vinify this exceptional Pinot with deeply-concentrated cherry-raspberry fruit, and fragrant cream, cinnamon, and berries in the scent. It's a steal at this price.

Kitchen Countertop Survivor™ Grade: A

Your notes:_____

_____

Meridian Pinot Noir California

PC	T	V
$	18	18

So many tasters pointed out that this wine is perfect for every day, especially for the price. The mouthwatering flavor "tastes like biting into fresh cherries."

Kitchen Countertop Survivor™ Grade: B

Your notes:_____

_____

Merry Edwards Russian River   **PC**   **T**   **V**
Valley Pinot Noir, California   **$$$**   **X**   **X**

✗ "They don't make much," but this is "one to watch if you're a Pinot lover." It's "lush, full—yet elegant." The texture is silky but very rich and plump, with flavors of cola, dark cherry, and chocolate.

Kitchen Countertop Survivor™ Grade: B

Your notes:_____

_____

Morgan Pinot Noir   **PC**   **T**   **V**
California   **$$**   **24**   **22**

Morgan's Pinot Noirs are known for their ripe cherry fruit and exotic, smoky character. Their consistency and quality, year after year, are something very few Pinot Noir producers achieve. Bravo!

Kitchen Countertop Survivor™ Grade: B+

Your notes:_____

_____

Pepperwood Grove Pinot Noir   **PC**   **T**   **V**
California   **$**   **X**   **X**

✗ You get a lot of "spicy and smoky" complexity that's "totally unexpected at this price." The smoothness and "lively cherry fruit" make it "easy to sip and to match with food."

Kitchen Countertop Survivor™ Grade: Avg

Your notes:_____

_____

Rex Hill Willamette Valley   **PC**   **T**   **V**
Pinot Noir, Oregon   **$$$**   **X**   **X**

✗ The "cherry and earthy flavors" are a great introduction to the Willamette Valley, Oregon, Pinot style— one that trades on elegance and a spicy-earthiness that's best showcased with earthy foods like mushroom dishes and smoked meats.

Kitchen Countertop Survivor™ Grade: Avg

Your notes:_____

_____

Price Ranges: **$** = $12 or less; **$$** = 12.01–20; **$$$** = 20.01–35; **$$$$** = > $35

Kitchen Fridge/Countertop Survivor™ Grades: *Avg.* = a "one-day wine," tastes noticeably less fresh the next day; *B* = holds its freshness for 2–3 days after opening; *B+* = holds *and gets better* over 2–3 days after opening; *A* = a 3- to 4-day "freshness window"; *A+* = holds *and gets better* over 3–4 days

Robert Mondavi Private Selection	PC	T	V
Pinot Noir, California	$$	22	16

One of the best varietals in the Mondavi Private Selection line, and true to the grape with its silky berry fruit. It's one of the better Pinots at this price point.

Kitchen Countertop Survivor™ Grade: B

Your notes:_____

_____

Robert Mondavi Napa Pinot Noir	PC	T	V
California	$$$	21	19

Although this wine could benefit from a bit of bottle age, if you can't wait, a few swirls in a large wine glass with plenty of air space usually does the trick. The style is quite distinctive, with "gorgeous cherry fruit," plus a lot of smoky spice and complexity. Delicious.

Kitchen Countertop Survivor™ Grade: B

Your notes:_____

_____

Robert Sinskey Napa Pinot Noir	PC	T	V
California	$$$	24	20

For a time I had felt the Sinskey style was over-oaked, but no more—the spicy, supple, dark berry fruit now shines, and the complexity develops in the glass.

Kitchen Countertop Survivor™ Grade: B

Your notes:_____

_____

Saintsbury Carneros Pinot Noir	PC	T	V
California	$$$	X	X

✗ This "Carneros stalwart" is all about elegance: cranberry, rhubarb, and spice scents and flavors, and an "endless finish." My experience is that it improves for a year or two in bottle, too.

Kitchen Countertop Survivor™ Grade: B+

Your notes:_____

_____

Turning Leaf Pinot Noir	PC	T	V
California	$	18	22

This wine made a big leap in quality. It's got real Pinot flavors—cherry and spice—at a super price.

Kitchen Countertop Survivor™ Grade: Avg

Your notes:_____

_____

| **Wild Horse Pinot Noir** | PC | T | V |
| **California** | $$ | 24 | 23 |

Many of my trade tasters cited this as a "standard-bearer" in an increasingly prominent Pinot region, namely Santa Barbara. The cherry-cola aromas and plump berry fruit—hallmarks of this regional style—are in abundance here.

Kitchen Countertop Survivor™ Grade: B

Your notes:_____

_____

| **Willakenzie Willamette Valley** | PC | T | V |
| **Pinot Noir, Oregon** | $$$ | 24 | 20 |

The Willakenzie name comes from the distinctive soil type in this growing area, which itself is named for the two rivers that converge there: the Willamette and the McKenzie. The wine is consistently tasty and elegant and a value for this quality. From "luscious black cherry fruit" to "lovely cedar and herbal nuances," it's clearly a home run. They also make an outstanding Pinot Gris.

Kitchen Countertop Survivor™ Grade: B

Your notes:_____

_____

| **Willamette Valley Vineyards Pinot** | PC | T | V |
| **Noir, Oregon** | $$ | 23 | 22 |

This winery delivers consistent quality every year in a cherry-and-spice-scented style that's subtle and doesn't hit you over the head with too much wood.

Kitchen Countertop Survivor™ Grade: Avg

Your notes:_____

_____

Price Ranges: **$** = $12 or less; **$$** = 12.01–20; **$$$** = 20.01–35; **$$$$** = > $35

Kitchen Fridge/Countertop Survivor™ Grades: *Avg.* = a "one-day wine," tastes noticeably less fresh the next day; *B* = holds its freshness for 2–3 days after opening; *B+* = holds *and gets better* over 2–3 days after opening; *A* = a 3- to 4-day "freshness window"; *A+* = holds *and gets better* over 3–4 days

Chianti and Sangiovese

Category Profile: Remember the days when "Chianti" meant those kitschy straw-covered bottles? Tuscany's signature red has come a long way in quality since then, pulling much of the Italian wine world with it. But let me clear up some understandable confusion about the labels and styles. As quality has improved, Chianti has "morphed" into three tiers of wine—varietal Sangiovese (san-joe-VAY-zay), labeled with the grape name; traditional Chianti in a range of styles; and the luxury tier, which includes top regional wines like Brunello, and the so-called "Super Tuscan" reds. Many of the major Tuscan wineries produce wines in all three categories. The basic Sangioveses largely populate the one-dollar-sign price tier, and many offer good value. Chianti itself now spans the entire price and quality spectrum from budget quaff to boutique collectible, with the top-quality *classico* and *riserva* versions worthy of aging in the cellar. Finally, the Super Tuscans emerged because wineries wanted creative license to use international grapes outside the traditional Chianti "recipe" (and, I guess, with fantasy names like Summus, Sassicaia, and Luce, poetic license, too!). What they all have in common is that Italian "zest"—savory spice in the scent, plus vibrant acidity and texture that seems "alive" in the mouth. It's a flavor profile that truly sings with food, and, coming from the joyously food-frenzied Italians, would you expect anything less?

Serve: Room temperature (the varietal Sangioveses are also nice with a light chill); the "bigger" wines—classicos, riservas, and Super Tuscans—benefit from aeration (pour into the glass and swirl, or decant into a pitcher or carafe with plenty of air space).

When: Any food occasion, from snack to supper to celebration.

With: Especially great wherever tomato sauce, cheese, olive oil, or savory herbs (rosemary, basil, oregano) are present.

In: An all-purpose wineglass or larger-bowled red wine stem.

Antinori (Marchese) (*ahn-tee-NORE-ee mar-KAY-zee*) Chianti Classico Riserva, Italy	PC $$$	T 25	V 22

From the "King of Chianti" comes this well-made wine, whose flavor concentration and balance earn it serious raves from my tasters. The classic strawberry fruit, tannic grip, and peppery spice shine through now, but will also reward aging.

Kitchen Countertop Survivor™ Grade: B+

Your notes:_____

_____

Banfi Brunello di Montalcino Italy	PC $$$$	T 27	V 23

This "beautiful" Brunello is a rarity: fairly easy to find, consistently classy, and true to the Brunello character. The palate-coating tannin and dense fig and mocha flavors form a package that's big but balanced. Decant or aerate in the glass to soften it up.

Kitchen Countertop Survivor™ Grade: A

Your notes:_____

_____

Barone Ricasoli 1141 Chianti Classico, Italy	PC $	T X	V X

✗ What a great Chianti Classico for the money! It's a perfect rendering of the Chianti character—leathery-berry scent, strawberry-spice flavors, mouthwatering acidity, and a little "grip" in the mouth that creates a fabulous backdrop for food.

Kitchen Countertop Survivor™ Grade: B

Your notes:_____

_____

Price Ranges: **$** = $12 or less; **$$** = 12.01–20; **$$$** = 20.01–35; **$$$$** = > $35

Kitchen Fridge/Countertop Survivor™ Grades: *Avg.* = a "one-day wine," tastes noticeably less fresh the next day; *B* = holds its freshness for 2–3 days after opening; *B+* = holds *and gets better* over 2–3 days after opening; *A* = a 3- to 4-day "freshness window"; *A+* = holds *and gets better* over 3–4 days

Castello di Brolio Chianti Classico | PC | T | V
Italy | $$ | 22 | 22

If you're invited to dinner, this is the wine to bring: it's from a winery with pedigree; it's got the spice, zing, and fruit to go with any food and please a lot of palates, and the quality for the price is super.

Kitchen Countertop Survivor™ Grade: B

Your notes:_____

_____

Castello di Gabbiano Chianti | PC | T | V
Italy | $ | 16 | 18

A soft, light Chianti, with red cherry flavors and spicy nuances. It's a versatile food partner and, as my tasters point out, can't be beat for the price.

Kitchen Countertop Survivor™ Grade: B

Your notes:_____

_____

Castello di Gabbiano Chianti | PC | T | V
Classico Riserva, Italy | $$ | 24 | 15

My tasters call it "textbook Chianti Classico Riserva," with a cornucopia of red fruit, lively acidity, and a nice tug of tannin. They point out "it's gotten pricey," too.

Kitchen Countertop Survivor™ Grade: B

Your notes:_____

_____

Castello di Volpaia (*cass-TELL-oh* | PC | T | V
***dee vole-PYE-uh*) Chianti Classico** | $$$ | X | X
Riserva, Italy

✗ Spice, earth, leather, fig fruit—this is a classy Riserva that's "worth the price." If you've got the patience, it ages well. Otherwise, decant for aeration to open up the scent and flavors.

Kitchen Countertop Survivor™ Grade: A

Your notes:_____

_____

Cecchi (*CHECK-ee*) Chianti Classico | PC | T | V
Italy | $$ | 22 | 20

My tasters "love the quality for the price," and the soft berry fruit, tinged with a bit of spice.

Kitchen Countertop Survivor™ Grade: Avg

Your notes:_____

_____

Felsina (*FELL-si-nuh*) Chianti Classico, Italy

PC	T	V
$$$	22	22

It's "worth the price," and "ageable," as my tasters point out. Subtle, strawberry-raspberry fruit, balanced with savory-earthy notes, make it a wonderful food wine.

Kitchen Countertop Survivor™ Grade: B+

Your notes:_____

Frescobaldi Chianti Rufina (*ROO-fin-uh*) Riserva, Italy

PC	T	V
$$$	24	29

Lots of raves for Frescobaldi's whole lineup—budget to luxury. Though fans say the riserva is hard to find, you'll be rewarded with plenty of ripe cherry fruit and peppery nuances. It's a "great value compared to riservas from the Classico zone."

Kitchen Countertop Survivor™ Grade: B+

Your notes:_____

Monte Antico (*MOHN-tay ann-TEE-coh*) Toscana, Italy

PC	T	V
$	X	X

✗ This "excellent value" Sangiovese-based wine shows what Tuscany does so well: a "rustic, and layered," wine that's "robust but not overpowering" for food or just sipping. The "plum fruit" and "moderate tannins" are "a tasty package."

Kitchen Countertop Survivor™ Grade: B+

Your notes:_____

Nozzole (*NOTES-oh-lay*) Chianti Classico Riserva, Italy

PC	T	V
$$	X	X

✗ Lots of raves for this one, due to its "outstanding length and balance," and "complexity as good as more expensive names." The "great acidity" and "savory spice" make it "ready to drink" and "great with food."

Kitchen Countertop Survivor™ Grade: A

Your notes:_____

Price Ranges: **$** = $12 or less; **$$** = 12.01–20; **$$$** = 20.01–35; **$$$$** = > $35

Kitchen Fridge/Countertop Survivor™ Grades: *Avg.* = a "one-day wine," tastes noticeably less fresh the next day; *B* = holds its freshness for 2–3 days after opening; *B+* = holds *and gets better* over 2–3 days after opening; *A* = a 3- to 4-day "freshness window"; *A+* = holds *and gets better* over 3–4 days

Rocca della Macie (*ROH-cuh dell-eh mah-CHEE-uh*) **Chianti Classico, Italy**

PC	T	V
$	X	X

✗ The "cherry and blackberry" flavor and "smooth" texture make this wine great for food, and at the price, it's "good value," too.

Kitchen Countertop Survivor™ Grade: B

Your notes:_____

_____

Rocca della Macie Chianti Classico Riserva, Italy

PC	T	V
$$	X	X

✗ This "full-bodied" Riserva offers great Chianti complexity, with "peppery, leathery" earthiness, concentrated fig fruit, and a long finish. If you've got the discipline, it will age nicely for a few years.

Kitchen Countertop Survivor™ Grade: A

Your notes:_____

_____

Ruffino Chianti Classico Riserva Ducale (*ri-ZUR-vuh doo-CALL-eh*) **Gold Label, Italy**

PC	T	V
$$$$	24	21

The "pricey" refrain endures, but in the same breath as "worth it," thanks to the "wow-level complexity and leathery-ness." The A+ survivor grade is well deserved: the open bottle of this wine gets increasingly complex over many days.

Kitchen Countertop Survivor™ Grade: A+

Your notes:_____

_____

Santa Cristina Sangiovese, Antinori Italy

PC	T	V
$	23	25

"What a deal" for this "easy to drink for everyday" wine. The tangy cranberry fruit makes it very food friendly.

Kitchen Countertop Survivor™ Grade: B

Your notes:_____

_____

Selvapiana (*SELL-vuh-pee-AH-nuh*) **Chianti Rufina, Italy**

PC	T	V
$$	29	29

✓ Wow! My tasters "love" this wine. And with its earthy mushroom and spice scents, bright cherry fruit,

and velvety texture, *it* loves food. Ages beautifully
(5–7 years), too.

Kitchen Countertop Survivor™ Grade: A

Your notes:_____

_____

Straccali Chianti	PC	T	V
Italy	$	12	18

"I'd buy it again," say my tasters of this soft, juicy
Chianti that's "a bargain for a big party."

Kitchen Countertop Survivor™ Grade: Avg

Your notes:_____

_____

Merlot

Grape Profile: When early nineties news reports
linked heart health and moderate red wine drinking, Merlot joined the ranks of go-to wine grapes that
inspire instant customer recognition. As with other
market-leading varietals like Chardonnay and Cabernet Sauvignon, Merlot can range both in price, from
budget to boutique, and in complexity, from soft and
simple to "serious." Across the spectrum, Merlot is
modeled on the wines from its home region of Bordeaux, France. At the basic level, that means medium
body and soft texture, with nice plum and berry fruit
flavor. The more ambitious versions have more body,
tannin, and fruit concentration and usually a good bit
of oakiness in the scent and taste. Washington state,
California's Sonoma and Napa regions, and Chile are
my favorite growing regions for varietal Merlot. Most
Merlot producers follow the Bordeaux practice of
blending in some Cabernet Sauvignon (or another of
the classic Bordeaux red grapes) to complement and
enhance the wines' taste and complexity.

Serve: *Cool* room temperature.

Price Ranges: **$** = $12 or less; **$$** = 12.01–20; **$$$** = 20.01–35;
$$$$ = > $35

Kitchen Fridge/Countertop Survivor™ Grades: *Avg.* = a "one-day
wine," tastes noticeably less fresh the next day; *B* = holds its freshness for 2–3 days after opening; *B+* = holds *and gets better* over 2–3
days after opening; *A* = a 3- to 4-day "freshness window"; *A+* =
holds *and gets better* over 3–4 days

MERLOT'S KISSING COUSINS: If you are looking for something new but similar to Merlot, check out two South American specialties. First, there's Argentinean Malbec (*MAHL-beck*), a red grape originally from Bordeaux. It's similar in body and smoothness to Merlot, with lots of smoky aromatic complexity. Some wineries to look for: Trapiche, Navarro Correas, Catena, and Chandon Terrazas. Second, from Chile, try Carmenere (*car-muh-NAIR-eh*), also a Bordeaux import that was originally misidentified as Merlot in many Chilean vineyards. Its smooth texture and plum fruit are complemented by an exotically spicy scent. Look for Carmeneres from Concha y Toro, Carmen, Veramonte Primus, and Arboleda. Check out the Other Reds for more on these.

When: With meals, of course; and the basic bottlings are soft enough to enjoy on their own as a cocktail alternative.

With: Anything with which you enjoy red wine, especially cheeses, roasts, fuller-bodied fish, and grilled foods.

In: An all-purpose wineglass or larger-bowled red wine stem.

	PC	T	V
Barton & Guestier (B&G) Merlot		17	21
France	$		

France is the traditional HQ for Merlot, and my tasters like the "bright, easy to drink" style and "cherry cobbler" flavors of this one.

Kitchen Countertop Survivor™ Grade: Avg

Your notes:_____

_____

	PC	T	V
Beaulieu Vineyard (BV) Coastal		21	20
Merlot, California	$		

This is among the best "coastal" Merlots on the market, earning high marks for its "rustic/classy" style and "rich fruit."

Kitchen Countertop Survivor™ Grade: Avg

Your notes:_____

_____

Beringer Founders' Estate Merlot	PC	T	V
California	$	21	24

Although a few tasters say it's "slipped recently," most say the "easy plum and berry flavor" are great for everyday drinking, and "the value is super."

Kitchen Countertop Survivor™ Grade: B

Your notes:_____

_____

Blackstone Merlot	PC	T	V
California	$	22	23

This wine's price dropped, and its fan club seems to have mushroomed, due to the "excellent value and smooth taste that pleases all."

Kitchen Countertop Survivor™ Grade: Avg

Your notes:_____

_____

Bogle Merlot	PC	T	V
California	$	24	25

Another popular brand whose price dropped—yay! The "soft cherry flavor" pleases even white wine drinkers, yet is "sturdy enough for grill fare."

Kitchen Countertop Survivor™ Grade: Avg

Your notes:_____

_____

Bolla Merlot	PC	T	V
Italy	$	12	6

The Bolla name keeps this wine selling, but the thinness of fruit flavor prompts tasters to note that they've "had better for the money."

Kitchen Countertop Survivor™ Grade: Avg

Your notes:_____

_____

Price Ranges: **$** = $12 or less; **$$** = 12.01–20; **$$$** = 20.01–35; **$$$$** = > $35

Kitchen Fridge/Countertop Survivor™ Grades: *Avg.* = a "one-day wine," tastes noticeably less fresh the next day; *B* = holds its freshness for 2–3 days after opening; *B+* = holds *and gets better* over 2–3 days after opening; *A* = a 3- to 4-day "freshness window"; *A+* = holds *and gets better* over 3–4 days

Burgess Merlot	PC	T	V
California	$$$	X	X

✗ This is incredibly sophisticated Merlot. It's deeply complex—chocolate, mint, cedar, and plum scents and flavors—yet elegant and not over-blown the way so many "serious" California reds are. It is beautiful now, but will cellar well, too.

Kitchen Countertop Survivor™ Grade: B+

Your notes:_____

_____

Casa Lapostolle Classic Merlot	PC	T	V
California	$	23	24

Plum and cherry flavors and a gentle tug of tannin make this a "good everyday drinking wine for the price."

Kitchen Countertop Survivor™ Grade: Avg

Your notes:_____

_____

Casa Lapostolle Cuvée Alexandre	PC	T	V
Merlot, Chile	$$$	21	21

With its sweet vanilla and coffee scents, extremely ripe and concentrated plum fruit, velvety tannins, and very long finish, it drinks "like top California Merlot, at half the price"—though some say "the budget bottling has the edge," and the scores (above) bear that out.

Kitchen Countertop Survivor™ Grade: Avg

Your notes:_____

_____

Château Ste. Michelle Columbia	PC	T	V
Valley Merlot, Washington	$$	29	23

✓ Year in and year out, this is one of the nicest Merlots coming out of Washington, whose "Bordeaux-style elegance" and smooth plum flavor "finds its place at the table with so many foods." Delicious!

Kitchen Countertop Survivor™ Grade: B

Your notes:_____

_____

Château Simard Bordeaux	PC	T	V
France	$$$	28	18

The entire world models its Merlots on the château wines from Bordeaux's so-called "right bank" villages—namely, Pomerol and St. Emilion, which is the source of this wine. The subtle scents of earth, cedar, and coffee cloaking the plum fruit and soft tannins are textbook St. Emilion. Tasters note it's a great way to try a red with some bottle age, since older vintages are available in the marketplace.

Kitchen Countertop Survivor™ Grade: B+

Your notes:_____

_____

Château Souverain Alexander	PC	T	V
Valley Merlot, California	$$	X	X

✗ Lots of tasters' plaudits for this wine's "exceptional quality for the price." It's got a deep, plummy scent touched with a "wet leaves" earthiness, concentrated, rich fruit on the palate, and a "very long finish."

Kitchen Countertop Survivor™ Grade: B

Your notes:_____

_____

Christian Moueix (*MWEXX*) Merlot	PC	T	V
France	$	23	26

"Unmistakably Bordeaux," say my tasters—meaning elegant, soft, best when paired with food.

Kitchen Countertop Survivor™ Grade: Avg

Your notes:_____

_____

CK Mondavi Merlot	PC	T	V
California	$$	18	18

This is a light and fruity crowd-pleaser Merlot, with berry flavors and a smooth finish. Good for the price; good for parties.

Kitchen Countertop Survivor™ Grade: Avg

Your notes:_____

_____

Price Ranges: **$** = $12 or less; **$$** = 12.01–20; **$$$** = 20.01–35; **$$$$** = > $35

Kitchen Fridge/Countertop Survivor™ Grades: *Avg.* = a "one-day wine," tastes noticeably less fresh the next day; *B* = holds its freshness for 2–3 days after opening; *B+* = holds *and gets better* over 2–3 days after opening; *A* = a 3- to 4-day "freshness window"; *A+* = holds *and gets better* over 3–4 days

Clos du Bois Sonoma Merlot　　　PC　　T　　V
California　　　　　　　　　　　　$$　　24　　25

Happily, the price has dropped for this very popular bottle that trade buyers call "a must on wine lists." I'm still underwhelmed by the fruit, but out-numbered by the many fans who say it's "yummy."

Kitchen Countertop Survivor™ Grade: Avg

Your notes:_____

_____

Columbia Crest Merlot　　　　　PC　　T　　V
Washington　　　　　　　　　　　　$　　21　　24

"Great for the money," say my tasters of this textbook "entry-level" Merlot: velvety texture, medium body, and subtle plum-berry fruit, layered with a bit of earth, all in balance. Yum!

Kitchen Countertop Survivor™ Grade: B

Your notes:_____

_____

Columbia Winery Merlot　　　　PC　　T　　V
Washington　　　　　　　　　　　　$$　　X　　X

✗ "Amazing for the money," captures my tasters' concensus. The "YUMMY fruit" gives a succulent, berry-rich palate, and the presence of a bit of Cabernet gives "great structure" and a long finish.

Kitchen Countertop Survivor™ Grade: B+

Your notes:_____

_____

Concha y Toro Frontera Merlot　　PC　　T　　V
Chile　　　　　　　　　　　　　　　$　　20　　18

Tasters love the "wonderful blackberry" flavor at "a price that's easy to swallow."

Kitchen Countertop Survivor™ Grade: Avg

Your notes:_____

_____

Corbett Canyon Merlot　　　　　PC　　T　　V
California　　　　　　　　　　　　$　　13　　15

This is a soft, pleasant wine, with nice berry flavors, that is "great for sipping with friends, either over a light meal or just by itself."

Kitchen Countertop Survivor™ Grade: Avg

Your notes:_____

_____

Duckhorn Napa Merlot   PC   T   V
California $$$$ 25   21

The full-throttle, blackberry fruit, toasty oak, and ample tannins are "for lovers of BIG Merlot," who are prepared for the fact that it's "pricey." It remains a benchmark against which the other CA Merlots are judged.

Kitchen Countertop Survivor™ Grade: B+

Your notes:_____

Dynamite Merlot   PC   T   V
California $$$ 18   18

This used to be Carmenet Dynamite. It also "used to have more fruit," though fans say there's "some black cherry flavor."

Kitchen Countertop Survivor™ Grade: Avg

Your notes:_____

Ecco Domani Merlot   PC   T   V
Italy $ 14   16

A budget-priced Italian Merlot whose light fruit flavor is meant to complement and not overpower a wide range of foods. There were mixed reviews, but I find it does that nicely.

Kitchen Countertop Survivor™ Grade: Avg

Your notes:_____

Ernest & Julio Gallo Twin Valley   PC   T   V
Merlot, California $ 16   17

At this price, I don't expect the wine to scream Merlot character, but it delivers what I do expect: a simple, soft quaffing red wine.

Kitchen Countertop Survivor™ Grade: Avg

Your notes:_____

Price Ranges: $ = $12 or less; $$ = 12.01–20; $$$ = 20.01–35; $$$$ = > $35

Kitchen Fridge/Countertop Survivor™ Grades: *Avg.* = a "one-day wine," tastes noticeably less fresh the next day; *B* = holds its freshness for 2–3 days after opening; *B+* = holds *and gets better* over 2–3 days after opening; *A* = a 3- to 4-day "freshness window"; *A+* = holds *and gets better* over 3–4 days

Fetzer Eagle Peak Merlot   PC   T   V
California $ 23   26

Still among the best basic California Merlots on the market, with "juicy" cherry berry flavors, and an impressive survivor grade that make it "always a favorite by the glass or bottle" in restaurants.

Kitchen Countertop Survivor™ Grade: B

Your notes:_____

_____

Forest Glen Merlot   PC   T   V
California $ 21   21

"Always a very safe bet," say fans of this soft, ripe, plummy Merlot that's "a good price for the quality."

Kitchen Countertop Survivor™ Grade: Avg

Your notes:_____

_____

Franciscan Oakville Estate Merlot   PC   T   V
California $$$ 28   22

You get quintessential Napa Merlot here—lush cherry fruit, plush tannins, and just enough light, toasty oak to give it "layers and layers," especially if you "let it breathe a little."

Kitchen Countertop Survivor™ Grade: B

Your notes:_____

_____

Francis Coppola Diamond Series   PC   T   V
Blue Label Merlot, California $$ 22   23

Coppola puts drama on the screen *and* in the bottle. This is textbook California Merlot—plum flavors and a mushroomy earthiness, soft vanilla-scented oak, velvety tannins.

Kitchen Countertop Survivor™ Grade: Avg

Your notes:_____

_____

Franzia Merlot   PC   T   V
California $ 12   13

"What you see is what you get": a simple, off-dry bag-in-a-box red, whose fruity style would be good in sangria.

Kitchen Countertop Survivor™ Grade: NA

Your notes:_____

_____

Frei Brothers Reserve Merlot	PC	T	V
California	$$	21	21

It's rare to get top-rank Merlot character and complexity for under $20. The plum-berry fruit is concentrated but subtle, the oak and tannins are beautifully integrated and plush, and the finish is long.

Kitchen Countertop Survivor™ Grade: B

Your notes:_____

_____

Frog's Leap Merlot	PC	T	V
California	$$$	24	21

Though it's expensive, devotees find the big, beautiful flavor of this Merlot "worth every penny." I give it extra points for balance—though the fruit is intense, the oak and alcohol are not.

Kitchen Countertop Survivor™ Grade: A

Your notes:_____

_____

Gallo of Sonoma Merlot	PC	T	V
California	$	24	28

The "very luscious" plum fruit flavor, sweet-scented oak, and satiny-smooth texture make it among the best Merlots on the market for the price. Bravo!

Kitchen Countertop Survivor™ Grade: A

Your notes:_____

_____

Glen Ellen Proprietor's Reserve	PC	T	V
Merlot, California	$	14	14

Although *reserve* in the name suggests a special quality status for the wine, in reality, the "nice fruit" makes this a "decent everyday red."

Kitchen Countertop Survivor™ Grade: B

Your notes:_____

_____

Price Ranges: **$** = $12 or less; **$$** = 12.01–20; **$$$** = 20.01–35; **$$$$** = > $35

Kitchen Fridge/Countertop Survivor™ Grades: *Avg.* = a "one-day wine," tastes noticeably less fresh the next day; *B* = holds its freshness for 2–3 days after opening; *B+* = holds *and gets better* over 2–3 days after opening; *A* = a 3- to 4-day "freshness window"; *A+* = holds *and gets better* over 3–4 days

Gossamer Bay Merlot   PC   T   V
California $ 11   12

Like so many California Merlots at this price point, it's soft, simple, and fruity.

Kitchen Countertop Survivor™ Grade: Avg

Your notes:_____

_____

Kendall-Jackson Vintner's Reserve   PC   T   V
Merlot, California $$ 20   20

This is Merlot in the luscious style—redolent with black cherry flavor and smooth texture.

Kitchen Countertop Survivor™ Grade: B+

Your notes:_____

_____

L'Ecole No. 41 Walla Walla Valley   PC   T   V
Merlot, Washington $$$ X   X

✗ I've been following this wine for years, and agree with tasters who note that, although it's "not cheap," there's "value for the quality." Its deep berry and cocoa scent and flavor are exotic without being over the top. The oaky vanilla character is prominent, but in balance.

Kitchen Countertop Survivor™ Grade: Avg

Your notes:_____

_____

Lindemans Bin 40 Merlot   PC   T   V
Australia $ 22   23

A huge fan club lauds the "easy drinking" plump plum and berry fruit flavor that makes it "a great house wine."

Kitchen Countertop Survivor™ Grade: Avg

Your notes:_____

_____

Markham Merlot   PC   T   V
California $$$ 27   21

Still a value compared to other high-end California Merlots. The rich plum fruit and silky texture say "serious Merlot," something for which you usually expect to pay a lot more.

Kitchen Countertop Survivor™ Grade: B+

Your notes:_____

_____

Meridian Merlot	PC	T	V
California	$	18	20

An "easy-drinking" Merlot whose plump flavor reminds me of black cherry Jell-O, balanced with a nice tang of vibrant acidity.

Kitchen Countertop Survivor™ Grade: B+

Your notes:_____

_____

Montes Merlot	PC	T	V
Chile	$	20	22

Montes remains a standard-bearer among Chilean Merlots: concentrated dark-berry flavors and cedar and earth scents—all on an elegant frame.

Kitchen Countertop Survivor™ Grade: B

Your notes:_____

_____

Mouton-Cadet Bordeaux	PC	T	V
France	$	17	16

Reviews are mixed on this "light," basic Bordeaux that pros say can be "soft and elegant when it's on, but thin tasting and one-dimensional when it's off." I suspect, however, that there may be some label snobbery at work here, as we used to serve it with the label hidden to our Windows on the World wine students—to generally positive responses. Look also for the Mouton-Cadet Reserve, which has a lot more flavor and complexity for just a little more money.

Kitchen Countertop Survivor™ Grade: Avg

Your notes:_____

_____

Price Ranges: **$** = $12 or less; **$$** = 12.01–20; **$$$** = 20.01–35; **$$$$** = > $35

Kitchen Fridge/Countertop Survivor™ Grades: *Avg.* = a "one-day wine," tastes noticeably less fresh the next day; *B* = holds its freshness for 2–3 days after opening; *B+* = holds *and gets better* over 2–3 days after opening; *A* = a 3- to 4-day "freshness window"; *A+* = holds *and gets better* over 3–4 days

Nathanson Creek Merlot	PC	T	V
California	$	14	14

While it used to be one of the best California value brands, Nathanson Creek has slipped a bit in my opinion. Still, this Merlot is a "no bells and whistles" kind of wine, with some "redeeming red-berry fruit."

Kitchen Countertop Survivor™ Grade: Avg

Your notes:_____

Pine Ridge Crimson Creek Merlot	PC	T	V
California	$$$$	18	18

Intense and concentrated, with beautifully balanced oak and alcohol. The "spicy blackberry" fruit, subtle earthiness, and long finish make it "good, but expensive."

Kitchen Countertop Survivor™ Grade: B+

Your notes:_____

Ravenswood Vintners Blend Merlot	PC	T	V
California	$$	22	19

It's got "jammy, smooth" plum and cherry fruit, but some say there are "better Merlots for the price."

Kitchen Countertop Survivor™ Grade: B+

Your notes:_____

Robert Mondavi Private Selection	PC	T	V
Merlot, California	$	20	20

This wine, formerly known as Robert Mondavi Coastal, gets mixed feedback—some say "bland," others "great for the price." I, too, have found some bottle-to-bottle quality variation.

Kitchen Countertop Survivor™ Grade: Avg

Your notes:_____

Rodney Strong Sonoma Merlot	PC	T	V
California	$$	26	26

"A big cut above other Merlots at this price" say my tasters, who laud the "cedar, spice, plum, berry, and earth" qualities. Yum!

Kitchen Countertop Survivor™ Grade: Avg

Your notes:_____

Rutherford Hill Merlot   PC   T   V
California $$$ X   X

✗ This "very rich Merlot" has been a wine list stalwart for years. Happily, it resisted the trend toward over-oaked, heavy Merlots, keeping its smoothness. The plum fruit and sweet spice from oakiness are the classic California Merlot style, and the quality for the price is impressive.

Kitchen Countertop Survivor™ Grade: Avg

Your notes:_____

_____

Shafer Merlot   PC   T   V
California $$$$ 28   18

If the occasion dictates a splurge, and "if you can find it," you will love this rich, classy wine in the lush, powerful "cult-quality" California style. "It cellars well," too.

Kitchen Countertop Survivor™ Grade: B+

Your notes:_____

_____

Stag's Leap Wine Cellars Napa   PC   T   V
Merlot, California $$$$ 24   18

To me the hallmark of this wine is complexity—earth, mocha, and mint in the scent; cassis and licorice flavors; and great balance. It is also age-worthy.

Kitchen Countertop Survivor™ Grade: B

Your notes:_____

_____

St. Francis Sonoma Merlot   PC   T   V
California $$$ 26   20

Yes, the price has gone up some, but this wine remains a relative value "year in and year out." The style is distinctly St. Francis—velvety texture, berry

Price Ranges: **$** = $12 or less; **$$** = 12.01–20; **$$$** = 20.01–35; **$$$$** = > $35

Kitchen Fridge/Countertop Survivor™ Grades: *Avg.* = a "one-day wine," tastes noticeably less fresh the next day; *B* = holds its freshness for 2–3 days after opening; *B+* = holds *and gets better* over 2–3 days after opening; *A* = a 3- to 4-day "freshness window"; *A+* = holds *and gets better* over 3–4 days

compote and fig flavors, clove, coconut, and eucalyptus scents, and a long finish.

Kitchen Countertop Survivor™ Grade: B

Your notes:_____

_____

Sterling Vineyards Napa Merlot	PC	T	V
California	$$$	22	20

"You can ever go wrong," say my tasters, with this "solid Napa Merlot." I agree the complex "cherry and tobacco" character is scrumptious.

Kitchen Countertop Survivor™ Grade: B+

Your notes:_____

_____

Sutter Home Merlot	PC	T	V
California	$	21	27

In the "friendly crowd-pleaser" category, the Sutter Home wines always impress me because they're well made. The soft plum flavor makes this a great everyday Merlot for the money.

Kitchen Countertop Survivor™ Grade: Avg

Your notes:_____

_____

Swanson Vineyards Merlot	PC	T	V
California	$$$	X	X

✗ This "big" and "luscious" Merlot with lavish vanilla-scented oak nevertheless manages to keep a good balance. A great choice for "a big steak" or just if you like the "monumental Merlot style."

Kitchen Countertop Survivor™ Grade: Avg

Your notes:_____

_____

Talus Merlot	PC	T	V
California	$$	15	16

Mixed reviews here, with some tasters calling it "great for the price" but others quite underwhelmed by the taste. In my opinion it's not a standout in this crowded price category.

Kitchen Countertop Survivor™ Grade: Avg

Your notes:_____

_____

Trinchero Mario's Special Reserve	PC	T	V
Merlot, California	$$	X	X

✗ The berry and coconut scent and plush, velvety texture make this wine a real treat to drink young, even though it's got tons of concentration—"a great steakhouse wine."

Kitchen Countertop Survivor™ Grade: B+

Your notes:_____

_____

Trinity Oaks Merlot	PC	T	V
California	$	18	19

This easy-drinking, smooth Merlot is a great everyday dinner wine. The price is affordable, and it pairs easily with anything from mac and cheese to Mexican food.

Kitchen Countertop Survivor™ Grade: Avg

Your notes:_____

_____

Turning Leaf Merlot	PC	T	V
California	$	18	18

Mixed reviews. Consumers credit the "drinkability at a great price," but note that the Coastal Reserve bottling, for not much more money, has a lot more fruit.

Kitchen Countertop Survivor™ Grade: Avg

Your notes:_____

_____

Vendange Merlot	PC	T	V
California	$	15	12

Consumers say this Merlot is a "crowd pleaser for big parties." I think other brands at the same price top it in flavor per dollar.

Kitchen Countertop Survivor™ Grade: Avg

Your notes:_____

_____

Price Ranges: **$** = $12 or less; **$$** = 12.01–20; **$$$** = 20.01–35; **$$$$** = > $35

Kitchen Fridge/Countertop Survivor™ Grades: *Avg.* = a "one-day wine," tastes noticeably less fresh the next day; *B* = holds its freshness for 2–3 days after opening; *B+* = holds *and gets better* over 2–3 days after opening; *A* = a 3- to 4-day "freshness window"; *A+* = holds *and gets better* over 3–4 days

Walnut Crest Merlot	PC	T	V
Chile	$	17	18

Mixed reviews. Some say "you can't beat the value," while others say it "just tastes cheap."

Kitchen Countertop Survivor™ Grade: Avg

Your notes:_____

_____

Woodbridge (Robert Mondavi)	PC	T	V
Merlot, California	$	16	18

Trade buyers call this Merlot "flavor-shy," saying it "has basic berry fruit" but "nothing special." Still, the Mondavi name and the price "make guests happy."

Kitchen Countertop Survivor™ Grade: Avg

Your notes:_____

_____

Cabernet Sauvignon and Blends

Grape Profile: Merlot may have been the *mucho*-trendy red of the late 1990s, but Cabernet Sauvignon remains a top-selling red varietal wine, I think for good reason. Specifically, Cabernet (for short) grows well virtually all over the wine world and gives excellent quality and flavor at every price level, from steal to splurge. Its flavor intensity and body can vary, based on the wine's quality level—from uncomplicated everyday styles to the superintense boutique and collector bottlings. Nearly every major wine-growing country produces Cabernets across that spectrum, but the most famous and plentiful sources are Bordeaux in France, California (especially Sonoma and Napa), Washington state, and Italy on the high end with its Super Tuscan versions. I think Chile shines in the mid-priced category, with some two-dollar-sign wines offering $$$ Cabernet character. Classically, that means a scent and taste of dark berries (blueberry, blackberry), plus notes of spice, earth, cocoa, cedar, and even mint that can be very layered and complex in the best wines. It also means medium to very full body and often more tannin—that bit of a tongue-gripping sensation that one of my waiters once described, perfectly I think, as "a slip-cover for the tongue, ranging from terry cloth to suede to velvet," depending on the wine in question.

Oakiness, either a little or a lot, depending on the growing region and price, is also a common Cabernet feature. Combined, these can make for a primo mouthful of a wine, which surely explains why Cabernet rules the red wine world.

A note about "blends": As described previously for Merlot, Cabernet Sauvignon wines follow the Bordeaux blending model, with one or more of the traditional Bordeaux red grapes—Merlot, Cabernet Franc, Petit Verdot, and Malbec—blended in for balance and complexity. Australia pioneered blending Cabernet Sauvignon with Shiraz—a delicious combination that the wine buying market has embraced. Those blends are listed either here or in the Shiraz section, according to which of the two grapes is dominant in the blend (it will be listed first on the label, too).

Serve: Cool room temperature; the fuller-bodied styles benefit from aeration—pour into the glass a bit ahead of time or decant into a carafe (but if you forget, don't sweat it; if you care to, swirling the glass does help).

When: With your favorite red wine meals, but the everyday bottlings are soft enough for cocktail-hour sipping.

With: Anything you'd serve alongside a red; especially complements beef, lamb, goat cheese, and hard cheeses, pesto sauce, and dishes scented with basil, rosemary, sage, or oregano.

In: An all-purpose wineglass or larger-bowled red wine stem.

Arrowood Cabernet Sauvignon	PC	T	V
Sonoma County, California	$$$$	26	22

This has been one of my favorite Sonoma Cabernets for years, and always true to the classic Sonoma Cab

Price Ranges: $ = $12 or less; $$ = 12.01–20; $$$ = 20.01–35; $$$$ = > $35

Kitchen Fridge/Countertop Survivor™ Grades: *Avg.* = a "one-day wine," tastes noticeably less fresh the next day; B = holds its freshness for 2–3 days after opening; B+ = holds *and gets better* over 2–3 days after opening; A = a 3- to 4-day "freshness window"; A+ = holds *and gets better* over 3–4 days style, with wild blackberry fruit, toasty-vanilla oak, and a long finish.

Kitchen Countertop Survivor™ Grade: B

Your notes:_____

_____

Barton & Guestier (B&G) Cabernet Sauvignon, France	PC $	T 16	V 17

This surprisingly nice French Cabernet has decent backbone and nice cherry and spice aromas; it "tastes peppery" and has a "pretty nice" finish.

Kitchen Countertop Survivor™ Grade: Avg

Your notes:_____

_____

Beaulieu Vineyard (BV) Coastal Cabernet Sauvignon, California	PC $	T 20	V 20

Retail buyers especially cite this wine as a "terrific value and huge seller." It's great that the varietal character comes through—even at this bargain price—with ripe blackberry fruit, a "lovely anise scent," and nice structure—but not too much tannin.

Kitchen Countertop Survivor™ Grade: B+

Your notes:_____

_____

Beaulieu Vineyard (BV) Rutherford Cabernet Sauvignon, California	PC $$$	T 23	V 20

In the face of price competition in the category of California Cabernet, the value score of this wine slipped a little. It still offers ripe, jammy Cabernet flavor with scents of mint, cedar, and wet earth, but at a "kind of high price."

Kitchen Countertop Survivor™ Grade: A

Your notes:_____

_____

Beringer Founders' Estate Cabernet Sauvignon, California	PC $	T 22	V 22

The first vintages of this wine disappointed me, but no more. Now it's among the top players in the value game, with real Cabernet character—blackberry fruit, cedar scent—acknowledged by a most intriguing array of tasters, from trade to consumer novice to collector. Everyone respects a value.

Kitchen Countertop Survivor™ Grade: A

Your notes:_____

_____

Beringer Knights Valley Cabernet Sauvignon, California	PC	T	V
	$$$	25	23

Lots of raves for this wine's "great quality for the price." The cedar and mint scent with dense, chewy cassis fruit cloaks an elegant but powerful frame, with vanilla-scented oak and alcohol in balance. "Let it age a little if you've got the discipline!"

Kitchen Countertop Survivor™ Grade: B+

Your notes:_____

_____

Black Opal Cabernet Sauvignon Australia	PC	T	V
	$	24	26

"You couldn't possibly find more for the money," as the T/V scores affirm. It's "juicy, yummy," and "available everywhere."

Kitchen Countertop Survivor™ Grade: B

Your notes:_____

_____

Black Opal Cabernet/Merlot Australia	PC	T	V
	$	20	20

This Cab/Merlot blend from Australia "goes with anything" and has "pretty berry" flavors.

Kitchen Countertop Survivor™ Grade: B

Your notes:_____

_____

Blackstone Cabernet Sauvignon, California	PC	T	V
	$$	X	X

✗ Tasters noted that although Blackstone is more famous for Merlot, this Cab is "pretty impressive for

Price Ranges: **$** = $12 or less; **$$** = 12.01–20; **$$$** = 20.01–35; **$$$$** = > $35

Kitchen Fridge/Countertop Survivor™ Grades: *Avg.* = a "one-day wine," tastes noticeably less fresh the next day; *B* = holds its freshness for 2–3 days after opening; *B+* = holds *and gets better* over 2–3 days after opening; *A* = a 3- to 4-day "freshness window"; *A+* = holds *and gets better* over 3–4 days

the price" with blackberry and cocoa scents and flavors.

Kitchen Countertop Survivor™ Grade: Avg

Your notes:_____

_____

Buena Vista Cabernet Sauvignon	PC	T	V
California	$	20	22

I've always thought of Buena Vista as a white wine specialist, but this Cabernet is nice. It's got lots of blackberry fruit, a coconut scent from oak, and a lot of concentration for a wine at this price point.

Kitchen Countertop Survivor™ Grade: Avg

Your notes:_____

_____

Cain Cuvée Bordeaux Style Red	PC	T	V
California	$$$	24	18

I agree with pro and consumer buyers who noted that this wine is "so much better" than many other, "higher-priced California blends" featuring the Bordeaux red grapes. Beautiful cassis fruit with cedar-oak aromas and a long finish.

Kitchen Countertop Survivor™ Grade: A

Your notes:_____

_____

Cakebread Napa Cabernet	PC	T	V
Sauvignon, California	$$$$	25	19

All the superpremium California wines in this book drew complaints about their high prices, and this one is no exception. Some tasters "love" the cassis fruit and soft vanilla oak, but others said they "just don't get what all the fuss is about."

Kitchen Countertop Survivor™ Grade: B+

Your notes:_____

_____

Caliterra Cabernet Sauvignon	PC	T	V
Chile	$	18	24

Here's a Cabernet with character that's "good and cheap," as my tasters commented. With its ripe berry fruit flavors and pleasant tannins, it's a great "crowd-pleaser."

Kitchen Countertop Survivor™ Grade: B+

Your notes:_____

_____

| Canyon Road Cabernet Sauvignon | PC | T | V |
| California | $ | 20 | 24 |

Buyers "thought it was a lot more expensive at first," and lauded the blackberry fruit and cedar-chocolate scent "for a great price."

Kitchen Countertop Survivor™ Grade: B

Your notes:_____

_____

| Casa Lapostolle Classic Cabernet | PC | T | V |
| Sauvignon, Chile | $ | 27 | 29 |

As Chilean Cabernets go, this one stands out for its ripe red fruit, rich texture, and overall elegance. It's "a steal" that my tasters raved about.

Kitchen Countertop Survivor™ Grade: B

Your notes:_____

_____

| Casa Lapostolle Cuvée Alexandre | PC | T | V |
| Cabernet Sauvignon, Chile | $$ | 20 | 22 |

This Cabernet has classic structure and flavors, modeled on French red Bordeaux, with Southern Hemisphere fruit vibrancy. The cedar, vanilla, cinnamon, dark dusky fruit, and earth scents all seem Old World. But on the palate, the richness and immediacy of the fruit are very modern.

Kitchen Countertop Survivor™ Grade: Avg

Your notes:_____

_____

| Château Gloria Bordeaux | PC | T | V |
| France | $$$$ | 24 | 24 |

A smooth, subtle expression of what Bordeaux does best—black currant fruit, touched with cedar, coffee, and mocha scents. It benefits a lot from aeration, so plan to decant.

Kitchen Countertop Survivor™ Grade: B+

Your notes:_____

_____

Price Ranges: **$** = $12 or less; **$$** = 12.01–20; **$$$** = 20.01–35; **$$$$** = > $35

Kitchen Fridge/Countertop Survivor™ Grades: *Avg.* = a "one-day wine," tastes noticeably less fresh the next day; *B* = holds its freshness for 2–3 days after opening; *B+* = holds *and gets better* over 2–3 days after opening; *A* = a 3- to 4-day "freshness window"; *A+* = holds *and gets better* over 3–4 days

Château Greysac Bordeaux	PC	T	V
France	$$	22	23

Even serious collectors and elite sommeliers rate this "one of the great Bordeaux values." In my experience the classic cedar spice scent and powerful but elegant plum fruit have fooled many in blind tastings into thinking it was one of the top châteaus.

Kitchen Countertop Survivor™ Grade: B

Your notes:_____

_____

Château Gruaud-Larose (*GROO-oh*	PC	T	V
lah-ROSE) Bordeaux, France	$$$$	26	20

It's "pricey," but still more affordable than many Bordeaux of comparable quality. The palate-coating tannins, the dark fruit, cedar, and toasty coffee scents and long finish, are the style model for Cabernet-based wine worldwide.

Kitchen Countertop Survivor™ Grade: A

Your notes:_____

_____

Château Larose-Trintaudon	PC	T	V
(*la-ROSE TRENT-oh-DOAN*)	$$	27	24
Bordeaux, France			

This wine combines classic Bordeaux characteristics and real-world virtues: rich, round tannins and deep plum fruit with a drink-it-young suppleness and affordable price that keep it accessible.

Kitchen Countertop Survivor™ Grade: A+

Your notes:_____

_____

Château Smith-Haut-Lafitte	PC	T	V
(*smith oh lah-FEET*) Bordeaux	$$$$	X	X
France			

✗ This wine, "affordable by Bordeaux standards," is one of my favorites year in and year out. It's got the tannic grip and cedar, blackcurrant, warm brick scent classic to its sub-region (Graves), and "ages beautifully."

Kitchen Countertop Survivor™ Grade: B+

Your notes:_____

_____

Chât. Ste. Michelle Columbia Valley   **PC**   **T**   **V**
Cabernet Sauvignon, Washington   **$$**   **23**   **26**

I think this Cabernet is one of the best coming from
Washington—especially for the price—with intense
black cherry aromas, concentrated blackberry flavors,
and a toasty-oak finish. It's big but not heavy-handed.

Kitchen Countertop Survivor™ Grade: A

Your notes:_____

_____

Château St. Jean Cinq Cepages   **PC**   **T**   **V**
(*sank seh-PAHJH*) **Cabernet**   **$$$$**   **28**   **18**
Blend, California

"Pricey but worth it," say tasters of this "big, oaky," yet
"balanced" wine. The full-throttle blackberry fruit and
vanilla-spice scent, and the way it coats your palate,
let you know it's "serious California Cab" that's
special, "even in off vintages." Decant it to open up
the scents and flavors.

Kitchen Countertop Survivor™ Grade: B+

Your notes:_____

_____

Clos du Bois Marlstone Proprietary   **PC**   **T**   **V**
Bordeaux Blend, California   **$$$$**   **X**   **X**

✗ This "bold, tannic" Cabernet-based wine has "dark
berry fruit" and a "cedary, spicy" complexity that
shines with a bit of aeration. Decant before serving.

Kitchen Countertop Survivor™ Grade: A

Your notes:_____

_____

Clos du Bois Sonoma Cabernet   **PC**   **T**   **V**
Sauvignon, California   **$$**   **22**   **21**

Although a few tasters called it "light" and "pricey,"
in my view this soft but solid Cabernet is textbook

Price Ranges: $ = $12 or less; $$ = 12.01–20; $$$ = 20.01–35;
$$$$ = > $35
Kitchen Fridge/Countertop Survivor™ Grades: *Avg.* = a "one-day
wine," tastes noticeably less fresh the next day; *B* = holds its freshness for 2–3 days after opening; *B+* = holds *and gets better* over 2–3
days after opening; *A* = a 3- to 4-day "freshness window"; *A+* =
holds *and gets better* over 3–4 days

"Sonoma," with a distinctive wild berry, anise, and eucalyptus character.

Kitchen Countertop Survivor™ Grade: B

Your notes:_____

_____

Columbia Crest Cabernet Sauvignon Washington

	PC	T	V
	$	25	28

"Delicious" and "a 'wow' at this price" sums up the raves for this plush Cab. I like it because with one taste you know where you are, Washington state, where Cabernets are always rich yet still elegant.

Kitchen Countertop Survivor™ Grade: B+

Your notes:_____

_____

Concha y Toro Sunrise Cabernet Sauvignon/Merlot, Chile

	PC	T	V
	$	18	20

For "the budget-minded host," this wine will do you proud. It's light-bodied and soft, but still tastes like the grapes used to make it—plummy and succulent. It even has that tinge of earthiness in the scent that says "Chile" to me.

Kitchen Countertop Survivor™ Grade: Avg

Your notes:_____

_____

Corbett Canyon Cabernet Sauvignon, California

	PC	T	V
	$	11	12

Corbett Canyon's Sauvignon Blanc fared better with my tasters than this Cabernet, which they found to be "lightweight" and "simple." Not a top performer in the price range.

Kitchen Countertop Survivor™ Grade: Avg

Your notes:_____

_____

Dynamite Cabernet Sauvignon, California

	PC	T	V
	$$$	24	22

This used to be called "Carmenet Dynamite"; the owners sold the Carmenet name. It's still got classic California Cabernet character—cassis fruit, cedar, spice and vanilla scents.

Kitchen Countertop Survivor™ Grade: B

Your notes:_____

_____

Ernest & Julio Gallo Twin Valley	PC	T	V
Cabernet Sauvignon, California	$	15	16

This simple, one-dimensional, fruity Cabernet is "priced right for experimentation," according to tasters, but since there are better Cabernets at the same price point, why not experiment with one of those?

Kitchen Countertop Survivor™ Grade: Avg

Your notes:_____

_____

Escudo Rojo Cabernet Blend,	PC	T	V
Baron Philippe de Rothschild, Chile	$$	24	26

Tasters "love the spice" and "earthy complexity" of this Chilean wine. Especially at this price, it would delight anyone—meaty-smokiness, dried spices, leather, coffee, figs, mint . . . on an elegant, balanced frame.

Kitchen Countertop Survivor™ Grade: A

Your notes:_____

_____

Estancia Alexander Valley Red	PC	T	V
Meritage, California	$$$	X	X

✗ Although this delicious Cabernet/Merlot blend's price has been rising, it still offers, "excellent value, wide availability." Its elegance and coffee/mocha scent are classic Alexander Valley attributes. There's so much great blackberry fruit I even like to match it with bittersweet chocolate!

Kitchen Countertop Survivor™ Grade: B

Your notes:_____

_____

Estancia Cabernet Sauvignon	PC	T	V
California	$$	23	24

"Real-deal California Cabernet" flavor—mint and cassis—at a "good price" that means "you can afford to drink it often."

Kitchen Countertop Survivor™ Grade: B+

Your notes:_____

_____

Price Ranges: $ = $12 or less; $$ = 12.01–20; $$$ = 20.01–35; $$$$ = > $35

Kitchen Fridge/Countertop Survivor™ Grades: *Avg.* = a "one-day wine," tastes noticeably less fresh the next day; *B* = holds its freshness for 2–3 days after opening; *B+* = holds *and gets better* over 2–3 days after opening; *A* = a 3- to 4-day "freshness window"; *A+* = holds *and gets better* over 3–4 days

Far Niente Cabernet Sauvignon	PC	T	V
California	$$$$	27	12

For California Cabernet lovers who like the classic, classy Napa style—big fruit and body without the overwhelming oak and alcohol that became trendy in the 1990s, this is a home-run choice. But it rates weak on the value front because the name "exacts a hefty price premium."

Kitchen Countertop Survivor™ Grade: A

Your notes:_____

_____

Ferrari-Carano Siena Sonoma	PC	T	V
County, California	$$$	X	X

✗ My tasters promise you'll "love this wine!" The Cabernet's blended with Sangiovese like a Super Tuscan wine, so you get the leathery-spiciness of the Italian grape, with "huge berry ripeness" from the Sonoma sun. The open bottle actually gets better after a day or two.

Kitchen Countertop Survivor™ Grade: A+

Your notes:_____

_____

Fetzer Valley Oaks Cabernet	PC	T	V
Sauvignon, California	$	21	24

Pros think that Fetzer offers exactly what a "bargain"-priced Cab should: "generous fruit" and "mild, food-friendly tannins."

Kitchen Countertop Survivor™ Grade: B

Your notes:_____

_____

Forest Glen Barrel Select Cabernet	PC	T	V
Sauvignon, California	$	18	18

The fruit and flavor are "soft, plummy, pleasant" for the money.

Kitchen Countertop Survivor™ Grade: Avg.

Your notes:_____

_____

Francis Coppola Diamond Series	PC	T	V
Black Label Claret (*CLARE-ett*)	$$	20	21
California			

English wine merchants' nickname for Bordeaux is Claret, a name sometimes used by California winemakers for their blends of the Bordeaux red grapes, chiefly Cabernet and Merlot. This one's got cedary, mocha scents and firm blackberry fruit and tannins. Nice!

Kitchen Countertop Survivor™ Grade: B

Your notes:_____

_____

| Franciscan Napa Cabernet | PC | T | V |
| Sauvignon, California | $$$ | 24 | 21 |

"It's gotten more pricey," note my tasters, but still offers real Napa Cabernet character—a whiff of mintiness, dark cassis fruit, a balanced oak profile of sweet vanilla and spice, and velvety tannins. The year-in and year-out consistency is impressive.

Kitchen Countertop Survivor™ Grade: B

Your notes:_____

_____

| Gallo of Sonoma Barelli Creek | PC | T | V |
| Cabernet Sauvignon, California | $$$ | X | X |

✗ The huge oak and black fig fruit yield a wine that's "almost overwhelmingly rich and concentrated." It "needs decanting," but is a great choice for "serious California Cabernet lovers."

Kitchen Countertop Survivor™ Grade: Avg

Your notes:_____

_____

| Gallo of Sonoma Cabernet | PC | T | V |
| Sauvignon, California | $ | 25 | 25 |

"You can't beat the price/value," say both trade and consumers. It's got "succulent," "big cassis fruit," though some point out "it's gotten more oaky." Many tasters love that, though.

Kitchen Countertop Survivor™ Grade: B+

Your notes:_____

_____

Price Ranges: **$** = $12 or less; **$$** = 12.01–20; **$$$** = 20.01–35; **$$$$** = > $35

Kitchen Fridge/Countertop Survivor™ Grades: *Avg.* = a "one-day wine," tastes noticeably less fresh the next day; *B* = holds its freshness for 2–3 days after opening; *B+* = holds *and gets better* over 2–3 days after opening; *A* = a 3- to 4-day "freshness window"; *A+* = holds *and gets better* over 3–4 days

Geyser Peak Cabernet Sauvignon | PC | T | V
California | $$ | X | X

✗ This "textbook Sonoma Cab" "hits all the right notes"—cedar, berry fruit, medium tannins, for the price. "A good wine list bet," too.

Kitchen Countertop Survivor™ Grade: B

Your notes:_____

_____

Glen Ellen Proprietor's Reserve | PC | T | V
Cabernet Sauvignon, California | $ | 14 | 14

A good wine for new red wine drinkers, because its fruity, almost-sweet, entry-level taste won't offend. And neither will the price.

Kitchen Countertop Survivor™ Grade: Avg

Your notes:_____

_____

Greg Norman Cabernet/Merlot | PC | T | V
Australia | $$ | 23 | 22

Tasters laud the plump, concentrated, silky style and mint, dark berry, and chocolate flavors. But some note they've "had other Aussie Cab/Merlots that are just as good, for less money."

Kitchen Countertop Survivor™ Grade: Avg

Your notes:_____

_____

Groth Napa Cabernet Sauvignon | PC | T | V
California | $$$$ | 24 | 18

Although it is "pricey," I think this wine remains fairly reasonable within the category of luxury Cabernets. And with its plush tannins and deep cassis fruit, elegantly framed with vanilla oak, it's a benchmark Napa Valley Cabernet. Although this wine improves with age, it's also nicely drinkable in youth.

Kitchen Countertop Survivor™ Grade: B+

Your notes:_____

_____

Guenoc Cabernet Sauvignon | PC | T | V
California | $$ | 23 | 23

This is real California Cabernet flavor, yet silky smooth in texture—a rare breed, indeed. The high

quality for the money is also a rarity, making this easy
to enjoy with any food or no food—and often.

Kitchen Countertop Survivor™ Grade: B

Your notes:_____

_____

Heitz Napa Cabernet Sauvignon   PC   T   V
California $$$$ 28   14

Both pros and consumers give Heitz top marks for its
"fabulous earthy-minty qualities," and powerful dark
fruit. It scores weak for value, though I think it's
priced fairly compared to other luxury Napa Cabs.

Kitchen Countertop Survivor™ Grade: B+

Your notes:_____

_____

Hess Select Cabernet Sauvignon   PC   T   V
California $$ 21   23

My tasters "love" this "always-reliable" Cabernet. The
plum and blackberry flavors and touch of earthy spici-
ness offer lots of real Cab character for the money.

Kitchen Countertop Survivor™ Grade: B

Your notes:_____

_____

Jacob's Creek Cabernet Sauvignon   PC   T   V
Australia $ 21   24

Nice minty-berry varietal character, soft tannin, great
price. Hard to go wrong with this "amazing value for
the money."

Kitchen Countertop Survivor™ Grade: B

Your notes:_____

_____

J. Lohr 7 Oaks Cabernet Sauvignon   PC   T   V
California $$ 23   25

This is one of my favorite California Cabernets at
any price, so its affordability is, to me, a major bonus.

Price Ranges: **$** = $12 or less; **$$** = 12.01–20; **$$$** = 20.01–35;
$$$$ = > $35

Kitchen Fridge/Countertop Survivor™ Grades: *Avg.* = a "one-day
wine," tastes noticeably less fresh the next day; *B* = holds its freshness for 2–3 days after opening; *B+* = holds *and gets better* over 2–3
days after opening; *A* = a 3- to 4-day "freshness window"; *A+* =
holds *and gets better* over 3–4 days

The style—powerful, exotic berry fruit and luxurious coconut cream scent from American oak—is incredibly consistent from year to year.

Kitchen Countertop Survivor™ Grade: B+

Your notes:_____

_____

Jordan Cabernet Sauvignon California

	PC	T	V
	$$$$	23	17

This wine is always controversial, with some calling it "elegant," and "always reliable." Others are decidedly underwhelmed. I think this: the elegant, cedar-scented, silky style seems light compared to the huge "fruit and oak bomb" Cabs that are so popular. Still, Jordan is delicious to drink and ages quite well, too, so it's really a matter of what style you prefer. Personally, I love it.

Kitchen Countertop Survivor™ Grade: B+

Your notes:_____

_____

Joseph Phelps Napa Cabernet Sauvignon, California

	PC	T	V
	$$$$	27	22

This is real Napa Cabernet that, while not cheap, is priced fairly for what you get: great structure, mint, cedar, coffee-spice scents, and classic Cabernet fruit flavors—cassis and blackberry.

Kitchen Countertop Survivor™ Grade: B

Your notes:_____

_____

Kendall-Jackson Vintner's Reserve Cabernet Sauvignon, California

	PC	T	V
	$$	20	22

"Always a winner," say my tasters, and I agree. It's hard to find real varietal character—blackberry flavor, a touch of earth, and a tug of tannin—for this price.

Kitchen Countertop Survivor™ Grade: B

Your notes:_____

_____

Kenwood Cabernet Sauvignon   PC   T   V
California $$ 22   22

This is a good example of the Sonoma Cabernet style, emphasizing wild berry fruit with a touch of Asian spice and smooth tannin.

Kitchen Countertop Survivor™ Grade: Avg.

Your notes:_____

Los Vascos Cabernet Sauvignon   PC   T   V
Chile $ 29   27

Definitely a great value every year and one of Chile's most elegant, classically styled Cabernets. It's got dark cherry fruit and a cedary scent, with smooth but structured tannins. My tasters call it "a 'wow!' for the price."

Kitchen Countertop Survivor™ Grade: B

Your notes:_____

Meridian Cabernet Sauvignon   PC   T   V
California $ 21   23

This juicy wine is "always a great value," say my tasters. I say the in-your-face style has appealing aromas of black cherry and fruitcake and a soft texture.

Kitchen Countertop Survivor™ Grade: B

Your notes:_____

Mt. Veeder Napa Cabernet   PC   T   V
Sauvignon, California $$$$ 28   24

The Mt. Veeder district is a sub-appellation of Napa Valley. This Cab is "immense," with gripping tannins, dense figlike fruit, and great ageability. If you plan to drink it young, decant and invite a big steak or a fine cheese to the table.

Kitchen Countertop Survivor™ Grade: A

Your notes:_____

Price Ranges: $ = $12 or less; $$ = 12.01–20; $$$ = 20.01–35; $$$$ = > $35

Kitchen Fridge/Countertop Survivor™ Grades: *Avg.* = a "one-day wine," tastes noticeably less fresh the next day; *B* = holds its freshness for 2–3 days after opening; *B+* = holds *and gets better* over 2–3 days after opening; *A* = a 3- to 4-day "freshness window"; *A+* = holds *and gets better* over 3–4 days

Mystic Cliffs Cabernet Sauvignon	PC	T	V
California	$	12	18

I find this wine shy on fruit, but my tasters rate it "ok for a budget choice."

Kitchen Countertop Survivor™ *Grade: Avg*

Your notes:_____

_____

Napa Ridge Lodi Cabernet	PC	T	V
Sauvignon, California	$	15	21

This wine "was better before they switched to Lodi fruit" from the Central Valley (it used to be a Coastal appellation). But it still scores "ok for value."

Kitchen Countertop Survivor™ *Grade: Avg*

Your notes:_____

_____

Pahlmeyer Meritage Napa Valley	PC	T	V
California	$$$$	X	X

✗ This "hard-to-find" boutique Cabernet has "great fruit flavors of wild dark berries," "massive oak" and a "great finish." Collector-types find the "very high price" "worth it."

Kitchen Countertop Survivor™ *Grade: B*

Your notes:_____

_____

Penfolds Bin 389 Cabernet	PC	T	V
Sauvignon/Shiraz, Australia	$$$	25	23

This "awesome" wine delivers on all counts: complexity, density of flavor, the "yum" factor, and value. It is one of my favorite wines. The vivid raspberry fruit and pepper/cedar/spice/coconut scent are delicious young, but the wine also develops breathtaking complexity with age.

Kitchen Countertop Survivor™ *Grade: A+*

Your notes:_____

_____

Penfolds Koonunga Hill Cabernet	PC	T	V
Merlot, Australia	$	20	21

This blend gives you the cedar scent and structure of Cabernet, the plummy softness of Merlot, and thus lots of pleasure at a good price. A great everyday dinner wine.

Kitchen Countertop Survivor™ *Grade: B*

Your notes:_____

_____

Pride Mountain Vineyards	PC	T	V
Cabernet Sauvignon, California	$$$$	26	19

Major raves for this wine's "gorgeous aromas," "dense, incredible dark fruit," and "great quality price ratio when you compare it against some of the hard-to-find CA cult wines." I agree. I think it tastes as complex and intense as cult Cabs at three times the price. (I hope it stays that way!)

Kitchen Countertop Survivor™ *Grade: B*

Your notes:_____

_____

Raymond Napa Cabernet Sauvignon	PC	T	V
California	$$	24	24

The Raymond family puts quality in the bottle for a good price. It's "minty and elegant," balanced and not heavy.

Kitchen Countertop Survivor™ *Grade: B*

Your notes:_____

_____

Robert Mondavi Private Selection	PC	T	V
Cabernet Sauvignon, California	$	17	19

I'd have expected Mondavi, longtime leader in California's signature red grape, to be easily among the best in this price point. It is not. It's "drinkable," but others at this price beat it for flavor and quality.

Kitchen Countertop Survivor™ *Grade: Avg*

Your notes:_____

_____

Price Ranges: **$** = $12 or less; **$$** = 12.01–20; **$$$** = 20.01–35; **$$$$** = > $35

Kitchen Fridge/Countertop Survivor™ Grades: *Avg.* = a "one-day wine," tastes noticeably less fresh the next day; *B* = holds its freshness for 2–3 days after opening; *B+* = holds *and gets better* over 2–3 days after opening; *A* = a 3- to 4-day "freshness window"; *A+* = holds *and gets better* over 3–4 days

Robert Mondavi Napa Cabernet	PC	T	V
Sauvignon, California	$$$	25	24

This is a "consistently great Cab" which, compared to others of its quality, remains "good value for the money." The deeply concentrated cassis and licorice flavor and cedary, spicy, minty scent are consistent style signatures and a benchmark for the category.

Kitchen Countertop Survivor™ Grade: B

Your notes:_____

_____

Rodney Strong Sonoma Cabernet	PC	T	V
Sauvignon, California	$$	24	23

My tasters "love" the coconutty oak scent and "huge fruit" that "tastes more expensive than it is."

Kitchen Countertop Survivor™ Grade: B

Your notes:_____

_____

Rosemount Diamond Label	PC	T	V
Cabernet Sauvignon, Australia	$	22	25

My tasters rave that this "jammy," "very-well-made" Aussie Cab is "simply one of the best buys in wine." I agree and love the minty, cedary varietal character, too. And of course anyone could love the price.

Kitchen Countertop Survivor™ Grade: B

Your notes:_____

_____

Rosemount Diamond Label	PC	T	V
Cabernet Sauvignon/Merlot	$	22	26
Australia			

An absolutely "fantastic value" that I'd recommend by the glass and for everyday drinking. The juicy, dark, plummy fruit is delicious.

Kitchen Countertop Survivor™ Grade: B

Your notes:_____

_____

Santa Rita 120 Cabernet Sauvignon	PC	T	V
Chile	$	27	24

It is indeed "a price that's hard to believe" for the quality and flavor punch it delivers. The nice tannic grip and meaty-spicy scent and flavor show the rustic Chilean Cabernet character that I love.

Kitchen Countertop Survivor™ Grade: B
Your notes:_____

_____

Silverado Napa Cabernet	PC	T	V
Sauvignon, California	$$$$	22	19

This wine is "the reason I love Cabernet, the perfect balance of soft and tough, sorta like your favorite leather jacket," writes one aficionado. Silverado's elegant but firm style is classy, with cassis flavor scented with sweet oak and earthiness.

Kitchen Countertop Survivor™ Grade: A
Your notes:_____

_____

Silver Oak Alexander Valley	PC	T	V
Cabernet Sauvignon, California	$$$$	25	20

Whether in auction rooms, on wine lists, or in the boutique wine shops that score a few bottles, this wine counts a sea of die-hard devotees who find its consistency and quality "worth the price." But more than just "yummy" to drink, it is utterly original, known for really intense wild berry fruit, velvety-thick tannins, a coconut-dill scent coming from American oak barrels, and density in the mouth that seizes your senses unforgettably.

Kitchen Countertop Survivor™ Grade: B
Your notes:_____

_____

Simi Sonoma Cabernet Sauvignon	PC	T	V
California	$$	24	24

Simi's blue chip reputation, now more than ever, offers excellent value for the money and classy, true California Cabernet flavors: blackberry, earth, and spice.

Kitchen Countertop Survivor™ Grade: B+
Your notes:_____

_____

Price Ranges: $ = $12 or less; $$ = 12.01–20; $$$ = 20.01–35; $$$$ = > $35
Kitchen Fridge/Countertop Survivor™ Grades: *Avg.* = a "one-day wine," tastes noticeably less fresh the next day; *B* = holds its freshness for 2–3 days after opening; *B+* = holds *and gets better* over 2–3 days after opening; *A* = a 3- to 4-day "freshness window"; *A+* = holds *and gets better* over 3–4 days

Stag's Leap Wine Cellars Napa | PC | T | V
Cabernet Sauvignon, California | $$$$ | 28 | 24

Although it's "pricey," this wine's "incredible complexity"—with dark spices, mint, and berry character, make it "worth the splurge." It "ages great," too.

Kitchen Countertop Survivor™ Grade: B

Your notes:_____

Sterling Vineyards Napa Cabernet | PC | T | V
Sauvignon, California | $$$ | 25 | 23

The price dropped, bumping up scores for this classic name in Cabernet. Tasters praise its "concentrated," "jammy fruits." I think it is good but outperformed of late by many old Napa neighbors, as well as new names from Sonoma, Paso Robles, and beyond.

Kitchen Countertop Survivor™ Grade: B

Your notes:_____

Stonestreet Alexander Valley | PC | T | V
Cabernet Sauvignon, California | $$$ | 23 | 21

This is very classy California Cabernet, unencumbered by excessive oak and alcohol, but with plenty of power and concentration. The scents of vanilla, damp earth, crushed mint, and blackberry are classic Alexander Valley.

Kitchen Countertop Survivor™ Grade: Avg

Your notes:_____

Sutter Home Cabernet Sauvignon | PC | T | V
California | $ | 15 | 16

Though not particularly expressive of Cabernet character, this is "just tasty red wine" that's a "crowd pleaser."

Kitchen Countertop Survivor™ Grade: Avg

Your notes:_____

Talus Cabernet Sauvignon | PC | T | V
California | $ | 18 | 21

Though it's not a star in this Cabernet price range, this is the best varietal in the Talus line, with some good fruit flavor and a soft texture.

Kitchen Countertop Survivor™ *Grade: Avg*
Your notes:_____
_____

Terra Rosa Cabernet Sauvignon	PC	T	V
Chile/Argentina	$	20	25

This "Best Buy-plus" Cabernet is made by Laurel Glen Winery's Patrick Campbell. Year in and year out it offers "great fruit flavor" at a great price, and even boasts a bit of the Chilean earthy/smokiness that I think is classic to the region.

Kitchen Countertop Survivor™ *Grade: B*
Your notes:_____
_____

Turning Leaf Cabernet Sauvignon	PC	T	V
California	$	20	22

This Cab made big strides in both taste and value with my tasters, who call it "soft and tasty for the money." The leftovers hold up well, too.

Kitchen Countertop Survivor™ *Grade: B*
Your notes:_____
_____

Vendange Cabernet Sauvignon	PC	T	V
California	$	12	12

Neither taste nor value held their own with my tasters, who note "there are better options at this price."

Kitchen Countertop Survivor™ *Grade: Avg*
Your notes:_____
_____

Veramonte Cabernet Sauvignon	PC	T	V
Chile	$	17	19

Retail buyers tag this a "real value find for consumers," and I agree. It's got great color, good concentration,

Price Ranges: **$** = $12 or less; **$$** = 12.01–20; **$$$** = 20.01–35; **$$$$** = > $35

Kitchen Fridge/Countertop Survivor™ Grades: *Avg.* = a "one-day wine," tastes noticeably less fresh the next day; *B* = holds its freshness for 2–3 days after opening; *B+* = holds *and gets better* over 2–3 days after opening; *A* = a 3- to 4-day "freshness window"; *A+* = holds *and gets better* over 3–4 days

and some substance—licorice-berry fruit, some chewy tannin, and a savory spice note.

Kitchen Countertop Survivor™ Grade: Avg

Your notes:_____

_____

Viader Napa Valley Cabernet blend, California	PC	T	V
	$$$$	X	X

✗ A "wonderfully smooth" classic Napa Cab blend whose "glorious fruit," soft vanilla-coffee scent of oak and awesome complexity are "as good as any of the cult Cabs" but with a sense of proportion and elegance that's rare in the category. "A wine to actually enjoy with dinner," as my one of my tasters put it so well.

Kitchen Countertop Survivor™ Grade: A

Your notes:_____

_____

Viña Carmen Cabernet Sauvignon Chile	PC	T	V
	$	17	19

So cheap and so drinkable, with "nice berry aromas" and a tug of tannin. What's not to love?

Kitchen Countertop Survivor™ Grade: B

Your notes:_____

_____

Walnut Crest Cabernet Sauvignon Chile	PC	T	V
	$	18	21

"Tastes more expensive than it is," say tasters, who rank it accordingly for both taste and value. The peppery, fruity, and crowd-pleasing style is at once smooth and savory.

Kitchen Countertop Survivor™ Grade: Avg

Your notes:_____

_____

Woodbridge (Robert Mondavi) Cabernet Sauvignon, California	PC	T	V
	$	17	18

Both pros and consumers rate Woodbridge as reliable and "pleasant" for everyday drinking.

Kitchen Countertop Survivor™ Grade: Avg

Your notes:_____

_____

Wynn's Coonawarra Estate	PC	T	V
Cabernet Sauvignon, Australia	$$	20	25

The "smooth blackcurrant fruit" and cedary, "minty" scent are classic characteristics of Coonawarra Cab. The soft oak and sleek texture make for an elegant Cab that "drinks nicely young."

Kitchen Countertop Survivor™ Grade: A

Your notes:_____

Rioja, Ribera del Duero, and Other Spanish Reds

Category Profile: Haven't tried one? Busted! You see, if I were chief of the "wine police," I'd put all wine drinkers on probation until they'd tried at least one Spanish red. If, like so many Americans, your kitchen table is presently a "crime scene" (as described here), you can quickly destroy the evidence by trying any one of these wines or another that your favorite store or restaurant recommends. (One look at the across-the-board great reviews for this category should convince you it's a low-risk bet!) There aren't many familiar grapes on the label, so you'll just have to go with them as classical, wholesome, centuries-old products of nature. (Can you say that about the other things you ingest regularly?) Now, for the background: Red Rioja (*ree-OH-huh*) and Ribera del Duero (*ree-BEAR-uh dell DWAIR-oh*) are Spain's two most famous wines and regions—like other classic Euro wines, it's the place rather than the grape on the label. Both are made mainly from the local Tempranillo (*temp-rah-NEE-oh*) grape. Depending on quality level, Rioja ranges from easy-drinking and spicy to seriously rich, leathery/toffee in character— never ho-hum. The other Spanish reds here are from Priorat (*pre-oh-RAHT*), known for strong, inky-dark

---

Price Ranges: **$** = $12 or less; **$$** = 12.01–20; **$$$** = 20.01–35; **$$$$** = > $35

Kitchen Fridge/Countertop Survivor™ Grades: *Avg.* = a "one-day wine," tastes noticeably less fresh the next day; *B* = holds its freshness for 2–3 days after opening; *B+* = holds *and gets better* over 2–3 days after opening; *A* = a 3- to 4-day "freshness window"; *A+* = holds *and gets better* over 3–4 days

cellar candidates (some made from Cabernet and/or Grenache). Though not represented in the top red wine sellers, Penedes (*pen-eh-DESS*), which is better known for Cava sparkling wines, is also an outstanding source of values in every style and color.

Serve: Cool room temperature; as a rule Spanish reds are exemplary food wines, but basic reds from Penedes and Rioja (with the word Crianza on the label), and emerging regions like Navarra, Toro, and Somontano, are good "anytime" wines and tasty on their own.

When: Rioja Crianza is my personal "house" red wine. Also, if you dine out often in wine-focused restaurants, Spanish reds are *the* red wine category for world-class drinking that's also affordable.

With: Your next pig roast (!) . . . Seriously, the classic matches are pork and lamb, either roasted or grilled; also amazing with slow-roasted chicken or turkey and hams, sausages, and other cured meats. Finally, if you enjoy a cheese course in lieu of dessert, or are interested in trying one of the world's great pairings that's also easy to pull off, try a Spanish Ribera del Duero, Priorat, or Rioja Reserva or Gran Reserva with good-quality cheese. (Spanish Manchego is wonderful and available in supermarkets.)

In: An all-purpose wineglass or larger-bowled red wine stem.

	PC	T	V
Alvaro Palacios Les Terrasses			
(*ALL-vahr-oh puh-LAH-see-os lay tear-AHSS*) Priorat, Spain	**$$$**	**26**	**24**

For sheer drama it's hard to top this dark, brooding beauty from Priorat, the tiny Spanish wine region that has sommeliers and fine wine buyers buzzing. This one from Alvaro Palacios, a premier producer, is lush, intense, and inky, with beautiful black cherry flavors, toasty oak, and a finish that seems hours long.
Kitchen Countertop Survivor™ Grade: B
Your notes:_____
_____

Arzuaga (*ahr-ZWAH-guh*) **Crianza**

Ribera del Duero, Spain

	PC	T	V
	$$$	22	22

My tasters gave this high taste and value marks for its power, concentration, ripeness, and complexity. Though it's "expensive," most tasters felt the gorgeous, rich flavor and length do deliver the goods.

Kitchen Countertop Survivor™ Grade: Avg

Your notes:_____

Faustino (*fau-STEEN-oh*) **Rioja**

Crianza, Spain

	PC	T	V
	$	26	29

✓ The rustic, earthy scent, chewy cherry-berry flavor and full-on tannins are complex, making this a "steal for the price."

Kitchen Countertop Survivor™ Grade: A

Your notes:_____

Marqués de Cáceres (*mahr-KESS deh CAH-sair-ess*) **Rioja Crianza Spain**

	PC	T	V
	$$	22	23

With "lots of cherry fruit" and "typical toffee-spice," this Rioja Crianza is true to type—delicious, drinkable, and food friendly. It is among my very favorite widely available, basic Riojas.

Kitchen Countertop Survivor™ Grade: A

Your notes:_____

Marqués de Riscal (*mahr-KESS deh ree-SKALL*) **Rioja Crianza, Spain**

	PC	T	V
	$	21	18

Although its value reviews slipped, this wine still earns praise for its lovely spicy nose, silken texture, and savory-strawberry flavor.

Kitchen Countertop Survivor™ Grade: B+

Your notes:_____

Price Ranges: **$** = $12 or less; **$$** = 12.01–20; **$$$** = 20.01–35; **$$$$** = > $35

Kitchen Fridge/Countertop Survivor™ Grades: *Avg.* = a "one-day wine," tastes noticeably less fresh the next day; *B* = holds its freshness for 2–3 days after opening; *B+* = holds *and gets better* over 2–3 days after opening; *A* = a 3- to 4-day "freshness window"; *A+* = holds *and gets better* over 3–4 days

Montecillo (*mohn-teh-SEE-yoh*)   PC   T   V
Rioja Crianza, Spain $ 24   24

Another favorite of wine aficionados, for its Old World savory spiciness and long finish. Very nice indeed.
Kitchen Countertop Survivor™ Grade: Avg
Your notes:_____

_____

Muga (*MOO-guh*) Rioja Reserva   PC   T   V
Spain $$$ 25   22

This classic, sturdy Rioja is a world class wine, and a relative value in that realm. The stunningly generous fig, prune, and dried cherry fruit and dense but suede-smooth tannins make it "a brooding red" that's fabulous with cheese, lamb, and game. "Cellar it if you can," say my tasters.
Kitchen Countertop Survivor™ Grade: A+
Your notes:_____

_____

Pesquera (*pess-CARE-uh*) Ribera   PC   T   V
del Duero, Spain $$$ 22   20

For years Pesquera's quality and gorgeous cherry fruit with firm tannins were legendary. Sadly, I share the new consensus among tasters that the wine has declined, and is getting "over-oaked for the fruit."
Kitchen Countertop Survivor™ Grade: B
Your notes:_____

_____

Vega Sindoa (*VAY-guh sin-*   PC   T   V
***DOUGH-uh*) Tempranillo/Merlot** $ 18   24
Navarra Tinto, Spain

The rustic, spicy note and soft fruit make this a "great crowd pleaser," especially for the money.
Kitchen Countertop Survivor™ Grade: B
Your notes:_____

_____

Vinicola del Priorat Onix   PC   T   V
(*veen-EE-co-lah dell PREE-oh-raht* $$$ 20   22
***OH-nix*), Spain**

A great entrée to Spain's big, inky Priorat wines, because this one's "more affordable than most." It's not as teeth-staining as some, but still has the deep berry fruit, tarry scent, and chewy tannins of the region. Decant, and serve it "with cheese or big meat." *Kitchen Countertop Survivor™ Grade: A*

Your notes:_____

_____

Other Reds

Category Profile: As with the whites, this isn't a cohesive category but rather a spot to put big-selling reds that don't neatly fit a grape or region category— namely, generic wines, proprietary blends, and uncommon varietals.

Generics—Recapping the definition in the white wine section, this category uses classic regional names like Chianti and Burgundy for basic bulk wines.

Proprietary blends—These may be tasty, inexpensive blends, or ambitious signature blends at luxury prices.

Uncommon varietals—These are quite exciting. I introduced Malbec and Carmenere in the Merlot section, because I think they are distinctive and delicious alternatives for Merlot lovers. Although the names and even the style (bold and a little peppery) are similar, Petite Sirah and Syrah (Shiraz) are not the same grape.

Serve: Cool room temperature, or even slightly chilled.

When: Anytime you need an uncomplicated, value-priced red. Many tasters recommended generics for big parties, picnics (even with ice cubes), and other casual occasions. Quite a few pros also said they are a good-tasting and low-cost base for sangría and other wine-based punches.

Price Ranges: **$** = $12 or less; **$$** = 12.01–20; **$$$** = 20.01–35; **$$$$** = > $35

Kitchen Fridge/Countertop Survivor™ Grades: *Avg.* = a "one-day wine," tastes noticeably less fresh the next day; *B* = holds its freshness for 2–3 days after opening; *B+* = holds *and gets better* over 2–3 days after opening; *A* = a 3- to 4-day "freshness window"; *A+* = holds *and gets better* over 3–4 days

With: Snacks and everyday meals.

In: An all-purpose wineglass.

Ca'del Solo Big House Red
	PC	T	V
California	$$	22	19

This "spicy," juicy red offers "great value" and easy drinkability—a "fun for everyday" wine. The screwcap can't be beat for convenience.

Kitchen Countertop Survivor™ Grade: A

Your notes:_____

_____

Carlo Rossi Burgundy
	PC	T	V
USA	$	12	25

The assessments here clearly reflect the fact that Americans have traded up to varietal wines, but respect this value "for sangría" and "for cooking," and it is indeed widely used in restaurant kitchens in New York for just that. While the taste is as "simple as the twist-off cap it comes with," it is sound and competently made.

Kitchen Countertop Survivor™ Grade: B

Your notes:_____

Concannon Petite Sirah
	PC	T	V
California	$	21	24

Take a black pepper and berry scent, add explode-in-your-mouth fruit-pie flavor, chewy tannins, and a long licorice finish, and you've got this unique, fun, and utterly delicious wine.

Kitchen Countertop Survivor™ Grade: B+

Your notes:_____

Concha y Toro Terrunyo Carmenere
	PC	T	V
Chile	$$	18	18

You'll have to search a bit for this, but it's worth the trouble. The flavor is like the concentrated essence of wild berries (huckleberries, raspberries), with a velvety-plush texture and seductive sweet spice-cola scents.

Kitchen Countertop Survivor™ Grade: B

Your notes:_____

| **Coppola (Francis) Presents Rosso** | PC | T | V |
| California | $ | 22 | 22 |

"Just what an everyday wine should be," said tasters of this juicy, fruity, and simple Coppola wine (yes, *that* Coppola). It's delicious and "fun."

Kitchen Countertop Survivor™ Grade: B+

Your notes:_____

_____

| **Navarro Correas Malbec** | PC | T | V |
| Argentina | $ | 24 | 24 |

This is rustic but really inviting, with earthy, leathery, savory spice and dried fruits on the scent. The grip of tannin is followed by silky, subtle plum fruit and a smoky, earthy finish. But "look for the reserve," said some tasters.

Kitchen Countertop Survivor™ Grade: B+

Your notes:_____

_____

| **Terrazas Alto Malbec** | PC | T | V |
| Argentina | $ | 21 | 20 |

This "juicy, plummy, spicy" Malbec gets "great value" marks from my tasters. It's soft enough for sipping on its own, but with enough grip and concentration to compliment steak or cheese.

Kitchen Countertop Survivor™ Grade: Avg

Your notes:_____

_____

| **Veramonte Primus** | PC | T | V |
| Chile | $$ | 24 | 18 |

This, one of the first Chilean Carmeneres on the market, is still one of the best, with a lot of exotic berry fruit and both savory and sweet spices and flavors that almost mimic Asian flavors like hoisin or teriyaki. Yum!

Kitchen Countertop Survivor™ Grade: B

Your notes:_____

_____

Price Ranges: **$** = $12 or less; **$$** = 12.01–20; **$$$** = 20.01–35; **$$$$** = > $35

Kitchen Fridge/Countertop Survivor™ Grades: *Avg.* = a "one-day wine," tastes noticeably less fresh the next day; *B* = holds its freshness for 2–3 days after opening; *B+* = holds *and gets better* over 2–3 days after opening; *A* = a 3- to 4-day "freshness window"; *A+* = holds *and gets better* over 3–4 days

Italian Regional Reds

Category Profile: This group includes small Italian regions like Valpolicella and Lambrusco, whose market presence is dominated by a few big-selling, well-known brands.

Serve: Cool room temperature or slightly chilled.

When: As the Italians would, for everyday drinking.

With: Snacks and everyday meals.

In: An all-purpose wineglass.

	PC	T	V
Allegrini Valpolicella (*al-uh-GREE-nee val-pole-uh-CHELL-uh***), Italy**	**$$**	**22**	**23**

"Always a great choice" and "great with food," say my tasters. It's classic Valpolicella—dried cherry flavor, spicy scent, vibrant acidity.

Kitchen Countertop Survivor™ Grade: B

Your notes:_____

_____

	PC	T	V
Bolla Valpolicella Italy	**$**	**19**	**20**

This Valpolicella is fruity, soft, and a little spicy. A "no-brainer for casual pasta/pizza fare."

Kitchen Countertop Survivor™ Grade: Avg

Your notes:_____

_____

	PC	T	V
Citra Montepulciano d'Abruzzo (*CHEE-truh mon-teh-pool-CHAH-no dah-BROOT-so***), Italy**	**$**	**18**	**24**

This is just a yummy little wine for the money, whose fruity taste and touch of earthy spiciness make almost any dish taste better.

Kitchen Countertop Survivor™ Grade: B

Your notes:_____

_____

	PC	T	V
Falesco Vitiano (*fuh-LESS-co vee-tee-AH-no***), Italy**	**$**	**24**	**28**

✓ This wine gives you major yum for a song, something no one does better than the Italians. It's a spicy, plummy, lip-smacking blend of Merlot, Cabernet

Sauvignon, and Sangiovese, from the Umbria region of Italy.

Kitchen Countertop Survivor™ Grade: B

Your notes:_____

_____

Pio Cesare Barolo	PC	T	V
Italy	$$$$	X	X

✗ Here is a classy, real-deal Barolo with good availability, and a good price for the quality. The deep plum, cedar, and tar scent is textbook Barolo. The tannins are gripping but balanced, and the dusty berry-rhubarb flavor is mouthwatering. Definitely a cellar candidate. If you can't wait, serve it with game or rich cheeses.

Kitchen Countertop Survivor™ Grade: A

Your notes:_____

_____

Riunite Lambrusco (*ree-you-NEE-tee	PC	T	V
***lam-BROO-scoe*), Italy**	$	21	21

If you liked it as "Riunite on ice," you'll like it now, "for big parties" and as "a summer cooler."

Kitchen Countertop Survivor™ Grade: Avg

Your notes:_____

_____

Zenato Amarone Della Valpolicella	PC	T	V
Classico, Italy	$$$$	X	X

✗ This "delicious & decadent," deeply rich wine drips with ripe fig fruit, sweet spices and thick, mouth-coating tannins. It's incredible with game, strong cheeses, even chocolate—a "worthy splurge" that's still not crazy-expensive for what you get.

Kitchen Countertop Survivor™ Grade: A

Your notes:_____

_____

Price Ranges: **$** = $12 or less; **$$** = 12.01–20; **$$$** = 20.01–35; **$$$$** = > $35

Kitchen Fridge/Countertop Survivor™ Grades: *Avg.* = a "one-day wine," tastes noticeably less fresh the next day; *B* = holds its freshness for 2–3 days after opening; *B+* = holds *and gets better* over 2–3 days after opening; *A* = a 3- to 4-day "freshness window"; *A+* = holds *and gets better* over 3–4 days

| Zenato Ripassa Valpolicella DOC | PC | T | V |
| Superiore, Italy | $$ | X | X |

✗ "Fruity but with real depth" is a great descriptor for this "mini Amarone" with luscious raisin-fig fruit and a smooth texture that's "irresistible." It's always been a hit when I've served it with strong cheeses and braised meats.

Kitchen Countertop Survivor™ Grade: A

Your notes:_____

_____

Syrah/Shiraz and Other Rhône-Style Reds

Category Profile: This category of reds continues as a sizzling seller—especially the varietal Shiraz, Australia's signature red, which is so hot that many pros say it has unseated Merlot as consumers' go-to grape. It is true that even at the one-dollar-sign level you get a scent of sweet spice and jammy, succulent fruit flavor that, in my opinion, dusts many of the popular reds out there based on Merlot and Cabernet Sauvignon. The same grape, under the French spelling *Syrah,* also forms the backbone for France's revered Rhône Valley reds with centuries-old reputations. These include Côtes-du-Rhône (*coat-duh-ROAN*), Côte-Rôtie (*ro-TEE*), Hermitage (*uhr-muh-TAHJ*), and Châteauneuf-du-Pape (*shah-toe-NUFF-duh-POP*). Like Shiraz, Côtes-du-Rhône, with its lovely spicy fruit character, is a one-dollar-sign wonder. The latter three are true French classics and in my view currently lead that elite group in quality for the money. They are full-bodied, powerful, peppery, earthy, concentrated, and oak-aged. Finally, most major American wineries, and many smaller players, are bottling California or Washington state versions, often labeled with the Aussie spelling *Shiraz* rather than the French *Syrah.*

Serve: Room temperature; aeration enhances the aroma and flavor.

When: Basic Shiraz and Côtes-du-Rhône are great everyday drinking wines; in restaurants, these are great go-to categories for relative value.

With: Grilled, barbecued, or roasted anything (including fish and vegetables); outstanding with steaks, fine cheeses, and other dishes that call for a full red wine; I also love these styles with traditional Thanksgiving fare.

In: An all-purpose wineglass or a larger-bowled red wine stem.

| Black Opal Shiraz | PC | T | V |
| Australia | $ | 21 | 23 |

"Always a great value," with juicy fruit and a soft texture that makes it a great "house red."
Kitchen Countertop Survivor™ Grade: Avg.
Your notes:_____

_____

| Château de Beaucastel | PC | T | V |
| Châteauneuf-du-Pape, France | $$$$ | 24 | 21 |

Although it's "expensive" and "hard to get," among the peer group of truly collectible, ageable, world-class wines, Beaucastel is a relative value. The Asian spice and leather scent and powerful fig and dark berry fruit are fabulous young, but it cellars beautifully, too.
Kitchen Countertop Survivor™ Grade: A+
Your notes:_____

_____

Château La Nerthe (*shah-TOE lah*	PC	T	V
NAIRT) Châteauneuf-du-Pape,	$$$$	28	18
France			

While trade buyers and serious wine devotees rave about this "lovely," "smooth" wine, some also rightly point out that all the really good Rhône juice around is giving it stiff competition, often at lower prices. The pepper/spicy/leathery scents, gripping tannins, and dried cranberry-anise flavors are textbook Châteauneuf, built for rich meats and stews.
Kitchen Countertop Survivor™ Grade: A
Your notes:_____

_____

Price Ranges: **$** = $12 or less; **$$** = 12.01–20; **$$$** = 20.01–35; **$$$$** = > $35
Kitchen Fridge/Countertop Survivor™ Grades: *Avg.* = a "one-day wine," tastes noticeably less fresh the next day; *B* = holds its freshness for 2–3 days after opening; *B+* = holds *and gets better* over 2–3 days after opening; *A* = a 3- to 4-day "freshness window"; *A+* = holds *and gets better* over 3–4 days

Cline Syrah   PC   T   V
California $ 22   24

Cline is a red wine wizard, putting vibrant berry fruit flavor and spicy-zingy scent in the bottle for a great price.

Kitchen Countertop Survivor™ Grade: B+

Your notes:_____

_____

Cockfighter's Ghost Hunter Valley   PC   T   V
Shiraz, Australia $$ 26   20

Special enough "for company," but with a price that's do-able for the host. The raspberry-vanilla fruit and succulent texture are delicious for just sipping, but also great with bold foods like barbecue or blackened chicken.

Kitchen Countertop Survivor™ Grade: B

Your notes:_____

_____

D'Arenberg The Footbolt Shiraz   PC   T   V
Australia $$ 22   25

I love this "intense and well balanced" wine whose flavors are so distinctive—meaty-smoky, tangy berries, savory and sweet spices. All the complexity for a "nice price."

Kitchen Countertop Survivor™ Grade: B

Your notes:_____

_____

Domaine Santa Duc Gigondas   PC   T   V
(*doh-MAIN santa duke* $$$ 23   21
JHEE-gohn-dahss), France

The "gorgeous berry and cherry fruit" are spiked with the peppery spice typical of Gigondas. The gripping tannins and rustic earthiness make it great with smoked fare, bean dishes, and mushroom dishes.

Kitchen Countertop Survivor™ Grade: B+

Your notes:_____

_____

Duboeuf (Georges) Côtes-du-Rhône   PC   T   V
(*du-BUFF coat-duh-ROAN*), France $ 20   22

Although Duboeuf is virtually synonymous with Beaujolais, his other French regional wines, like this

Côtes-du-Rhône, are consistently well made and often at best-deal prices. This wine delivers character for cheap: it is juicy and fresh tasting, with red cherry and a spicy pomegranate note. Yum!

Kitchen Countertop Survivor™ Grade: B

Your notes:_____

_____

E & M Guigal (*ghee-GALL*)	**PC**	**T**	**V**
Côtes-du-Rhône, France	**$$**	**23**	**25**

So many tasters, obviously enticed by the famous Guigal name, have discovered and enjoyed the cherry fruit and pepper-spice notes of this classic Côtes-du-Rhône. For consistency and flavor for the money, it's a solid bet.

Kitchen Countertop Survivor™ Grade: A

Your notes:_____

_____

E & M Guigal Cote-Rotie Brune et	**PC**	**T**	**V**
Blonde, France	**$$$$**	**26**	**25**

Is it the texture ("liquid velvet"), the scent ("pepper and lavender"), or flavor ("blackberry") that's most compelling? Any one or all of them will get your attention if you drink it now, but my tasters are right: it "will age 20 years."

Kitchen Countertop Survivor™ Grade: B+

Your notes:_____

_____

Elderton Shiraz	**PC**	**T**	**V**
Australia	**$$$**	**24**	**25**

A "top rank Aussie Shiraz" for the price, with buckets of fruit, oak, and alcohol and "just enough balance."

Kitchen Countertop Survivor™ Grade: B

Your notes:_____

_____

Price Ranges: **$** = $12 or less; **$$** = 12.01–20; **$$$** = 20.01–35; **$$$$** = > $35

Kitchen Fridge/Countertop Survivor™ Grades: *Avg.* = a "one-day wine," tastes noticeably less fresh the next day; *B* = holds its freshness for 2–3 days after opening; *B+* = holds *and gets better* over 2–3 days after opening; *A* = a 3- to 4-day "freshness window"; *A+* = holds *and gets better* over 3–4 days

Fetzer Valley Oaks Syrah   PC   T   V
California $ 24   24

Fetzer puts amazing quality in the bottle for the price, and this Syrah is no exception. Aside from being yummy, it does what few California Syrahs do: it captures the grape's wonderful character—wild raspberry fruit and peppery spice.

Kitchen Countertop Survivor™ *Grade: B*

Your notes:_____

_____

Hill of Content Grenache/Shiraz   PC   T   V
Australia $$ 24   27

The scent is of raspberry, while the taste offers ripe, jammy berry fruit and succulent texture. De-lish!

Kitchen Countertop Survivor™ *Grade: A*

Your notes:_____

_____

Jaboulet (*jhah-boo-LAY***)**   PC   T   V
Côtes-du-Rhône, France $ 22   23

While Jaboulet stakes its reputation on its luxurious and collectible Hermitage, this bottling is an equally impressive calling card in the budget price category with succulent red-berry fruit and smoky black pepper scents.

Kitchen Countertop Survivor™ *Grade: B*

Your notes:_____

_____

Jacob's Creek Shiraz/Cabernet   PC   T   V
Sauvignon, Australia $ 21   22

"This wine is tough to beat in the 'great taste and great value' category," said one of my tasters, and I have to agree. The exotic raspberry and eucalyptus notes and plump texture make it easy to see why Australia has been so successful at blending its signature Shiraz grape with Cabernet.

Kitchen Countertop Survivor™ *Grade: B+*

Your notes:_____

_____

Joseph Phelps Le Mistral	PC	T	V
California	$$$	26	22

Phelps was one of California's Rhone varietal pioneers, and this mainly Grenache-Syrah blend is still "excellent," with a beautiful balance between strawberry-rhubarb fruit and zippy spice. A love letter to food.

Kitchen Countertop Survivor™ Grade: B+

Your notes:_____

Kendall-Jackson Vintner's Reserve	PC	T	V
Syrah, California	$$	21	22

This tasty Syrah keeps the K-J family tradition of lots of fruit, in this case ripe, dark berry flavor, as well as savory spice that's super with grill fare and chili.

Kitchen Countertop Survivor™ Grade: Avg.

Your notes:_____

La Vieille Ferme (*lah vee-yay*	PC	T	V
FAIRM; means "the old farm")	$	27	27
Côtes-du-Ventoux, France			

✔ I wasn't the slightest bit surprised by tasters' comments that this raspberry-ripe, lively red is a favorite, with "great character" for the price and "great food-versatility." It has been that way for years.

Kitchen Countertop Survivor™ Grade: B+

Your notes:_____

Lindemans Bin 59 Shiraz	PC	T	V
Australia	$	19	22

The ripe raspberry fruit and a top note of black pepper scent, plus a plump and round mouthfeel, make this wine an all-around great drink and great buy.

Kitchen Countertop Survivor™ Grade: B+

Your notes:_____

Price Ranges: **$** = $12 or less; **$$** = 12.01–20; **$$$** = 20.01–35; **$$$$** = > $35

Kitchen Fridge/Countertop Survivor™ Grades: *Avg.* = a "one-day wine," tastes noticeably less fresh the next day; *B* = holds its freshness for 2–3 days after opening; *B+* = holds *and gets better* over 2–3 days after opening; *A* = a 3- to 4-day "freshness window"; *A+* = holds *and gets better* over 3–4 days

Lindemans Shiraz/Cabernet | PC | T | V
Sauvignon, Cawarra, Australia | $ | 21 | 21

This wine's got nice raspberry fruit and peppery spiciness. The soft plump texture makes it easy drinking.

Kitchen Countertop Survivor™ Grade: B

Your notes:_____

_____

Marquis Phillips Sarah's Blend | PC | T | V
Australia | $$ | X | X

✗ Take two favorites (Shiraz and Merlot), and put Dan Phillips of the Grateful Palate behind them. The result is "juicy, rich, velvety," and "such fun to drink" at a "great price."

Kitchen Countertop Survivor™ Grade: B

Your notes:_____

_____

Penfolds Coonawarra Shiraz | PC | T | V
Bin 128, Australia | $$$ | 25 | 21

"Smooth and polished" Shiraz with "rich but elegant" berry fruit, soft oak, and "chewy tannins" that "melt when you put it with food."

Kitchen Countertop Survivor™ Grade: Avg

Your notes:_____

_____

Penfolds Kalimna Shiraz Bin 28, | PC | T | V
Australia | $$$ | 26 | 22

As one taster put it: "In a good year, this stuff is crazy good. In a normal year, it is merely great." I couldn't agree more. I serve this to my students as an example of real-deal Aussie Shiraz—it's full of black pepper, plum compote flavors, and thick velvety tannins.

Kitchen Countertop Survivor™ Grade: B

Your notes:_____

_____

Penfolds Koonunga Hill Shiraz | PC | T | V
Cabernet, Australia | $ | 21 | 26

You can't beat this plummy, slightly spicy red for easy drinkability, yet with some nice grip to handle meat, barbecue, and other bold food flavors.

Kitchen Countertop Survivor™ Grade: Avg

Your notes:_____

_____

Reynolds Shiraz   PC   T   V
Australia $$ 24   29

With this Shiraz, you get ripe blackberry fruit and a "spicy peppery taste" that's great with burgers or barbecue.

Kitchen Countertop Survivor™ *Grade: Avg*

Your notes:_____

_____

Rosemount Diamond Label Shiraz   PC   T   V
Australia $ 24   25

This wine is just one big annual encore of delicious raspberry-vanilla fruit and a lively but succulent mouthfeel. Although "the price has gone up," it's still a "best buy" that counts legions of devotees.

Kitchen Countertop Survivor™ *Grade: B+*

Your notes:_____

_____

Rosemount Diamond Label Shiraz/   PC   T   V
Cabernet Sauvignon, Australia $ 22   27

This bottling really shows the virtues of blending the Cabernet and Shiraz grapes, with juicy, mouth-watering berry fruit, a touch of mint in the scent, and a gentle tug of tannin.

Kitchen Countertop Survivor™ *Grade: A*

Your notes:_____

_____

Rosemount GSM (Grenache-Shiraz-   PC   T   V
Mourvedre), Australia $$ 26   28

This exotic treat shows all the hallmarks of blends from these three Rhône red grapes—both savory and sweet spices, polished tannins, an irresistible smoky/meaty character in the scent, and rich, jammy black cherry and blueberry flavors.

Kitchen Countertop Survivor™ *Grade: A*

Your notes:_____

_____

Price Ranges: **$** = $12 or less; **$$** = 12.01–20; **$$$** = 20.01–35; **$$$$** = > $35

Kitchen Fridge/Countertop Survivor™ Grades: *Avg.* = a "one-day wine," tastes noticeably less fresh the next day; *B* = holds its freshness for 2–3 days after opening; *B+* = holds *and gets better* over 2–3 days after opening; *A* = a 3- to 4-day "freshness window"; *A+* = holds *and gets better* over 3–4 days

Wolf Blass President's Selection	PC	T	V
Shiraz, Australia	$$	22	24

The "intense blueberry and black pepper aromas" are surprising for the accessible price. It "tastes more expensive than it is."

Kitchen Countertop Survivor™ Grade: Avg

Your notes:_____

_____

Wyndham Bin 555 Shiraz	PC	T	V
Australia	$	21	21

Wyndham is an "always reliable" Aussie Shiraz, in the rich but balanced, smooth style. The "spicy plum" taste is "an easy match for lots of different foods."

Kitchen Countertop Survivor™ Grade: Avg

Your notes:_____

_____

Yellowtail Shiraz	PC	T	V
Australia	$	19	22

Although the consensus is that it's "not as good as their Chardonnay," most of my tasters call it a "good quaff" at an "unbeatable price."

Kitchen Countertop Survivor™ Grade: Avg

Your notes:_____

_____

Red Zinfandel

Category Profile: I'd say *groupie* is the apt moniker for devotees of this lovely red grape, a California specialty that ranges in style from medium-bodied, with bright and juicy raspberry flavors, to lush and full-bodied, with intense blueberry, licorice, and even chocolate scents and flavors. Many of the best vineyards are pre-Prohibition plantings, whose gnarled old vines, often interplanted with other grapes (formerly a common European practice, brought to California by Italian immigrants), produce some amazingly intense, complex wines. Along with their big, bold red wine fruit and body, the wines usually are oaky—a little or a lot depending on the intensity of the grapes used. The grape intensity is a function of the vineyard—its age and its location. California's most famous red Zinfandel areas are Sonoma (especially the Dry

Creek Valley subdistrict), Napa, Amador, and the Sierra foothills, whose most ambitious bottlings can be worthy of aging in the cellar. Lodi, in California's Central Valley, is also a good source. The value bottlings are usually regionally labeled as California or Lodi.

Serve: Room temperature; aeration enhances the aroma and flavor.

When: Value Zinfandels are excellent for everyday drinking; good restaurant lists (not necessarily the "big" ones) usually have a selection worth exploring across the price spectrum.

With: Burgers, pizza, lamb (especially with Indian or Moroccan spices), and quality cheeses are favorite matches. I have even enjoyed very rich, juicy Zinfandels with dark chocolate!

In: An all-purpose wineglass or a larger-bowled red wine stem.

Beaulieu Vineyard (BV) Coastal Zinfandel, California	PC $	T 24	V 24

This is a soft, pleasant, cherry-flavored Zinfandel in the lighter style. If you like soft reds with up-front fruit, skip the budget Merlots you'd normally turn to. This is the flavor you really want.

Kitchen Countertop Survivor™ *Grade: A*

Your notes:_____

_____

Beaulieu Vineyard Napa Valley Zinfandel, California	PC $$	T 24	V 24

I agree with tasters who recommend this wine's "jammy" fruit flavors (meaning the fruit tastes like jam—rich and juicy) "with grilled steaks." I'd also suggest it with cheeseburgers and pizza.

Kitchen Countertop Survivor™ *Grade: Avg*

Your notes:_____

_____

Price Ranges: **$** = $12 or less; **$$** = 12.01–20; **$$$** = 20.01–35; **$$$$** = > $35

Kitchen Fridge/Countertop Survivor™ Grades: *Avg.* = a "one-day wine," tastes noticeably less fresh the next day; *B* = holds its freshness for 2–3 days after opening; *B+* = holds *and gets better* over 2–3 days after opening; *A* = a 3- to 4-day "freshness window"; *A+* = holds *and gets better* over 3–4 days

Beringer North Coast Zinfandel
California

PC	T	V
$$	24	18

This fruity Zin, with cherry-berry flavors and soft tannins, is medium-bodied, so it won't overpower food.

Kitchen Countertop Survivor™ Grade: A

Your notes:_____

_____

Cline Zinfandel
California

PC	T	V
$	23	23

It is rare that you get "wow" wine for this price, but it is here. Cline is one of California's great producers, but keeps a lower profile in Contra Costa County, outside the spotlight of Napa and Sonoma. *Lots* of spice and fruit "for a great price" prompted tasters to describe it as "the perfect house wine."

Kitchen Countertop Survivor™ Grade: A+

Your notes:_____

_____

Clos du Bois Sonoma Zinfandel
California

PC	T	V
$$	23	23

This is Zin in the medium style, with sweet oak in the scent, raspberry fruit, and soft tannins. To me, it totally outshines their more popular Merlot, and it's cheaper.

Kitchen Countertop Survivor™ Grade: B

Your notes:_____

_____

Dancing Bull Zinfandel
California

PC	T	V
$	X	X

✗ This tasty little Zin is a great everyday red for sipping, and for pairing with bold foods. The "nice fruit and spice" prompted some to say it's "better than its sister label Zabaco." It's cheaper, too.

Kitchen Countertop Survivor™ Grade: Avg

Your notes:_____

_____

Dry Creek Vineyard Reserve
Zinfandel, California

PC	T	V
$$$	29	24

Old-vines Zinfandel, made from some of the earliest northern California plantings, is the signature wine of Sonoma's Dry Creek Valley. It's a style that wine insid-

ers cherish, and this wine is a perfect introduction—
"blueberries and chocolate," as one of my sommelier
colleagues describes the flavor, with thick and velvety
tannins. It's a mouthful that deserves a mouthful—
some great cheese or a top-shelf prime steak.
Kitchen Countertop Survivor™ Grade: A
Your notes:_____

_____

Fetzer Valley Oaks Zinfandel	PC	T	V
California	$	21	21

This juicy, spicy Zinfandel has nice cherry flavors and
the consistency you can count on from Fetzer's Valley
Oaks line. A great "house wine," say my tasters.
Kitchen Countertop Survivor™ Grade: B+
Your notes:_____

_____

Gallo of Sonoma Dry Creek Valley	PC	T	V
Zinfandel, California	$$	22	23

An outstanding example of the Dry Creek Valley Zin
style, whose hallmarks are complex wild-raspberry-
spice character and exuberant, packed-in flavor. As
tasters point out, it's quite impressive for the money.
This is one to try with dark chocolate.
Kitchen Countertop Survivor™ Grade: B+
Your notes:_____

_____

Gallo of Sonoma Frei Ranch	PC	T	V
Zinfandel, California	$$$	24	24

I sometimes find that California's monster Zins don't
seem balanced, but not in this case. The deep
blueberry and chocolate scents evolve beautifully
in the glass, and the deep, lush, dark fruit flavor and
velvety tannins are huge, but harmonious.
Kitchen Countertop Survivor™ Grade: B+
Your notes:_____

_____

Price Ranges: **$** = $12 or less; **$$** = 12.01–20; **$$$** = 20.01–35;
$$$$ = > $35
Kitchen Fridge/Countertop Survivor™ Grades: *Avg.* = a "one-day
wine," tastes noticeably less fresh the next day; *B* = holds its freshness for 2–3 days after opening; *B+* = holds *and gets better* over 2–3
days after opening; *A* = a 3- to 4-day "freshness window"; *A+* =
holds *and gets better* over 3–4 days

Grgich Hills Sonoma Zinfandel	PC	T	V
California	$$$	26	22

In keeping with the Grgich style, this wine's complexity, firm structure, and restraint deliver the power of Zinfandel, with a subtler expression of scent and flavor. The cherry fruit and very delicate spice are framed firmly in oak and tannin. Improves with bottle age, if you can wait. Definitely a food wine—preferably dinner for two!

Kitchen Countertop Survivor™ *Grade: A*

Your notes:_____

_____

Kendall-Jackson Vintner's Reserve	PC	T	V
Zinfandel, California	$$	20	19

Some mixed reviews here, but most tasters consider it "solid," as do I. It drinks nicely by itself and with bold food, especially anything from the grill.

Kitchen Countertop Survivor™ *Grade: B*

Your notes:_____

_____

Laurel Glen Reds	PC	T	V
California	$	23	26

One taster captured the consensus perfectly: "Fabulous flavor in a Zin 'field blend'. Great with food, great alone, great value." I'll add that the year-to-year consistency is excellent.

Kitchen Countertop Survivor™ *Grade: B*

Your notes:_____

_____

Monteviña Amador Zinfandel	PC	T	V
California	$	24	24

This wine will give you—at a bargain price—a taste of the Amador Zin style—specifically, a leathery, savory-spice scent (think cumin and cardamom), prune and licorice flavors, and a firm tannic grip. It's a nice combination with Moroccan- or Indian-spiced dishes, as well as Mediterranean flavors—oregano, thyme, garlic, olive.

Kitchen Countertop Survivor™ *Grade: B+*

Your notes:_____

_____

Rabbit Ridge Zinfandel | PC | T | V
California | $ | 18 | 17

Rabbit Ridge staked its reputation on this balanced, fruit-forward Zinfandel, which previously got better marks for taste and value. Some tasters noted there are "better Zins for the money."

Kitchen Countertop Survivor™ Grade: B

Your notes:_____

_____

Rancho Zabaco Dry Creek Valley | PC | T | V
Zinfandel, California | $$ | X | X

✗ This is my favorite bottling in the Zabaco line, because it's textbook Dry Creek Zin—blueberry compote flavors, sweet spice, thick and juicy texture.

Kitchen Countertop Survivor™ Grade: Avg

Your notes:_____

_____

Rancho Zabaco Heritage Vines | PC | T | V
Zinfandel, California | $$ | 21 | 22

This sizzling Zin seems to get better every year, but "the price went up," too. It's got concentrated, rustic flavor that's thick with dried-cherry fruit and tobacco spice scents.

Kitchen Countertop Survivor™ Grade: B

Your notes:_____

_____

Ravenswood Vintners Blend | PC | T | V
Zinfandel, California | $ | 23 | 23

Ravenswood has been a Zin leader for years. It gets high marks for taste and value, with blueberry and spice flavors and a "yummy juiciness" to the texture.

Kitchen Countertop Survivor™ Grade: A

Your notes:_____

_____

Price Ranges: **$** = $12 or less; **$$** = 12.01–20; **$$$** = 20.01–35; **$$$$** = > $35

Kitchen Fridge/Countertop Survivor™ Grades: *Avg.* = a "one-day wine," tastes noticeably less fresh the next day; *B* = holds its freshness for 2–3 days after opening; *B+* = holds *and gets better* over 2–3 days after opening; *A* = a 3- to 4-day "freshness window"; *A+* = holds *and gets better* over 3–4 days

| **Renwood Sierra Zinfandel** | PC | T | V |
| California | $$ | 25 | 19 |

The "flavors of raspberry and spice," meaty-leathery scent, and plump tannins are classic Amador Zin. All of Renwood's Zin's are lovely and distinctive, and this is a great intro.

Kitchen Countertop Survivor™ Grade: Avg

Your notes:_____

_____

| **Ridge Geyserville (Zinfandel)** | PC | T | V |
| California | $$$ | 29 | 22 |

This happens to be one of my favorite wines, period. Clearly, I am not alone, as this wine continues to garner raves from my tasters. The price is climbing with its success; however, I think it is a relative value for this sort of world-class, memorable wine. The scent is complex cedar, savory-sweet spice, and dark fruit that's very intense. The texture feels like the finest chamois upholstery for your mouth. It also cellars beautifully.

Kitchen Countertop Survivor™ Grade: A+

Your notes:_____

_____

| **Robert Mondavi Private Collection** | PC | T | V |
| **Zinfandel, California** | $ | 24 | 24 |

The Zinfandel is a standout in this re-named line (formerly Robert Mondavi Coastal). It's plump with cherry fruit and balanced with a lively acid/tannin structure that makes it versatile with food.

Kitchen Countertop Survivor™ Grade: Avg

Your notes:_____

_____

| **Seghesio Sonoma Zinfandel** | PC | T | V |
| California | $$ | 26 | 25 |

"What a great deal," say my tasters. This has long been on my list of favorite Zins, because it offers real Sonoma character—wild-berry fruit, dried spices—at an affordable price.

Kitchen Countertop Survivor™ Grade: Avg

Your notes:_____

_____

St. Francis Sonoma Zinfandel   PC   T   V
California $$ 28   26

✓ This classic Sonoma Zin is both consistent and very popular. The dark blackberry and fig fruit are framed by lots of American oak. Some tasters "prefer the Old Vines bottling," but I like the balance of this subtler version.

Kitchen Countertop Survivor™ Grade: B+

Your notes:_____

_____

Sutter Home Zinfandel   PC   T   V
California $ 18   24

My tasters give "great value" credit where it's due, calling this a "juicy quaff" that's "great for everyday drinking."

Kitchen Countertop Survivor™ Grade: Avg

Your notes:_____

_____

Turning Leaf Zinfandel   PC   T   V
California $ 13   14

This Zinfandel lags the category in both price and value, which is a shame considering the Gallo wine-making resources (which yield good Zin under other brands) behind it. As a supersoft red for use in punches and sangria, it would be fine. But for Zin character, there are better choices (like its sister brand, Rancho Zabaco).

Kitchen Countertop Survivor™ Grade: Avg

Your notes:_____

_____

Vendange Zinfandel   PC   T   V
California $ 12   18

Both trade and consumer tasters say this light, fruity wine is "just OK," and "a budget buy for big parties."

Kitchen Countertop Survivor™ Grade: Avg

Your notes:_____

_____

Price Ranges: **$** = $12 or less; **$$** = 12.01–20; **$$$** = 20.01–35; **$$$$** = > $35

Kitchen Fridge/Countertop Survivor™ Grades: *Avg.* = a "one-day wine," tastes noticeably less fresh the next day; *B* = holds its freshness for 2–3 days after opening; *B+* = holds *and gets better* over 2–3 days after opening; *A* = a 3- to 4-day "freshness window"; *A+* = holds *and gets better* over 3–4 days

Woodbridge (Robert Mondavi)	PC	T	V
Zinfandel, California	$	15	18

I agree with Chairman Michael Mondavi, who calls this a good wine for everyday drinking ("with pizza," he suggests). I also think this is the best varietal in the Woodbridge line, with nice ripe plump fruit, nice food versatility, and a very nice price.

Kitchen Countertop Survivor™ Grade: Avg

Your notes:_____

_____

DESSERT WINES

Category Profile: No, none of these have major market presence. The "dessert" wines (or at least those sweet enough to qualify) that are statistically the biggest sellers are unfortunately weak commercial products that fulfill purposes other than a fine ending to a meal. There are plenty of great and available dessert wines to choose from, many of them affordable enough to enjoy often, with or instead of dessert (they're fat free!). These are dessert selections written in by my tasters, and by me. I hope you'll try them, because they will really jazz up your wine and food life.

Serve: Serving temperature depends on the wine, so see the individual entries.

When: With dessert, or as dessert; the lighter ones also make nice aperitifs. If you like to entertain, they're great. Add fruit, cheese, or some cookies, and you have a very classy end to a meal with very low hassle.

With: Blue cheese, chocolate, or simple cookies (like biscotti or shortbread) are classic. I've given specific matches in the individual entries.

In: An all-purpose wineglass or a smaller wineglass (the standard serving is 3 ounces rather than the traditional 6 for most wines).

Baron Philippe de Rothschild	PC	T	V
Sauternes, France	$$$	22	25

You have to taste it to believe that real Sauternes character is available at this price. (Most are collectors' items, priced accordingly.) It has the classic and beau-

tiful honeyed, crème brûlée and peach scent
and flavors of Sauternes. The French serve it as an
aperitif, or with foie gras, or at meal's end with Roquefort cheese—a combo that has to be tasted to be
believed. It is also lovely with crème brûlée and even
cheesecake. Serve slightly chilled.
Kitchen Countertop Survivor™ Grade: A
Your notes:_____

Blandy's 10-Year-Old Malmsey PC T V
Madeira, Portugal $$$$ 24 24

✓ Oh, how I love this wine—its flavor is so tantaliz-
ingly "out there." There's caramel, burnt sugar, toffee,
burnt orange, toasted nuts, spice, and a cut of tangy
acidity that keeps your palate on edge. It goes well
with any nut or caramel dessert, chocolate, or just
vanilla ice cream. Serve at room temp. The open
bottle will not go bad.
Kitchen Countertop Survivor™ Grade: A+
Your notes:_____

Bonny Doon Muscat Vin de PC T V
Glacière (*van duh glahss-YAIR*) $$ 23 24
California

Although it's "a little too sweet" for some, dessert wine
lovers will be thrilled with the lush passion fruit and
peach flavor. It's sold in half bottles.
Kitchen Fridge Survivor™ Grade: A
Your notes:_____

Château Rabaud-Promis (*shah-TOE* PC T V
***rah-BOW pro-MEE*) Sauternes** $$$$ X X
France

"Like honey" is the perfect description for this rich,
classic Sauternes with the scent of flowers, honey,

Price Ranges: **$** = $12 or less; **$$** = 12.01–20; **$$$** = 20.01–35;
$$$$ = > $35
Kitchen Fridge/Countertop Survivor™ Grades: *Avg.* = a "one-day
wine," tastes noticeably less fresh the next day; *B* = holds its fresh-
ness for 2–3 days after opening; *B+* = holds *and gets better* over 2–3
days after opening; *A* = a 3- to 4-day "freshness window"; *A+* =
holds *and gets better* over 3–4 days

peach preserves, and a hint of earth. Try it with Roquefort cheese.

Kitchen Fridge Survivor™ Grade: B+

Your notes:_____

_____

Emilio Lustau Pedro Ximenez	PC	T	V
"San Emilio" (*eh-MEE-lee-oh LOO-stau Pedro Hee-MEN-ez san eh-MEE-lee-oh*) NV, Spain	$$$	X	X

A wonderful dessert-style sherry redolent with fig flavors that's "lovely with all chocolate desserts." Pros call Pedro Ximenez "PX" for short.

Kitchen Fridge Survivor™ Grade: A+

Your notes:_____

_____

Ferreira Doña Antonia Port NV	PC	T	V
Portugal	$$$	22	22

This is a tawny-style Port—all amber-gold color, toasted nut, cinnamon sugar, cappuccino, and maple scents and flavors. I love it with bread pudding, any banana dessert, spice cake, carrot cake, pumpkin pie, and just by itself. Serve at room temp. The open bottle will not go bad.

Kitchen Countertop Survivor™ Grade: A+

Your notes:_____

_____

Ficklin Tinta "Port" NV	PC	T	V
California	$$	21	23

"Port" is in quotes, because the real thing is from Portugal. But this is a very worthy version of the style. Chocolate, nuts, dried figs, and sweet spices permeate both the scent and the taste. Great with Stilton cheese (an English blue), dark chocolate desserts, or nut cookies. Serve at room temp.

Kitchen Countertop Survivor™ Grade: A+

Your notes:_____

_____

Michele Chiarlo Nivole ("Clouds")	PC	T	V
Moscato d'Asti, Italy	$$$	19	20

This delicately sparkling, honeysuckle-scented wine from the Piedmont region of Italy should completely replace the brunch mimosa. It's got the bubbles, is low in alcohol, high in fruit (apricot and tangerine) and refreshment, and so much better tasting. For dessert it is lovely with fruit—fresh or in crêpes Suzette, strawberry shortcake, and so on. It's also a beautiful, delicate aperitif. Serve chilled.

Kitchen Countertop Survivor™ Grade: B

Your notes:_____

_____

PJ Valckenberg Madonna Eiswein	PC	T	V
Germany	$$$	X	X

✗ It's difficult to find affordable ice wine, so jump on this one which is "like drinking nectar." Imagine honeysuckle nectar on steroids.

Kitchen Fridge Survivor™ Grade: B

Your notes:_____

_____

St. Supery Moscato	PC	T	V
California	$$	X	X

✗ "A wonderful dessert wine" with the scent of honey-suckles and the flavor of spiced apricots.

Kitchen Fridge Survivor™ Grade: B+

Your notes:_____

_____

Warre 10-Year-Old Otima Tawny	PC	T	V
Port NV, Portugal	$$$	X	X

✗ The "nut flavor" and "smooth, warming texture" are classic to tawny Port, which is a touch sweet but not at all cloying.

Kitchen Fridge Survivor™ Grade: A+

Your notes:_____

_____

Price Ranges: **$** = $12 or less; **$$** = 12.01–20; **$$$** = 20.01–35; **$$$$** = > $35

Kitchen Fridge/Countertop Survivor™ Grades: *Avg.* = a "one-day wine," tastes noticeably less fresh the next day; *B* = holds its freshness for 2–3 days after opening; *B+* = holds *and gets better* over 2–3 days after opening; *A* = a 3- to 4-day "freshness window"; *A+* = holds *and gets better* over 3–4 days

THE
GREAT WINE MADE SIMPLE
MINI-COURSE:
A WINE CLASS IN A GLASS

How do you go about choosing wine? Many buyers assume the quick answer is to "trade up"—if you spend more, the wine will be better, right? Not necessarily, because price and quality are rarely proportional, meaning you cannot assume that a twenty-dollar bottle is twice as good as a ten-dollar one. And more important, preferences are individual. So the best way to ensure you'll be happy with your wine choices is to learn your taste.

Here are two quick wine lessons, adapted from my book *Great Wine Made Simple*, that will let you do exactly that. You're probably thinking, Will there be a test? In a way, every pulled cork is a test, but for the *wine*: Are you happy with what you got for the price you paid, and would you buy it again? This mini-course will teach you to pick wines that pass muster by helping you learn what styles and tastes you like in a wine and how to use the label to help you find them.

If you want, you can complete each lesson in a matter of minutes. As with food, tasting impressions form quickly with wine. Then you can get dinner on the table, accompanied by your wine picks. Start by doing the first lesson, "White Wine Made Simple," one evening, and then Lesson 2, "Red Wine Made Simple," another time. Or you can invite friends over and make it a party. Everyone will learn a little bit about wine, while having fun.

Setup
Glassware: You will need three glasses per taster. A simple all-purpose wineglass is ideal, but clear disposables are fine, too.

Pouring: Start with a tasting portion (about an ounce of each wine). Tasters can repour more of their favorite to enjoy with hors d'oeuvres or dinner.

Flights: Taste the Lesson 1 whites first and then the Lesson 2 reds (pros call each sequence of wine a *flight*). There is no need to wash or rinse the glasses.

To Taste It Is to Know It

Tasting is the fastest way to learn about wine. My restaurant guests tell me this all the time: they know what wines they like when they try them. The trick is in understanding the style and knowing how to ask for it and get it again: "I'd like a Chardonnay with lots of buttery, toasty oak and gobs of creamy, tropical fruit flavors." If you don't know what it means, you might feel silly offering a description like that when wine shopping. But those words really are in the glass, and these easy-to-follow tasting lessons will help you recognize the styles and learn which ones are your favorites.

The Lessons

What You'll Do:

For Lesson 1, "White Wine Made Simple," you will comparison-taste three major white wine grapes: Riesling, Sauvignon Blancs and Chardonnay. For Lesson 2, "Red Wine Made Simple," you will compare three major reds: Pinot Noir, Merlot, and Cabernet Sauvignon. Follow these easy steps:

1. Buy your wines. Make your choice from the varietal sections of this book. It's best to choose wines in the same price category—for example, all one-dollar-sign wines. To make the most of the lesson, choose wines from the region(s) suggested in each grape's "tasting notes."
2. Chill (whites only), pour, and taste the wines in the order of body, light to full, as shown in the tasting notes.
3. Use the tasting notes below as a guide, and record your own if you want.

What You'll Learn:

Body styles of the major grapes—light, medium, or full. You'll see that Riesling is lighter (less heavy) than

Chardonnay, in the same way that, for example, skim milk is lighter than heavy cream.

What the major grapes taste like—When tasted side by side, the grapes are quite distinctive, just as a pear tastes different from an apple, a strawberry tastes different from a blueberry, and so on.

What other wine flavor words taste like—Specifically, you'll experience these tastes: oaky, tannic, crisp, and fruity. Knowing them is helpful because they're used a lot in this book, on wine bottle labels, and by sellers of wine—merchants, waiters, and so on.

Getting comfortable with these basics will equip you to describe the wine styles you like to a waiter or wine merchant and to use the information on a bottle label to find those styles on your own. In the "Buying Lingo" section that follows, I've defined lots of other style words and listed some wine types you can try to experience them.

Tasting Lesson 1
WHITE WINE MADE SIMPLE

Instructions: Taste the wines in numbered order. Note your impressions of:

Color: Which is lightest and which is darkest? Whites can range from pale straw to deep yellow-gold. The darker the color, the fuller the body.

Scent: While they all smell like white wine, the aromas differ, from delicate and tangy to rich and fruity.

Taste and Body: In the same way that fruits range from crisp and tart (like apples) to ripe and lush (like mangoes), the wine tastes will vary along with the body styles of the grapes, from light to full.

Which grape and style do you like best? If you like more than one style, that's great, too!

The White Wines

Grape 1: Riesling (any region)—Light-bodied

Description: Crisp and refreshing, with vibrant fruit flavor ranging from apple to peach.

Brand Name: _____

Your notes: _____

_____

Grape 2: Sauvignon Blanc (France or New Zealand)—Medium-bodied

Description: Very distinctive! The smell is exotically pungent, the taste tangy and mouthwatering, like citrus fruit (lime and grapefruit).

Brand Name: _____

Your notes: _____

_____

Grape 3: Chardonnay (California)—Full-bodied

Description: The richest scent and taste, with fruit flavor ranging from ripe apples to peaches to tropical fruits. You can feel the full-bodied texture, too. "Oaky" scents come through as a sweet, buttery, or toasty impression.

Brand Name: _____

Your notes: _____

_____

Tasting Lesson 2
RED WINE MADE SIMPLE

Instructions: Again, taste the wines in numbered order and note your impressions.

Color: Red wines range in color from transparent ruby, like the Pinot Noir, to inky dark purple—the darker the color, the fuller the body.

Scent: In addition to the smell of "red wine," you'll get the cherrylike smell of Pinot Noir, perhaps plum character in the Merlot, and a rich dark berry smell in the Cabernet. There are other scents, too, so enjoy them. You can also compare your impressions with those included in the reviews section of the book.

Taste and Body: Like white wines, red wines range from light and delicate to rich and intense. You'll note the differences in body from light to full and the distinctive taste character of each grape. As you can see, tasting them side by side makes it easy to detect and compare the differences.

The Red Wines

Grape 1: Pinot Noir (any region)—Light-bodied

Description: Delicate cherrylike fruit flavor, silky-smooth texture, mouthwatering acidity, all of which make Pinot Noir a versatile wine for most types of food.

Brand Name: _____

Your notes: _____

_____

Grape 2: Merlot (California, Chile, or Washington)—Medium-bodied

Description: More intense than Pinot Noir: rich "red wine" flavor, yet not too heavy. That's probably why it's so popular!

Brand Name: _____

Your notes: _____

_____

Grape 3: Cabernet Sauvignon (Chile or California)—Full-bodied

Description: The fullest-bodied, most intense taste. Notice the drying sensation it leaves on your tongue? That's tannin, a natural grape component that, like color, comes from the skin. As you can see, more color and more tannin come together. Tasting high-tannin wines with fat or protein counters that drying sensation (that's why Cabernet and red meat are considered classic partners). In reds, an "oaky" character comes through as one or more of these scents: spice, cedar, smoke, toastiness, vanilla, and coconut. No wonder buyers love it!

Brand Name: _____

Your notes: _____

_____

Buying Lingo

Here are the meanings of other major wine style words that you see in this book and on wine bottles.

Acidity—The tangy, tart, crisp, mouthwatering component in wine. It's a prominent characteristic of Riesling, Sauvignon Blanc, and Pinot Grigio whites and Pinot Noir and Chianti/Sangiovese reds.

Bag-in-a-Box—A box with a wine-filled bag inside that deflates as the wine is consumed.

Balance—The harmony of all the wine's main components: fruit, alcohol, and acidity, plus sweetness (if any), oak (if used in the winemaking), and tannin (in reds). As with food, balance in the wine is important to your enjoyment, and a sign of quality. But it's also a matter of taste—the dish may taste "too salty" and the wine "too oaky" for one person but be fine to another.

Barrel aged—The wine was fermented or aged (or both) in oak barrels. The barrels give fuller body, as well as an "oaky" character to the wine's scent and flavor, making it seem richer. "Oaky" scents are often in the sweet family—but *not* sugary. Rather, *toasty, spicy, vanilla, buttery,* and *coconut* are the common wine words to describe "oaky" character. Other label signals that mean "oaky": Barrel Fermented, Barrel Select, Barrel Cuvée, Cask Fermented.

Bouquet—All of the wine's scents, which come from the grape(s) used, the techniques (like oak aging), the age of the wine, and the vineyard characteristics (like soil and climate).

Bright—Vivid and vibrant. Usually used as a modifier, like "bright fruit" or "bright acidity."

Buttery—Literally, the creamy-sweet smell of butter. One by-product of fermentation is an ester that mimics the butter smell, so you may well notice this in some wines, especially barrel-fermented Chardonnays.

Creamy—Can mean a smell similar to fresh cream or a smooth and lush texture. In sparkling wines, it's a textural delicacy and smoothness of the bubbles.

Crisp—See Acidity.

Dry—A wine without sweetness (though not without fruit; see Fruity for more on this).

Earthy—As with cheeses, potatoes, mushrooms, and other good consumables, wines can have scents and flavors reminiscent of, or owed to, the soil. The "earth" terms commonly attributed to wine include *mushrooms, truffles, flint, dusty, gravely, wet leaves,* and even *barnyard.*

Exotic—Just as it applies to other things, this description suggests unusual and alluring characteristics in wine. Quite often refers to wines with a floral or spicy style or flavors beyond your typical fruit bowl, such as tropical fruits or rare berries.

Floral—Having scents that mimic flower scents, whether fresh (as in the honeysuckle scent of some Rieslings) or dried (as in the wilted rose petal scent of some Gewürztraminers).

Food-friendly—Food-friendly wines have taste characteristics that pair well with a wide variety of foods without clashing or overpowering—namely, good acidity and moderate (not too heavy) body. The food-friendly whites include Riesling and Sauvignon Blanc; the reds include Chianti, Spanish Rioja, red Rhône, and Pinot Noir wines.

Fruity—Marked by a prominent smell and taste of fruit. In whites the fruit tastes can range from lean and tangy (like lemons and crisp apples) to medium (like melons and peaches) to lush (like mangoes and pineapples). In reds, think cranberries and cherries, plums and blueberries, figs and prunes. Note that *fruity* doesn't mean "sweet." The taste and smell of ripe fruit are perceived as sweet, but they're not sugary. Most wines on the market are at once dry (meaning not sweet) and fruity, with lots of fruit flavor.

Grassy—Describes a wine marked with scents of fresh-cut grass or herbs or even green vegetables (like green pepper and asparagus). It's a signature of Sauvignon Blanc wines, especially those grown in New Zealand and France. *Herbal* and *herbaceous* are close synonyms.

Herbal, herbaceous—See Grassy.

Legs—The drips running down the inside of the wineglass after you swirl it. Not a sign of quality (as in "good legs") but of viscosity. Fast-running legs indicate a low-viscosity wine and slow legs a high-viscosity wine. The higher the viscosity, the richer and fuller the wine feels in your mouth.

Nose—The smell of the wine. Isn't it interesting how wines have a nose, legs, and body? As you've no doubt discovered, they have personalities, too!

Oaky—See Barrel aged.

Off-dry—A lightly sweet wine.

Old vines—Refers to wine from vines significantly older than average, usually at least thirty years old and sometimes far older. Older vines yield a smaller, but often more intensely flavored, crop of grapes.

Regional wine—A wine named for the region where the grapes are grown, such as Champagne, Chianti, Pouilly-Fuissé, etc.

Spicy—A wine with scents and flavors reminiscent of spices, both sweet (cinnamon, ginger, cardamom, clove) and savory (pepper, cumin, curry).

Sweet—A wine that has perceptible sugar, called *residual sugar* because it is left over from fermentation and not converted to alcohol. A wine can be lightly sweet like a Moscato or very sweet like a Port or Sauternes.

Tannic—A red wine whose tannin is noticeable—a little or a lot—as a drying sensation on your tongue ranging from gentle (lightly tannic) to velvety (richly tannic) to harsh (too tannic).

Terroir—The distinctive flavors, scents, and character of a wine owed to its vineyard source. For example, the terroir of French red Burgundies is sometimes described as *earthy*.

Toasty—Wines with a toasty, roasted, caramelized, or smoky scent reminiscent of coffee beans, toasted nuts or spices, or burnt sugar.

Unfiltered—A wine that has not been filtered before bottling (which is common practice). Some say filtering the wine strips out flavor, but not everyone agrees. I think most tasters cannot tell the difference.

Varietal wine—A wine named for the grape used to make it, such as Chardonnay or Merlot.

Handling Wine Leftovers

I developed the Kitchen Countertop Survivor™ and Kitchen Fridge Survivor™ grades to give you an idea of how long each wine stays in good drinking condition if you don't finish the bottle. In the same way that resealing the cereal box or wrapping and refrigerating leftovers will extend their freshness window, you can do the same for wine by handling the leftovers as follows:

Still Wines

Recork—At a minimum, close the bottle with its original cork. Most wines will stay fresh a day or two. To extend that freshness-window, purchase a vacuum-sealer (available in kitchenware shops and wine shops). You simply cork the bottle with the purchased rubber stopper, which has a one-way valve. The accompanying plastic vacuum pump is then placed on top of the stopper; you pump the handle repeatedly until the resistance tightens, indicating the air has been pumped out of the bottle. (Note: A few wine experts don't think rubber stoppers work, but I have used them for years. In my restaurants, I have found they extended the life of bottles opened for by-the-glass service two days longer than just sealing with the original cork.)

Refrigerate stoppered (and vacuum-sealed) bottles, whether white, pink, or red. Refrigeration of anything slows the spoilage, and your red wine, once removed from the fridge and poured in the glass, will quickly come to serving temperature.

For even longer shelf-life, you can preserve partial bottles with inert gas. I recommend this especially for more expensive wines. Wine Life and Private Preserve are two brands that I have used (sold in wine shops and accessories catalogs). They come in a can that feels light, as if it's empty. Inside is an inert gas mixture that is heavier than air. The can's spray nozzle is inserted into the bottle. A one-second sprays fills the empty bottle space with the inert gas, displacing the air inside, which is the key because no air in contact with the wine means no oxidation. Then you quickly replace the cork (make sure the fit is tight). My experience in restaurants using gas systems for very upscale wines by the glass is that they keep well for a week or more.

Sparkling Wines

Your best bet is to purchase "clam shell" Champagne stoppers, with one or two hinged metal clamps attached to a stopper top that has a rubber or plastic gasket for a tight seal. You place the stopper on top, press down, and then anchor the clamps to the bottle lip. If you open your sparkler carefully and don't "pop" the cork, losing precious carbonation, a stoppered partial bottle will keep its effervescence for at least a few days, and sometimes much longer.

SAVVY SHOPPER: RETAIL WINE BUYING

Supermarkets, pharmacies, price clubs, catalogs, state stores, megastores, dot.coms, and boutiques . . . where you shop for wine depends a lot on the state where you live, because selling wine requires a state license. What many people don't realize is how much the wine laws vary from one state to the next.

In most states, the regulations affect the prices you pay for wine, what wines are available, and how you get your hands on them (ideally, they are delivered to your door or poured at your table, but this isn't always legal). Here is a quick summary of the retail scene to help you make the most of your buying power wherever you live.

Wine Availability The single biggest frustration for every wine buyer and winery is bureaucracy. To ensure the collection of excise taxes, in nearly all states every single wine must be registered and approved in some way before it can be sold. If a wine you're seeking isn't available in your area, this is probably the reason. For many small boutique wineries, it just isn't worth the bother and expense to get legal approval for the few cases of wine they would sell in a particular state. One extreme example is Pennsylvania, a "control state" where wine is sold exclusively by a state-run monopoly that, without competition, has little incentive to source a lot of boutique wines. By contrast, California, New York, and Chicago, with high demand and competition, are good markets for wine availability.

Wine Prices and Discounts Wine prices can vary from one state to the next due to different tax rates. And in general, prices are lower in competitive markets, where stores can use discounts, sale prices, and so on to vie for your business.

Where they are legal, case discounts of 10 to 15 percent are a great way to get the best possible prices for your favorite wines. On the more expensive wines, many people I know coordinate their buying with friends and family so they can buy full cases and get these discounts.

Delivery and Wine-by-Mail In many states, it is not legal for stores or other retailers to deliver wine to the purchaser.

Many catalogs and websites sell wine by mail. Some are affiliated with retail stores or wineries, while others are strictly virtual stores. The conveniences include shopping on your own time and terms, from home or office, helpful buying recommendations and information, and usually home delivery. But the laws governing such shipping are complex, and vary from state to state (in some states it is completely prohibited). When you add in shipping costs, there may not be a price advantage to shopping online, but many people swear by the convenience and buying advice it offers. It is also an easy way to send wine gifts.

Where Should I Shop? That depends on what you're buying. If you know what you want, then price is your main consideration, and you'll get your best deals at venues that concentrate on volume sales—discount stores, price clubs, and so on. If you want buying advice, or are buying rare wines, you're better off in a wine shop or merchant specializing in collectible wines. These stores have trained buyers who taste and know their inventory well; they can help you with your decision. The better stores also have temperature-controlled storage for their rare wines, which is critical to ensure you get a product in good condition. There are also web-based fine and rare wine specialists, but that is a fairly new market. I suggest you purchase fine and rare wines only through sources with a good track record of customer service. In that way, if you have problems with a shipment, you will have some recourse.

Can I Take That Bottle on the Wine List Home with Me? In most states, restaurants' wine licenses allow for sale and consumption "on-premise" only, meaning they cannot sell you a bottle to take home.

Burgundy Buyers, Beware With the exception of volume categories such as Beaujolais, Macon, and Pouilly-Fuissé, buyers of French white and red Burgundy should shop only at fine wine merchants, preferably those that specialize in Burgundy, for two reasons. First, Burgundy is simply too fragile to handle the storage conditions in most stores. Burgundy specialists ensure temperature-controlled storage. Second, selection is a major factor, because quality varies a lot from one winery to the next, and from one vintage to the next. Specialist stores have the needed buying expertise to ensure the quality of their offerings.

Is That a Deal or a Disaster? Floor stacks, "end caps," private labels, and bin ends can be a boon for the buyer, or a bust, depending on where you are shopping. Here's what you need to know about them:

"Floor Stacks" of large-volume categories and brands (e.g., branded varietal wines)—These are a best bet in supermarkets and other volume-based venues, where they're used to draw your attention to a price markdown. Take advantage of it to stock up for everyday or party wines.

"End Cap" wine displays featured at the ends of aisles—A good bet, especially in fine wine shops. You may not have heard of the wine, but they're usually "hidden gems" that the buyer discovered and bought in volume, to offer you quality and uniqueness at a savings.

"Bin Ends"—Retailers often clear out the last few bottles of something by discounting the price. In reputable retail stores, they are usually still good quality, and thus a good bet. Otherwise, steer clear.

Private labels—These are wines blended and bottled exclusively for the retailer—again, good bets in reputable stores, who stake their reputation on your satisfaction with their private labels.

"Shelf-talkers"—Written signs, reviews, and ratings. Good shops offer their own recommendations in lieu of, or along with, critics' scores. If the only information is a critic's score, check to be sure that the vintage being sold matches that of the wine that was reviewed.

Buying Wine in Restaurants

Wine List Strategy Session

A lot of us have a love-hate relationship with the wine list. On the one hand, we know it holds the potential to enhance the evening, impress the date or client, broaden our horizons, or all three. But it also makes us feel intimidated, inadequate, overwhelmed, and . . .

Panicked by prices—That goes for both the cheapest wines *and* the most expensive ones; we're leery of extremes.

Pressured by pairing—Will this wine "go with" our food?

Overwhelmed by options—Can this wine I've never heard of possibly be any good? Does my selection measure up? (Remember, the restaurant is supposed to impress *you,* not the other way around.) This "phone book" wine list makes me want to dial 911.

Stumped by Styles—Food menus are easy because we understand the key terms: appetizer, entree, dessert, salad, soup, fish, meat, and so on. But after *white* and *red,* most of us get lost pretty quickly with wine categories. (Burgundy . . . is that a style, a color, a place, or all three?)

Let's deal with the first three above. For the lowdown on wine list terms, use the decoder that follows to pinpoint the grapes and styles behind all the major wine names.

Wine List Prices

The prices on wine lists reflect three things:

- *The dining-out experience*—The restaurant wine markup is higher than in retail stores because the decor is (usually) nicer, and you get to stay awhile, during which time they open the wine, serve it in a nice glass, and clean up afterward. They also may have invested in the cost and expertise to select and store the wine properly. Consequently those who enjoy drinking wine in restaurants are accustomed to being charged more for the wine than you would pay to drink the same bottle at home. That said, exorbitant markups are, in my opinion, the biggest deterrent to more guests enjoying wine in restaurants (which is both good for the guests and good for business). You can always vote with your wallet and dine in restaurants with guest-friendly wine pricing.

- *Location*—Restaurants in exclusive resorts, in urban centers with a business clientele, or with a star chef behind them, tend toward higher wine markups, because they can get away with it. The logic, so to speak, is that if you're on vacation, it's on the company, or it's just the "in" place, high markups (on everything) are part of the price of admission. However, I don't really think that's right, and I do think these places would sell more wine with lower markups.

- *The rarity of the wine*—Often, the rarer the wine (either because it's in high demand due to critics' hype or because it's old and just a few bottles remain), the higher the markup. It's a form of rationing in the face of high demand/low supply. Food can be the same way (lobsters, truffles, caviar, etc.).

Getting the Most Restaurant Wine for Your Money

Seeking value doesn't make you a cheapskate. Here are the best strategies to keep in mind:

1. Take the road less traveled—Chardonnay and Cabernet Sauvignon are what I call "comfort wines" because they're so well known. But their prices often reflect a "comfort premium" (in the same way that a name-brand toothpaste costs more than the store brand). These spectacular wine styles often give better value for the money, because they're less widely known:

Whites

Riesling

Sauvignon Blanc and Fumé Blanc

Sancerre (a French Loire Valley wine made
from the Sauvignon Blanc grape)

Anything from Washington State or New
Zealand

Reds

Côtes-du-Rhône and other French Rhône
Valley reds

Red Zinfandel from California

Spanish Rioja and other reds from Spain

Cabernet Sauvignon from Chile

2. Savvy Splurging—There's no doubt about it:
nothing commemorates, celebrates, or im-
presses better than a special wine. Since splurging on wine in a restaurant can mean especially
big bucks, here are the "trophy" wine styles that
give you the most for your money on wine lists:

French Champagne—I think that Champagne (the real stuff from France's Champagne region) is among the most affordable
luxuries on the planet, and its wine list
prices are often among the best of all the
"badge" wine categories (such as French
Bordeaux and Burgundy, cult California
Cabernets, and boutique Italian wines).

California's Blue Chip Cabernets—I don't
mean the tiny-production cult-movement
Cabernets but rather the classics that have
been around for decades, and still make
world-class wine at a fair price. Names
like Beringer, BV, Cakebread, Jordan, Mt.
Veeder, Robert Mondavi, Silver Oak, Simi,
and Stag's Leap all made the survey, and for
good reason: they're excellent and available.

Italian Chianti Classico Riserva—This
recommendation may surprise you, but I
include it because the quality for the price
is better than ever, and recent vintages
have been great. I also think that across the
country a lot of people celebrate and do

business in steak houses and Italian restaurants, which tend to carry this wine category because it complements their food.

3. The Midprice/Midstyle "Safety Zone"—This is a strategy I first developed not for dining guests but for our *waiters* trying to help diners choose a bottle, usually with very little to go on (many people aren't comfortable describing their taste preference, and they rarely broadcast their budget for fear of looking cheap). The midprice/midstyle strategy is this: in any wine list category (e.g., Chardonnays, Italian reds, and so on), if you go for the midprice range in that section, odds are good the wine will be midstyle. Midstyle is my shorthand for the most typical, crowd-pleasing version, likely to satisfy a high proportion of guests and to be sticker shock free. The fact is that the more expensive the wine is, the more distinctive and even unusual its style is likely to be. If it's not to your taste *and* you've spent a lot, you're doubly disappointed.

4. Ask—With wine more popular than ever, restaurants are the most proactive they've ever been in seeking to put quality and value on their wine lists. So ask for it: "What's the best red wine deal on your list right now?" Or, if you have a style preference, say something like "We want to spend $XX. Which of these Chardonnays do you think is the best for the money?"

Pairing Wine and Food

Worrying a lot about this is a big waste of time, because most wines complement most foods, regardless of wine color, center-of-the-plate protein, and all that other stuff. How well? Their affinity can range from "fine" to "Omigod." You can pretty much expect at least a nice combination every time you have wine with food and great matches from time to time (of course, frequent experimentation ups your odds). The point is, your style preference is a lot more important than the pairing, per se, because if you hate the dish or the wine, you're hardly likely to enjoy the pairing. That said, here is a list of wine styles that are especially favored by sommeliers and chefs for their exceptional food affinity and versatility, along with a few best-bet food recommendations:

Favorite "Food Wines" White	Best-Bet Food Matches
Champagne and Sparkling Wine—So many people save bubbly just for toasts, but it's an amazing "food wine"	Sushi All shellfish Cheeses (even stinky ones) Omelets and other egg dishes Mushroom sauces (on risotto, pasta or whatever)
Riesling from Germany, Alsace (France), America, Australia	Mexican, southwestern, and other spicy foods Shellfish Cured meats and sausages
Alsace (France) White Wines—Riesling, Pinot Gris, and Gewürztraminer	Pacific Rim foods—Japanese, Thai, Korean, Chinese Indian food Smoked meats and char-cuterie Meat stews (really!)
Sauvignon Blanc and wines made from it (French Sancerre, Pouilly-Fumé, and white Bordeaux)	Goat cheese Salads Herbed sauces (like pesto) Tomato dishes (salads, soups, sauces)

Red	
Beaujolais (from France)	Mushroom dishes
Pinot Noir	Fish (especially rich ones like tuna, salmon, and cod) Smoked meats Grilled vegetables Duck
Chianti, Rosso di Montalcino, and other Italian reds made from the Sangiovese grape	Pizza, eggplant parmigiana (and other Italian-American–inspired tastes) Cheesy dishes Spicy sausages
Rioja from Spain	Roasted and grilled meats

Choosing from the Wine List

You've got the wine list. Unless you know a lot about wine, you now face at least one of these dilemmas:

- You've never heard of any of the wines listed or at least none of those in your price range (OK, maybe you've heard of Dom Pérignon, but let's be real). Or the names you do recognize don't interest you.

- You have no idea how much a decent selection should cost. But you *do* know you want to keep to your budget, without broadcasting it to your guests and the entire dining room.
- The wine list is so huge you don't even want to open it.

Wine List Playbook

Remember, you're the buyer. Good restaurants want you to enjoy wine and to feel comfortable with the list, your budget, and so on. As far as the wine-snobby ones go, what are you doing there anyway? (OK, if you took a gamble on a new place or somebody else picked it, the strategies here can help.)

The basics:

1. *Don't worry if you haven't heard of the names.* There are literally thousands of worthy wines beyond the big brand names, and many restaurants feature them to spice up their selection.

2. *Determine what you want to spend.* I think most people want the best deal they can get. With that in mind, here are some price/value rules of thumb. In most restaurants the wine prices tend to relate to the food prices, as follows:

   - Wines by-the-glass: The price window for good-quality wines that please a high percentage of diners usually parallels the restaurant's mid- to top-priced appetizers. So if the Caesar salad (or wings or whatever) is $5.95, expect to spend that, plus or minus a dollar or two, for a good glass of wine. This goes for dessert wine, too. Champagne and sparkling wines can be more, due to the cost of the product and greater waste because it goes flat.

   - Bottles: This is far more variable, but in general most restaurants try to offer an ample selection of good-quality bottles priced in what I call a "selling zone" that's benchmarked to their highest entree price, plus a margin. That's the variable part. It can range from $5–10 on average in national chain restaurants and their peers to at least $10–20 in luxury and destination restaurants. So if the casual chain's steak-and-shrimp-scampi combo costs $17.95, the $20–30 zone on their wine list will likely hold plenty of good bottle choices. In an urban restaurant where the star chef's signature herb-crusted lamb costs $28, you could expect a cluster of worthy bottles in the $35–55 range.

We in the trade find it funny, and nearly universal, that guests shy away from the least expensive wines on our lists, suspicious that there's something "wrong" with the wine. But any restaurant that's committed to wine, whether casual chain or destination eatery, puts extra effort into finding top-quality wines at the lowest price points. They may come from grapes or regions you don't know, but my advice is to muster your sense of adventure and try them. In the worst-case scenario, you'll be underwhelmed, but since tastes vary, this can happen with wine at any price. I think the odds are better that you'll enjoy one of the best deals on the wine list.

The wine list transaction: You've set your budget. Now it's time to zero in on a selection. You've got two choices—go it alone or ask for help. In either case, here's what to do:

1. Ask for the wine list right away. It's a pet peeve of mine that guests even *need* to ask (rather than getting the list automatically with the food menus), because that can cause both service delays and anxiety. Many people are scared to request the list for fear it "commits" them to a purchase, before they can determine whether they'll be comfortable with the prices and choices available. As you're being handed the menus, say "We'll take a look at the wine list, too" to indicate you want a copy to review, not a pushy sales job. Tip: I always ask that the wine-by-the-glass list be brought, too. Since many places change them often, they may be

on a separate card or a specials board. (I think verbal listings are the worst, because often key information, like the price or winery, can get lost in translation.)

2. Determine any style particulars you're in the mood for:
   - White or red?
   - A particular grape, region, or body style?

   If the table can't reach a consensus, look at wine-by-the-glass and half-bottle options. This can happen when preferences differ or food choices are all over the map ("I'm having the oysters, he's having the wild boar, we want one wine . . ." is a stumper I've actually faced!).

3. Find your style zone in the list. Turn to the section that represents your chosen category—e.g., whites, the wine-by-the-glass section, Chardonnays, Italian reds, or whatever—or let the server know what style particulars you have in mind.

4. Match your budget. Pick a wine priced accordingly, keeping in mind these "safety zones":
   - The wines recommended in this book
   - Winery or region names that you remember liking or hearing good things about (e.g., Chianti in Italy or a different offering from your favorite white Zinfandel producer)
   - The midprice/midstyle zone (as I explained earlier, many lists have this "sweet spot" of well-made, moderately priced offerings)
   - Featured wine specials, if they meet your price parameters

   You can communicate your budget while keeping your dignity with this easy trick I teach waiters:
   - Find your style zone—e.g., Pinot Grigios—in the wine list.
   - With both you and the server looking at the list, *point to the price* of a wine that's close to what you want to spend and then say, "We were looking at this one. What do you think?"
   - Keep pointing long enough for the server to see the price, and you'll be understood

without having to say (in front of your date or client), "No more than thirty bucks, OK?"

I ask my waiters to point to the price, starting at a moderate level, with their first wine suggestion. From there the guest's reaction shows his or her intentions, without the embarrassment of having to talk price.

There's no formula, but the bottom line is this: whether glass or bottle, it's hard to go wrong with popular grapes and styles, moderate prices, the "signature" or featured wine(s) of the restaurant, and/or the waiter's enthusiastic recommendation. If you don't like it, chalk it up to experience—the same could happen with a first-time food choice, right? Most of the time, experimentation pays off. So enjoy!

Wine List Decoder

Wine is like food—it's easy to choose from among the styles with which you're familiar. That's why wines like Pinot Grigio, Chardonnay, Chianti, and Merlot are such big sellers. But when navigating other parts of the list, namely less-common grape varieties and the classic European regional wines, I think many of us get lost pretty quickly. And yet these are major players in the wine world, without which buyers miss out on a whole array of delicious options, from classic to cutting edge.

This decoder will give you the tools you need to explore them. It reveals:

The grapes used to make the classic wines—If it's a grape you've tried, then you'll have an idea of what the wine tastes like.
The body styles from light to full of every major wine category—The waiters and wine students with whom I work always find this extremely helpful, because it breaks up the wine world into broad, logical categories that are easy to understand and similar to the way we classify other things. With food, for example, we have vegetables, meat, fish, and so on.
The taste profile, in simple terms—The exact taste of any wine is subjective (I say apple, you say pear), but knowing how the tastes *compare* is a great tool to help you identify your preferred style.

The names are set up just as you might see them on a wine list, under the key country and region headings, and in each section they are arranged by body style from light to full. (For whites, Italy comes before France in body style, overall. Their order is reversed for reds.) Finally, where applicable I've highlighted the major grapes in italics in the column on the left to help you quickly see just how widely used these grapes are and thus how much you already know about these heretofore mystifying wine names.

Sparkling Wines

- **Italy**

Asti Spumante	Muscat (Moscato)	Light; floral, hint of sweetness
Prosecco	Prosecco	Delicate; crisp, tangy, the wine used in Bellini cocktails

- **Spain**

Cava	Locals: Xarel-lo, Parellada, Macabeo plus Chardonnay	Light; crisp, refreshing

- **France**

Champagne	The red (yes!) grapes Pinot Noir and Pinot Meunier, plus Chardonnay	To me, all are heavenly, but check the style on the label: Blanc de Blancs—delicate and tangy Brut NV, vintage and luxury—range from soft and creamy to rich and toasty

White Wines

- **Italy**

Frascati	Trebbiano, Malvasia	As you've noticed, mostly local grapes are used in Italy's whites. But the style of all these is easy to remember: light, tangy, and refreshing. Pinot Grigio, the best known, is also more distinctive—pleasant pear and lemon flavors, tasty but not heavy. The less common Pinot Bianco is similar.
Soave	Garganega, Trebbiano	
Orvieto	Grechetto, Procanico, and many others	
Gavi	Cortese	
Vernaccia	Vernaccia	
Pinot Grigio		

- **Germany**

  Riesling

	Riesling rules Germany's quality wine scene	Feather-light but flavor-packed: fruit salad in a glass

- **France**

  - **Alsace—Grape names are on the label:**

	Pinot Blanc	Light; tangy, pleasant
Riesling	Riesling	Fuller than German Riesling but not heavy; citrus, apples, subtle but layered
	Pinot Gris	Smooth, richer texture; fruit compote flavors
	Gewürztraminer	Sweet spices, apricots, lychee fruit

  - **Loire Valley**

Vouvray	Chenin Blanc	Look for the style name: Sec—dry and tangy; Demisec—baked apple, hint of sweetness; Moelleux—honeyed dessert style

  Sauvignon Blanc

Sancerre and Pouilly-Fumé	Sauvignon Blanc	Light to medium; subtle fruit, racy acidity

  - **White Bordeaux**

  Sauvignon Blanc & Semillon

Entre-Deux-Mers	Sauvignon Blanc and Semillon	Tangy, crisp, light
Graves Pessac-Leognan		Medium to full; ranging from creamy lemon-lime to lush fig flavors; pricey ones are usually oaky

  - **Burgundy White**

  Chardonnay

Macon St.-Veran Pouilly-Fuissé	Every Chardonnay in the world is modeled on white French Burgundy	Light; refreshing, citrus-apple flavors
Chablis		Subtle, mineral, green apple

St. Aubin

Meursault

Puligny-
Montrachet

Chassagne-
Montrachet

Corton-
Charlemagne

Medium; pear,
dried apple, nutty;
complexity ranging
from simple to
sublime

Red Wines

- **France**
  - **Red Burgundy**

Beaujolais Beaujolais- Villages	Gamay	Uncomplicated, light; fruity, pleasant

Beaujolais
Cru:
  Morgon,
  Moulin-à-
Vent, etc.
		More complex,
		plum-berry taste,
		smooth (the wines
		are named for their
		village)

Pinot Noir

Côte de Beaune Santenay Volnay Pommard Nuits-St.- Georges Vosne- Romanée Gevrey- Chambertin Clos de Vougeot, etc.	Pinot Noir	Ranging from light body, pretty cherry taste to extraordinary com- plexity: captivating spice, berry and earth scents, silky texture, berries and plums flavor

  - **Red Bordeaux**

Merlot

Pomerol St. Emilion	Merlot, plus Cabernet Franc and Cabernet Sauvignon	Medium to full; oaky-vanilla scent, plum flavor

Cabernet Sauvignon

Médoc Margaux Pauillac St-Estèphe	Cabernet Sauvignon, plus Merlot, Cabernet Franc, and Petit Verdot	Full; chunky-velvety texture; cedar- spice-toasty scent; dark berry flavor

- ***Rhône Red***

Syrah, aka Shiraz

Côtes-du-Rhône	Mainly Grenache, Syrah, Cinsault, Mourvedre	Medium to full; juicy texture; spicy raspberry scent and taste
Côte-Rôtie	Syrah, plus a splash of white Viognier	Full; brawny texture; peppery scent; plum and dark berry taste
Hermitage	Syrah, plus a touch of the white grapes Marsanne and Roussane	Similar to Côte-Rôtie
Châteauneuf-du-Pape	Mainly Syrah, Grenache, Cinsault, Mourvedre	Full; exotic leathery-spicy scent; spiced fig and berry compote taste

(Red Zinfandel is here in the light-to-full body spectrum)

- **Spain**
  - ***Rioja***

Rioja Crianza, Reserva and Gran Reserva	Tempranillo, plus Garnacha, aka Grenache, and other local grapes	Ranging from soft and smooth, juicy strawberry character (Crianza); to full, caramel-leather scent, spicy-dried fruit taste (Reserva and Gran Reserva)

  - ***Ribera del Duero***

	Mostly Tempranillo	Full; mouth-filling texture; toasty-spice scent; anise and plum taste

  - ***Priorat***

Sometimes Cabernet Sauvignon

Priorat	Varied blends may include Cabernet Sauvignon, Garnacha, and other local grapes	Full; gripping texture; meaty-leathery-fig scent; superconcentrated plum and dark berry taste

- **Italy**

  As you'll notice from the left column, Italy's classic regions mostly march to their own *belissimo* beat.

  - ***Veneto***

Valpolicella	Corvina plus other local grapes	Light; mouthwatering, tangy cherry taste and scent

Amarone della Valpolicella	Corvina; same vineyards as Valpolicella	Full; rich, velvety texture; toasted almond/prune scent; intense dark raisin and dried fig taste (think Fig Newtons)

- ### *Piedmont*

Dolcetto d'Alba (the best known of the Dolcettos, but others are good, too)	Dolcetto	Light; zesty, spicy, cranberry-sour cherry taste
Barbera d'Alba (look for Barbera d'Asti and others)	Barbera	Medium; licorice-spice-berry scent; earth and berry taste
Barolo Barbaresco	Nebbiolo	Full; "chewy" texture; exotic earth, licorice, tar scent; strawberry-spice taste

- ### *Tuscany*

Chianti/ Chianti Classico	Sangiovese	Ranges from light, easy, lip-smacking strawberry-spice character to intense, gripping texture; plum, licorice, and earth scent and taste
Vino Nobile di Monte-pulciano	Prugnolo (a type of Sangiovese)	Medium-to-full; velvety texture, earth-spice, stewed plum taste
Brunello di Montalcino	Brunello (a type of Sangiovese)	Very full; "chewy" in the mouth; powerful dark-fruit flavor

Sometimes Cabernet Sauvignon

"Super Tuscans"— not a region but an important category	Usually a blend of Sangiovese and Cabernet Sauvignon	Modeled to be a classy cross between French red Bordeaux and Italian Chianti; usually full, spicy, and intense, with deep plum and berry flavors

The bottom line on restaurant wine lists: In my opinion, it's not the size of the list that matters but rather the restaurant's effort to make enjoying wine as easy as possible for its guests. How? As always, it comes down to the basics:

Top Ten Tip-Offs You're in a Wine-Wise Restaurant

1. You're *never* made to feel you have to spend a lot to get something good.
2. Wine by the glass is taken as seriously as bottles, with a good range of styles and prices, listed prominently so you don't have to "hunt" to find them.
3. The wine list is presented automatically, so you don't have to ask for it (and wait while the waiter searches for a copy).
4. There are lots of quality bottle choices in the moderate price zone.
5. Wine service, whether glass or bottle, is helpful, speedy, and proficient.
6. Waiters draw your attention to "great values" rather than just the expensive stuff.
7. *Affordable* wine pairings are offered for the signature dishes—either on the menu or by servers.
8. You can ask for a taste before you choose a wine by the glass if you're not sure which you want.
9. It's no problem to split a glass, or get just a half-glass, of by-the-glass offerings. (Great for situations when you want only a little wine or want to try a range of different wines.)
10. There's no such thing as no-name "house white and red." (House-featured wines are fine, but they, and you, merit a name or grape and a region.)

IMMER BEST BETS

Sometimes you just need quick recommendations for the buying occasion at hand. Here are my picks.

Best Restaurant Wineries

The following list of wineries probably includes some names that are familiar to you. These wineries are what we in the restaurant wine list business call *anchors*—the core names around which to build a well-balanced, high-quality wine list that pleases a lot of people. It's not a comprehensive anchor list. Rather, it is my personal list of the benchmark names that I've featured on wine lists for years because, in addition to name recognition with guests, they consistently deliver quality and value across their product line and are generally priced at a relative value compared to the competition in their categories. You can choose your favorite grape or style with extra confidence when it's made by one of these producers.

Antinori, Italy
Beringer, California
Cakebread, California
Calera, California
Cambria, California
Château St. Jean, California
Clos du Bois, California
Estancia, California
Ferrari-Carano, California
Franciscan, California
Hugel, France
Jolivet, France
Jordan, California
Joseph Phelps, California
Kendall-Jackson, California
King Estate, Oregon
Louis Jadot, France

Moët & Chandon, France
Morgan, California
Penfolds, Australia
Ravenswood, California
Ridge, California
Robert Mondavi, California
Rosemount Estate, Australia
Ruffino, Italy
Silverado, California
St. Francis, California
Taittinger, France
Trimbach, France
Veuve Clicquot, France

Best Wine List Values

Although wine list pricing varies widely, I regularly see these wines well priced in restaurants around the country and thus offering great value for the money.

White	Red
Bonny Doon Pacific Rim Riesling, USA/Germany	Firesteed Pinot Noir, Oregon
Alois Lageder Pinot Grigio, Italy	Cambria Julia's Vineyard Pinot Noir, California
King Estate Pinot Gris, Oregon	Fetzer Eagle Peak Merlot, California
Jolivet Sancerre, France	Franciscan Oakville Estate Merlot, California
Geyser Peak Sauvignon Blanc, California	Château Larose-Trintaudon Bordeaux, France
Casa Lapostolle Sauvignon Blanc, Chile	Guenoc Cabernet Sauvignon, California
Estancia Pinnacles Chardonnay, California	Penfolds Bin 389 Cabernet/ Shiraz, Australia
Gallo of Sonoma Chardonnay, California	Cline Zinfandel, California
Simi Chardonnay, California	J. Lohr 7 Oaks Cabernet Sauvignon, California
Château St. Jean Chardonnay, California	

Best "House" Wines for Every Day— Sparkling, White, and Red

(*House* means *your* house.) These are great go-to wines to keep around for every day and company too, because they're tasty, *very* inexpensive, and go with everything from takeout to Sunday dinner. They're also wines that got high Kitchen Countertop/Fridge Survivor™ grades, so you don't have to worry if you don't finish the bottle right away. (Selections are listed by body style—lightest to fullest.)

Sparkling
Aria Cava Brut Sparkling, Spain
Domaine Ste. Michelle Cuvée Brut Sparkling, Washington

House Whites
Ca' del Solo Big House White, California
Columbia Winery Cellarmaster's Reserve Riesling, Washington
Beringer Founders' Estate Sauvignon Blanc, California
Penfolds Semillon-Chardonnay, Australia
Camelot Chardonnay, California
Lindemans Bin 65 Chardonnay, Australia
Gallo of Sonoma Chardonnay, California

Reds
Echelon Pinot Noir, California
Duboeuf (Georges) Côtes-du-Rhône, France
Montecillo Rioja Crianza, Spain
Columbia Crest Merlot, Washington
Rosemount Estates Cabernet/Merlot, Australia
Casa Lapostolle Classic Cabernet Sauvignon, Chile

Impress the Date—Hip Wines

White
Bonny Doon Pacific Rim Riesling, USA/Germany
Frog's Leap Sauvignon Blanc, California
Brancott Reserve Sauvignon Blanc, New Zealand
Yellowtail Chardonnay, Australia
R.H. Phillips Toasted Head Chardonnay, California

Red
Coppola (Francis) Presents Rosso, California
Firesteed Pinot Noir, Oregon
Hill of Content Grenache/Shiraz, Australia
Monteviña Amador Zinfandel, California
Escudo Rojo Cabernet blend, Chile
Navarro Correas Malbec, Argentina
Penfolds Cabernet/Shiraz Bin 389, Australia

Impress the Client—Blue Chip Wines

Sparkling/White

Taittinger Brut La Française NV Champagne, France

Cloudy Bay Sauvignon Blanc, New Zealand

Ferrari-Carano Fumé Blanc, California

Robert Mondavi Fumé Blanc, California

Cakebread Chardonnay, California

Talbott (Robert) Sleepy Hollow Vineyard Chardonnay, California

Red

Etude Pinot Noir, California

Domaine Drouhin Pinot Noir, Oregon

Duckhorn Napa Merlot, California

Ridge Geyserville (Zinfandel), California

Stag's Leap Wine Cellars Napa Cabernet Sauvignon, California

Jordan Cabernet Sauvignon, California

You're Invited—Unimpeachable Bottles to Bring to Dinner

(You *do* still have to send a note the next day.)

Trimbach Riesling, Alsace, France

Simi Sauvignon Blanc, California

St. Supéry Sauvignon Blanc, California

Louis Jadot Pouilly-Fuissé, France

Beringer Napa Chardonnay, California

Calera Central Coast Pinot Noir, California

Ruffino Chianti Classico Riserva Ducale Gold Label, Italy

Penfolds Cabernet/Shiraz Bin 389, Australia

St. Francis Sonoma Merlot, California

Franciscan Napa Cabernet Sauvignon, California

Robert Mondavi Napa Cabernet Sauvignon, California

Cellar Candidates

These wines have consistently proven age-worthy throughout my restaurant career. The time window shown for each is the number of years' aging in reasonably cool cellar conditions to reach peak drinking condition. But this "peak" is in terms of *my* taste— namely when the wine's texture has softened and enriched, the aromas have become more layered, but the fruit remains vibrant. You may need to adjust your cellar regimen according to your taste. Generally, longer aging gradually trades youthful fruit and acidity for a whole new spectrum of aromas, many of which you might not instantly associate with grapes or wine. In whites, aging commonly leads to softened acidity and a nutty/caramel character; in reds, softened tannins and a leathery/spicy character.

White

Trimbach Riesling, France (3–4 yrs)

Trimbach Pinot Gris, France (4–5 yrs)

Didier Dagueneau Silex Pouilly-Fumé, France (6–8 yrs)

Edna Valley Vineyard Chardonnay, California (4–5 yrs)

Grgich Hills Chardonnay, California (5–7 yrs)

Cakebread Chardonnay, California (4–5 yrs)

Château Montelena Chardonnay, California (5–7 yrs)

Leflaive (Domaine) Puligny-Montrachet, France (5–6 yrs)

Leflaive (Olivier) Puligny-Montrachet, France (2–4 yrs)

Red

Calera Central Coast Pinot Noir, California (3–4 yrs)

Etude Pinot Noir, California (5–6 yrs)

Robert Mondavi Napa Pinot Noir, California (4–5 yrs)

Felsina Chianti Classico, Italy (3–4 yrs)

Frescobaldi Chianti Rufina Riserva, Italy (3–5 yrs)

Ruffino Chianti Classico Riserva Ducale Gold Label, Italy (5–7 yrs)

Selvapiana Chianti Rufina, Italy (3–5 yrs)

Banfi Brunello di Montalcino, Italy (6–8 yrs)

Duckhorn Napa Merlot, California (5–7 yrs)

Shafer Merlot, California (4–5 yrs)

Château Greysac Bordeaux, France (3–4 yrs)

Cakebread Napa Cabernet Sauvignon, California (4–5 yrs)

Château Gruaud-Larose Bordeaux, France (6–8 yrs)

Groth Napa Cabernet Sauvignon, California
(4–5 yrs)

Heitz Napa Cabernet Sauvignon, California
(5–6 yrs)

Mt. Veeder Cabernet Sauvignon, California
(5–7 yrs)

Penfolds Bin 389 Cabernet/Shiraz, Australia
(6–8 yrs)

Silver Oak Alexander Valley Cabernet Sauvignon,
California (6–8 yrs)

Stag's Leap Wine Cellars Napa Cabernet Sauvignon,
California (4–5 yrs)

Muga Rioja Reserva, Spain (7–9 yrs)

Pesquera Ribera del Duero, Spain (7–9 yrs)

Château de Beaucastel Châteauneuf-du-Pape,
France (6–8 yrs)

Grgich Hills Sonoma Zinfandel, California (4–5 yrs)

Ridge Geyserville (Zinfandel), California (5–7 yrs)

Would You Drink It on a Plane?

Disregard the package (screw-capped splits)—if you
see these wineries on the beverage cart, you can take
heart. They won't be the greatest wine you ever
drank, but they are often the only redeeming feature
of flying coach.

Glen Ellen Proprietor's Reserve
Sutter Home
Georges Duboeuf
CK Mondavi

CUISINE COMPLEMENTS

Whether you're dining out, ordering in, or whipping it up yourself, the following wine recommendations will help you choose a wine to flatter the food in question. If your store doesn't carry that specific wine bottle, ask for a similar selection.

Thanksgiving Wines

More than any other meal, the traditional Thanksgiving lineup features a pretty schizo range of flavors—from gooey-sweet yams to spicy stuffing to tangy cranberry sauce and everything in between. These wines are like a group hug for all the flavors at the table and the guests around it. My tip: choose a white and a red, put them on the table, and let everyone taste and help themselves to whichever they care to drink. (Selections are listed by body style—lightest to fullest.)

	White	Red
S T E A L	Cavit Pinot Grigio, Italy Château Ste. Michelle Johannisberg Riesling, Washington Geyser Peak Sauvignon Blanc, California Marqués de Riscal White Rueda, Spain Fetzer Echo Ridge Gewürztraminer, California Gallo of Sonoma Chardonnay, California	Louis Jadot Beaujolais-Villages, France Coppola (Francis) Presents Rosso, California Duboeuf Côtes-du-Rhône, France Marqués de Cáceres Rioja Crianza, Spain Cline Zinfandel, California Rosemount Diamond Label Shiraz, Australia
S P L U R G E	Martin Codax Albariño, Spain Trimbach Riesling, France Robert Mondavi Napa Fumé Blanc, California Hugel Gewürztraminer, France Kendall-Jackson Grand Reserve Chardonnay, California	Morgan Pinot Noir, California Château de Beaucastel Châteauneuf-du-Pape, France Penfolds Bin 389 Cabernet/Shiraz, Australia Pesquera Ribera del Duero, Spain Ridge Geyserville (Zinfandel), California

Barbecue
Penfolds Semillon-Chardonnay, Australia
Ca' del Solo Big House White, California
Dry Creek Fumé Blanc, California
Black Opal Shiraz, Australia
Coppola (Francis) Presents Rosso, California
Jaboulet Côtes-du-Rhône, France
Monteviña Amador Zinfandel, California

Chinese Food
Hugel Pinot Blanc, France
Jolivet Sancerre, France
Sutter Home Gewürztraminer, California
Echelon Pinot Noir, California
Marqués de Cáceres Rioja Crianza, Spain
Ravenswood Merlot, California
Louis Jadot Beaujolais-Villages, France
Allegrini Valpolicella, Italy

Nuevo Latino (Cuban, Caribbean, South American)
Freixenet Brut de Noirs Rosé Sparkling, Spain
Monteviña Pinot Grigio, Italy
Marqués de Riscal White Rueda, Spain
Santa Rita 120 Cabernet Sauvignon, Chile
Los Vascos Cabernet Sauvignon, Chile
Woodbridge (Robert Mondavi) Zinfandel, California

Picnics
CAVIT Pinot Grigio, Italy
Domaine Ste. Michelle Cuvée Brut Sparkling, Washington
Beringer White Zinfandel, California
Fetzer Sundial Chardonnay, California
Riunite Lambrusco, Italy
Citra Montepulciano d'Abruzzo, Italy
Duboeuf (Georges) Beaujolais-Villages, France

Sushi
Moët & Chandon White Star Champagne, France
Trimbach Riesling, France
Burgans Albariño, Spain
Jolivet Sancerre, France
Villa Maria Sauvignon Blanc, New Zealand

Frog's Leap Sauvignon Blanc, California
Louis Jadot Pouilly-Fuissé, France
B&G Beaujolais-Villages, France
Beringer Founders' Estate Pinot Noir, California
Calera Central Coast Pinot Noir, California

Clambake/Lobster Bake
Kendall-Jackson Vintner's Reserve Sauvignon Blanc,
 California
Murphy-Goode Fumé Blanc, California
Gallo of Sonoma Chardonnay, California
Beringer Napa Chardonnay, California
Sterling North Coast Chardonnay, California
Coppola (Francis) Presents Rosso, California
Beaulieu (BV) Coastal Zinfandel, California

Mexican Food
Ecco Domani Pinot Grigio, Italy
King Estate Pinot Gris, Oregon
Meridian Sauvignon Blanc, California
Hugel Gewürztraminer, France
Buena Vista Sauvignon Blanc, California
Beringer White Zinfandel, California
Dry Creek Fumé Blanc, California
Duboeuf (Georges) Côtes-du-Rhône, France
Cline Zinfandel, California
Ravenswood Vintners Blend Zinfandel, California

Pizza
Citra Montepulciano d'Abruzzo, Italy
Santa Cristina Sangiovese, Antinori, Italy
Montecillo Rioja Crianza, Spain
Viña Carmen Cabernet Sauvignon, Chile
Monteviña Amador Zinfandel, California
Woodbridge (Robert Mondavi) Zinfandel, California
Penfolds Koonunga Hill Shiraz/Cabernet Sauvignon,
 Australia

The Cheese Course
Frescobaldi Chianti Rufina Riserva, Italy
Penfolds Bin 389 Cabernet/Shiraz, Australia
Château de Beaucastel Châteauneuf-du-Pape,
 France
Muga Rioja Reserva, Spain
Pesquera Ribera del Duero, Spain

St. Francis Sonoma Zinfandel, California
Ridge Geyserville (Zinfandel), California
Rosemount GSM (Grenache-Shiraz-Mourvedre),
  Australia
Grgich Hills Sonoma Zinfandel, California
Mt. Veeder Cabernet Sauvignon, California
Château Gruaud-Larose Bordeaux, France
Banfi Brunello di Montalcino, Italy
Alvaro Palacios Les Terrasses Priorat, Spain

Steak

Ferrari-Carano Chardonnay, California
Talbott (Robert) Sleepy Hollow Vineyard
  Chardonnay, California
Morgan Pinot Noir, Oregon
Domaine Drouhin Pinot Noir, Oregon
Ruffino Chianti Classico Riserva Ducale Gold
  Label, Italy
Banfi Brunello di Montalcino, Italy
Shafer Merlot, California
Cakebread Napa Cabernet Sauvignon, California
Beringer Knights Valley Cabernet Sauvignon,
  California
Robert Mondavi Napa Cabernet Sauvignon,
  California
Groth Napa Cabernet Sauvignon, California
Stag's Leap Wine Cellars Napa Cabernet Sauvignon,
  California
Joseph Phelps Napa Cabernet Sauvignon, California
St. Francis Sonoma Zinfandel, California

Salad

Ruffino Orvieto, Italy
Hugel Pinot Blanc, France
Trimbach Riesling, France
Lucien Crochet Sancerre, France
Henri Bourgeois Pouilly-Fumé, France
Fetzer Echo Ridge Sauvignon Blanc, California
Louis Jadot Mâcon-Villages Chardonnay, France
Allegrini Valpolicella, Italy
Calera Central Coast Pinot Noir, California

Vegetarian

Folonari Pinot Grigio, Italy
Trimbach Pinot Gris, France

Rodney Strong Charlotte's Home Sauvignon Blanc, California
Hess Select Chardonnay, California
Estancia Pinnacles Pinot Noir, California
Gabbiano Chianti, Italy
Jaboulet Côtes-du-Rhône, France

WINERY INDEX

Blandy's, Portugal
  10-Year-Old Malmsey Madeira $$$$ 199

Blue Nun, Germany
  Liebfraumilch $ 103

Bogle, California
  Merlot $ 137

Bolla, Italy
  Merlot $ 137
  Pinot Grigio $ 52
  Soave $ 104
  Valpolicella $ 180

Bollinger, Champagne, France
  Special Cuvée Brut $$$$ 41

Bonny Doon, California
  Muscat Vin de Glaciere $$ 199
  Pacific Rim Riesling (USA/Germany) $ 57
  Vin Gris de Cigare Pink Wine $$ 112

Bouvet, Loire Valley, France
  Brut NV $$ 42

Brancott, New Zealand
  Reserve Pinot Noir $$ 119
  Reserve Sauvignon Blanc $$ 65

Buehler, California
  White Zinfandel $ 112

Buena Vista, California
  Cabernet Sauvignon $ 154
  Carneros Pinot Noir $$ 119
  Chardonnay $ 82
  Sauvignon Blanc $ 66

Burgans (Bodegas Vilarino-Cambados), Spain
  Albariño $ 104

Burgess, California
  Chardonnay $$$ 82
  Merlot $$$ 138

Byron, California
  Santa Maria Valley Pinot Noir $$$ 120

Ca' del Solo, California
  Big House Red $ 178
  Big House White $ 104

Cain, California
  Cain Cuvée Bordeaux Style Red $$$ 154

Cakebread, California
  Napa Cabernet Sauvignon $$$$ 154
  Napa Chardonnay $$$$ 82
  Sauvignon Blanc $$$ 66

Calera, California
  Central Coast Pinot Noir $$$ 120

Edna Valley Vineyard, California
Chardonnay **$$**   87

Elderton, Australia
Shiraz **$$$**   185

Elk Cove, Oregon
Pinot Noir **$$**   123

Emilio Lustau, Spain
Pedro Ximenez "San Emilio" Sherry **$$$**   200

Ernest & Julio Gallo, California
Twin Valley Cabernet Sauvignon **$**   159
Twin Valley Chardonnay **$**   87
Twin Valley Merlot **$**   141
Twin Valley Sauvignon Blanc **$**   70
Twin Valley White Zinfandel **$**   112

Eroica, Washington
Riesling **$$$**   58

Escudo Rojo (Baron Philippe de Rothschild), Chile
Cabernet Blend **$$**   159

Estancia, California
Alexander Valley Red Meritage **$$$**   159
Cabernet Sauvignon **$$**   159
Pinnacles Chardonnay **$$**   88
Pinnacles Pinot Noir **$$**   123

Etude, California
Carneros Pinot Noir **$$$$**   123

Falesco, Italy
Vitiano **$**   180

Far Niente, California
Cabernet Sauvignon **$$$$**   160

Faustino, Spain
Rioja Crianza **$**   175

Felluga (Livio), Italy
Pinot Grigio **$$**   53

Felsina, Italy
Chianti Classico **$$$**   133

Ferrari-Carano, California
Fumé Blanc **$$**   70
Siena Sonoma County **$$$**   160
Sonoma Chardonnay **$$$**   88

Ferreira, Portugal
Doña Antonia Port NV **$$$**   200

F. E. Trimbach, Alsace, France
See Trimbach

Fetzer, California
Barrel Select Chardonnay **$$**   88
Eagle Peak Merlot **$**   142

Echo Ridge Gewürztraminer $ 105
Echo Ridge Johannisberg Riesling $ 58
Echo Ridge Sauvignon Blanc $ 70
Sundial Chardonnay $ 88
Valley Oaks Cabernet Sauvignon $ 160
Valley Oaks Syrah $ 186
Valley Oaks Zinfandel $ 193

Ficklin, California
Tinta "Port" NV $$ 200

Firesteed, Oregon
Pinot Noir $ 123

Folonari, Italy
Pinot Grigio $ 52

Forest Glen, California
Cabernet Sauvignon $ 160
Chardonnay $ 88
Merlot $ 142

Franciscan, California
Napa Cabernet Sauvignon $$$ 161
Oakville Chardonnay $$ 89
Oakville Estate Merlot $$$ 142

Francis Coppola
See Coppola

Franzia, California
Blush $ 112
Chablis $ 105
Chardonnay $ 89
Merlot $ 142
White Zinfandel $ 113

Frei Brothers Reserve, California
Merlot $$ 143
Pinot Noir $$ 124

Freixenet, Spain
Brut de Noirs Sparkling Cava NV Rosé $ 44
Cordon Negro Brut NV $$ 44

Frescobaldi, Italy
Chianti Rufina Riserva $$$ 133

Frog's Leap, California
Merlot $$$ 143
Sauvignon Blanc $$ 70

Gallo of Sonoma, California
Barelli Creek Cabernet Sauvignon $$$ 161
Cabernet Sauvignon $ 161
Chardonnay $ 89
Dry Creek Valley Zinfandel $$ 193
Frei Ranch Zinfandel $$$ 193
Merlot $ 143
Pinot Noir $ 124

Hugel, Alsace, France
Gewürztraminer $$ 106
Pinot Blanc $ 106

Indigo Hills, California
Pinot Noir $ 124

Inglenook, California
Chardonnay $ 90
White Zinfandel $ 113

Iron Horse, California
Wedding Cuvée Brut $$$ 45

Jaboulet, France
Côtes-du-Rhône $ 186

Jacob's Creek, Australia
Cabernet Sauvignon $ 163
Chardonnay $ 91
Shiraz/Cabernet $ 186

Jekel, California
Riesling $ 59

J. Lohr, California
7 Oaks Cabernet Sauvignon $$ 163
Bay Mist White Riesling $ 59
Riverstone Chardonnay $$ 91

Jolivet (Pascal), France
Sancerre $$ 73

Jordan, California
Cabernet Sauvignon $$$$ 164
Chardonnay $$$ 91

Joseph Drouhin, France
Chorey-les-Beaune $$$$ 124
Pouilly-Fuissé $$ 91

Joseph Phelps, California
Le Mistral $$$ 187
Napa Cabernet Sauvignon $$$$ 164
Sauvignon Blanc $$ 73

J Wine Co., California
Russian River Pinot Noir $$$ 124
Vintage Brut $$$ 45

Kendall-Jackson, California
Grand Reserve Chardonnay $$ 92
Vintner's Reserve Cabernet Sauvignon $$ 164
Vintner's Reserve Chardonnay $$ 92
Vintner's Reserve Merlot $$ 144
Vintner's Reserve Pinot Noir $$ 125
Vintner's Reserve Riesling $ 59
Vintner's Reserve Sauvignon Blanc $ 73
Vintner's Reserve Syrah $$ 187
Vintner's Reserve Zinfandel $$ 194

Lingenfelder, Germany
   Bird Label Riesling **$$**   60

Livingston Cellars, California
   Chablis **$**   107
   Chardonnay **$**   94

Livio Felluga, Italy
   Pinot Grigio **$$**   53

Los Vascos, Chile
   Cabernet Sauvignon **$**   165

Louis Jadot, France
   Beaujolais-Villages **$**   116
   Bourgogne Pinot Noir **$$**   126
   Mâcon-Villages Chardonnay **$**   94
   Pouilly-Fuissé **$$**   95

Louis Latour, France
   Nuits-St.-Georges **$$$$**   126

Lucien Crochet, France
   Sancerre **$$**   74

Luna di Luna, Italy
   Chardonnay/Pinot Grigio **$**   95

MacMurray Ranch, California
   Sonoma Coast Pinot Noir **$$**   126

Mâcon-Lugny, France
   "Les Charmes" **$**   95

Macrostie, California
   Chardonnay **$$**   95

Markham, California
   Merlot **$$$**   144

Marqués de Cáceres, Spain
   Rioja Crianza **$$**   175
   Rioja Rosado **$**   113

Marqués de Riscal, Spain
   Rioja Crianza **$**   175
   Rueda White **$**   107

Marquis Phillips, Australia
   Sarah's Blend **$$**   188

Martin Codax, Spain
   Albariño **$$**   107

Mason, California
   Sauvignon Blanc **$$**   74

Matua, New Zealand
   Sauvignon Blanc **$**   74

McDowell, California
   Grenache Rosé **$**   114

Meridian, California
   Cabernet Sauvignon **$**   165

Chardonnay $	96
Merlot $	145
Pinot Grigio $	53
Pinot Noir $	126
Sauvignon Blanc $	74

Merry Edwards, California
   Russian River Valley Pinot Noir $$$ — 127

Merryvale, California
   Starmont Chardonnay $$$ — 96

MezzaCorona, Italy
   Pinot Grigio $ — 53

Michele Chiarlo, Italy
   Moscato d'Asti Nivole (Clouds) $$$ — 200

Michel Laroche, Burgundy, France
   Chablis St. Martin $$$ — 96

Michel Redde, France
   Pouilly-Fumé $$ — 75

Miguel Torres, Spain
   Viña Sol White $ — 108

Mionetto, Italy
   DOC Prosecco $$ — 46

Moët & Chandon, Champagne, France
   Brut Imperial NV $$$$ — 46
   White Star Champagne $$$$ — 47

Mondavi (Robert), California
   See Robert Mondavi

Monte Antico, Italy
   Toscana Red $ — 133

Montecillo, Spain
   Rioja Crianza $ — 176

Montes, Chile
   Merlot $ — 145

Monteviña, California
   Amador Zinfandel $ — 194
   Pinot Grigio $ — 54

Morgan, California
   Pinot Noir $$ — 127

Mouton-Cadet, France
   Bordeaux $ — 145

Mt. Veeder, California
   Napa Cabernet Sauvignon $$$$ — 165

Muga, Spain
   Rioja Reserva $$$ — 176

Mumm Cuvée, Napa, California
   Brut Prestige Sparkling $$ — 47

Piper-Heidsieck, France
Brut Cuvée $$$$ 48

Piper-Sonoma, California
Brut $$ 48

PJ Valckenberg, Germany
Madonna Eiswein $$$ 201

Pol Roger, Champagne, France
Blanc de Chardonnay Brut $$$$ 48
Brut Reserve NV $$$$ 48

Pommery, Champagne, France
Brut Royal Champagne NV $$$ 49

Pride Mountain Vineyards, California
Cabernet Sauvignon $$$$ 167

Puiatti, Italy
Pinot Grigio $$ 54

Rabbit Ridge, California
Zinfandel $ 195

Rancho Zabaco, California
Dry Creek Valley Zinfandel $$ 195
Heritage Vines Sonoma County Zinfandel $$ 195
Pinot Grigio $$ 54

Ravenswood, California
Vintners Blend Merlot $$ 146
Vintners Blend Zinfandel $ 195

Raymond Estates, California
Napa Cabernet Sauvignon $$ 167
Napa Chardonnay $$ 97

Regaleali, Italy
See Tasca D'Almerita

Renwood, California
Sierra Zinfandel $$ 196

Rex Hill, Oregon
Willamette Valley Pinot Noir $$$ 127

Reynolds, Australia
Shiraz $ 189

R.H. Phillips, California
Dunnigan Hills Chardonnay $ 97
Dunnigan Hills Sauvignon Blanc $ 75
Toasted Head Chardonnay $$ 97

Ridge, California
Geyserville (Zinfandel) $$$ 196

Riunite, Italy
Lambrusco $ 181

Robert Mondavi, California
Private Selection Cabernet Sauvignon $ 167
Private Selection Chardonnay $ 98

Private Selection Merlot **$** 146
Private Selection Pinot Noir **$$** 128
Private Selection Sauvignon Blanc **$** 75
Private Selection Zinfandel **$** 196
Napa Cabernet Sauvignon **$$$** 168
Napa Chardonnay **$$$** 98
Napa Fumé Blanc **$$** 76
Napa Pinot Noir **$$$** 128

Robert Sinskey, California
Napa Pinot Noir **$$$** 128

Robert Talbott, California
Sleepy Hollow Vineyard Chardonnay **$$$$** 100

Rocca delle Macie, Italy
Chianti Classico **$** 134
Chianti Classico Riserva **$$** 134

Rodney Strong, California
Cabernet Sauvignon **$$** 168
Chalk Hill Estate Bottled Chardonnay **$$** 98
Chardonnay **$$** 98
Charlotte's Home Sauvignon Blanc **$$** 76
Merlot **$$** 146

Roederer Estate, California
Brut Sparkling **$$$** 49

Rombauer, California
Chardonnay **$$$** 98

Rosemount, Australia
Chardonnay/Semillon **$** 109
Diamond Label Cabernet Sauvignon **$** 168
Diamond Label Cabernet Sauvignon/Merlot **$** 168
Diamond Label Chardonnay **$** 99
Diamond Label Shiraz **$** 189
Diamond Label Shiraz/Cabernet Sauvignon **$** 189
GSM (Grenache-Shiraz-Mourvedre) **$$** 189

Ruffino, Italy
Gold Label Chianti Classico Riserva Ducale **$$$$** 134
Orvieto **$** 109

Ruinart, France
Brut NV **$$$$** 49

Rutherford Hill, California
Merlot **$$$** 147

Saintsbury, California
Carneros Pinot Noir **$$$** 128

Santa Cristina Sangiovese, Antinori, Italy
See Antinori

Santa Margherita, Italy
Pinot Grigio **$$$** 54

Santa Rita, Chile
120 Cabernet Sauvignon **$** 168

Strub, Germany
Niersteiner Paterberg Riesling Spätlese $$ 61

Sutter Home, California
Cabernet Sauvignon $ 170
Chardonnay $ 100
Gewürztraminer $ 110
Merlot $ 148
Sauvignon Blanc $ 77
White Zinfandel $ 114
Zinfandel $ 197

Swanson Vineyards, California
Merlot $$$ 148

Taittinger, Champagne, France
Brut La Française NV $$$$ 51

Talbott (Robert), California
Sleepy Hollow Vineyard Chardonnay $$$$ 100

Talus, California
Cabernet Sauvignon $ 170
Chardonnay $ 100
Merlot $$ 148

Tasca D'Almerita, Italy
Regaleali Rosato $ 114

Terra Rosa, Chile/Argentina
Cabernet Sauvignon $ 171

Terrazas Alto, Argentina
Malbec $ 179

"TJ" Riesling, Selbach-Oster, Germany
See Selbach-Oster $

Trimbach, Alsace, France
Pinot Gris $$ 55
Riesling $$ 61

Trinchero, California
Mario's Special Reserve Merlot $$ 149

Trinity Oaks, California
Merlot $ 149

Turning Leaf, California
Cabernet Sauvignon $ 171
Chardonnay $ 100
Merlot $ 149
Pinot Grigio $ 55
Pinot Noir $ 128
Zinfandel $ 197

Vega Sindoa Navarra, Spain
Tempranillo/Merlot Tinto $ 176

Vendange, California
Cabernet Sauvignon $ 171
Merlot $ 149

White Zinfandel $ 114
Zinfandel $ 197

Veramonte, Chile
Cabernet Sauvignon $ 171
Chardonnay $ 101
Primus $$ 179

Veuve Clicquot, Champagne, France
Yellow Label NV $$$$ 51

Viader, California
Cabernet blend $$$$ 172

Villa Maria, New Zealand
Private Bin Sauvignon Blanc $$ 78

Viña Carmen, Chile
Cabernet Sauvignon $ 172

Vinicola del Priorat, Spain
Onix $$$ 176

Walnut Crest, Chile
Cabernet Sauvignon $ 172
Merlot $ 150

Walter Glatzer, Austria
Gruner Veltliner Kabinett $ 110

Warre, Portugal
10 year-old-Old Otima Tawny Port NV $$$ 201

Weingärtner, Austria
Gruner Veltliner Federspiel $ 110

Weingut Louis Guntrum, Germany
'Royal Blue' Riesling $ 62

Wente, California
Riesling $ 62

Wild Horse, California
Pinot Noir $$ 129

Willakenzie, Oregon
Willamette Valley Pinot Noir $$$ 129

Willamette Valley Vineyards, Oregon
Pinot Noir $$ 129

Wolf Blass, Australia
President's Selection Shiraz $$ 190

Woodbridge (Robert Mondavi), California
Cabernet Sauvignon $ 172
Chardonnay $ 101
Merlot $ 147
Sauvignon Blanc $ 78
Zinfandel $ 198

Wyndham, Australia
Bin 555 Shiraz $ 190

THANKS TO . . .

The tasting panel! You've made buying and drinking wine better and more fun for everyone who picks up this book. Thanks for sharing your hidden gems, and for telling it like it is. Keep tasting!

The trade insiders, for their view of the wines leading the market—especially Tylor Field at Morton's, Greg Duppler and the Target team, and Alan Gordon at Marshall-Fields.

Emily Bajus, who crunched all the numbers, and Kacy Henderson, who proofread like a pro.

Angela Miller and Broadway Books, especially Jennifer Josephy and Steve Rubin, for believing in the book.

DEDICATED TO . . .

My family.

In loving tribute to the memory of the missing from Windows on the World, where wine really was for everyone.

PLEASE JOIN MY TASTING PANEL

To share your comments on wines you like (or dislike), visit www.greatwinemadesimple.com or e-mail andrea@greatwinemadesimple.com. Or to request a paper survey by mail, please fill out and return this card to Great Wine Made Simple Tasting Panel, 160 Rockrimmon Road, Stamford CT 06903.

☐ Mr.   ☐ Mrs.   ☐ Ms.

_____

Your Name (and company if applicable)

_____

Street Address   Apt./Suite #

_____

City   State   Zip

Optional

_____

E-mail address

_____

Occupation

To order *Andrea Immer's Wine Buying Guide for Everyone,* check all that apply, and we will contact you by e-mail, mail, or phone:

☐ Customized copies
☐ Bulk order
☐ Signed copies
☐ Single copies/small quantities (help me find a store in my area)

Please contact me by (choose one):

☐ Phone (   ) _____-_____
☐ E-mail ⟩ Please fill in the above form.
☐ Mail